"...a loving tribute...profusely illustrated...liberally sprinkled with sidebars and anecdotes about Canadian amateur sport, and the place of women in it throughout the years."
Montreal Gazette

"This is a fascinating history of two wonderful athletes and their times. It will be of particular interest to anyone interested in the development of amateur sport in Canada, especially those familiar with the important initiatives coming from Montreal and the Laurentians."
Richard W. Pound

"Rempel's account of the twins' charmed lives and their impact on Canadian ski history is definitely a must-read in front of the fire this season."
Canadian Ski Magazine

"*No Limits* is a book that matters...it shapes the stories of two great Canadian athletes and lays those stories over decades when huge changes occurred."
Literary Review of Canada

"...a great read for anyone interested in inspiring confidence in themselves or others."
changinggears.ca

"As a ski reporter for the Montreal Gazette in the 1940s, I watched Rhona and Rhoda win race after race. They were truly phenomenal as they tamed the wildest hills. But I knew nothing about their later lives until I read this book. It led me to further admiration as I learned how the twins overcame many hardships and brought up, between them, seven children, all of whom have had outstanding careers. The book is much more than a chronicle of spsorting achievement; with its revealing sidelights it is also a valuable contribution to the social history of Canada in the Twentieth Century. "
William Weintraub

The first edition received the prestigious Ullr Award, International Skiing History Association, and was a finalist for the Mavis Gallant Prize for Non-fiction, Quebec Writers' Federation.

no limits

The Amazing Life Story
of Rhona and Rhoda Wurtele

NO LIMITS
The Amazing Life Story of Rhona and
Rhoda Wurtele, Canada's Olympian Skiing Pioneers

All unaccredited photos in this publication are from
the private collections of Rhona Gillis and Rhoda Eaves.

Library and Archives Canada Cataloguing in Publication
Includes selected bibliography and index.

First edition: Twinski Publications.
Revised (2012)
ISBN: 978-0-9783890-0-0
Legal deposit Bibliothèque et archives nationales du Québec (2007)
Legal deposit National Archives of Canada (2007)

A second edition was published by Les Éditions Histoire Québec,
Collection Société d'histoire et de généalogie des Pays-d'en-Haut
and Twinski Publications.
ISBN: 978-2-89586-055-6
Legal deposit Bibliothèque et archives nationales du Québec (2009)
Legal deposit National Archives of Canada (2009)

1. Sports biography (Rhona and Rhoda Wurtele)
2. Skiing history (Quebec)
3. Skiing history (Canada)
4. History of Women (Quebec)

Printed and bound in Canada
www.twinski.com

no limits

The Amazing Life Story
of Rhona and Rhoda Wurtele

Canada's Olympian Skiing Pioneers

By Byron Rempel

Author: Byron Rempel

Graphic Designer: Janou Fleury

Cover design: Jean-François Pigeon

Index: Sheila Eskenazi

Development and coordination: Nancy Robinson

Produced and Published by: Ronald K. Walker

Many thanks to Rhoda Wurtele Eaves and
Rhona Wurtele Gillis for making themselves
available for questions and interviews.
Also to their families and to all the Twinskiers past
and present for their enthusiasm and support.

Grateful acknowledgement is made to all
those who have granted permission to reprint
copyrighted material and those who have
provided personal photos.

Special thanks to Ronald K. Walker and Margaret
Lefebvre for their continued support of this project.

Contents

The twins Rhoda and Rhona at age eleven on the gully on Westmount hill: "We weren't courageous. Courage is when you're afraid to do something."

PREFACE

Winter tests us every year, but human ingenuity and élan have transformed the numbing cold and snow- and ice-crusted landscapes into the sliding sports and the joys, camaraderie and communities that surround them. The acrobatics of the skier, the artistry of the skater, the shouts of the bonspiel and the end-to-end rushes of hockey bring us out of ourselves and turn the metaphorical season of death into dances of life. These sports embroider our most memorable and sustaining narratives of self-discovery and possibility and shape our identities as Canadians.

Few Canadians have given us more defining chapters in our encounters with ice and snow, nor have helped more of us discover the joys of winter than the Wurtele twins, Rhoda and Rhona. In their youth, they were synonymous with daring, skill and accomplishment. They took on bigger and bigger challenges with big smiles on their faces, telling reporters that 'we weren't scared; we were just having fun', showing the skeptics that women could take up, excel in and enjoy any sport. For two decades, they dominated the North American alpine events, representing Canada in the 1948 and 1952 Olympics, the first serious female skiers to do so. After their Olympic careers, they became coaches and organizers, inspiring and aiding the next generation of successful Canadian female racers. But they also shared their love of sport with anyone who was interested. Starting with the Ski Jays, in 1956, and the Twinski Club, begun in 1962 and continuing to this day, they have been helping women and men of all ages and abilities learn, perfect and enjoy skiing for more than half a century. At 87, they still exude a joie de vivre and love of effort that is infectious. They are exemplars of the very best in Canadian sport.

Byron Rempel has done an excellent job with the Wurteles' remarkable story. It's a fascinating read, with just the right balance between biography and context. It's an important contribution to the social history of Canada, illuminating the lives and times of these extraordinary champions and the networks they have created. And it captures the thrills and pleasures of the winter sports. I write this on a hot, humid day in August, and I can't wait until the first snowfall.

Bruce Kidd, O.C., Ph.D
Professor and Dean
Faculty of Physical Education and Health
University of Toronto

Introduction
Learning to Fly

If you could choose what to come back as in your next life, what would it be?

Rhona: A bird.

Rhoda: An eagle.

The twins' brother Edgar going off the Côte des Neiges ski jump, 1932: you don't get to brag until you've gone off the senior jump.

On a clear winter day in the heart of Montreal, two identical girls stood at the top of a hill on ponderous seven-foot hickory skis and dreamed of flight. It wasn't the first time. In 1933, the eleven-year-old twins were already veteran skiers. Rhoda and Rhona Wurtele had been strapping their brothers' skis to their leather lace-up boots and skiing the Gully, a half-mile slope down Westmount hill, since they were five years old. The hill was a short walk from the front door of their family's Elizabethan home, and they had hiked the distance many times. The Gully was a bumpy, two-tracked *piste* that seemed tailor-made to train skiers for any eventuality. Today the track has become Summit Circle, a toney street winding past magnolias and fortresses of the wealthy, a place where people like to think they can keep the unpredictable at bay. But the twins weren't thinking of any of that, and especially not of the future. The Gully was only the means to an end. And the end was a massive wooden structure that rose from the mountainside: beside the junior ski jump, where skiers took off from a jump built into the hill, towered the 125-foot-high senior ski jump.

The jumps had the allure of forbidden fruit. The twins' older brothers, future air force aces Edgar and George, both regularly flew off the end of the things in the same long, four-inch-wide glorified barrel staves with four grooves on the bottom. It was a wonder they got any air at all. But professional male jumpers could wing it for 148 feet before gravity remembered them. Upon landing, skiers had to turn fast so they wouldn't jump again over the big snowdrift at the end of the run—and come down through the roof of a tennis clubhouse.

That afternoon, watching Edgar soar off the rickety jump, Rhoda and Rhona asked each other if today was the day to make the leap, take that jump. That was the danger and delight of being twins: you always had an alter ego to push you further or pull you back. They soon found themselves at the top of the junior jump and, before they knew it, off its ramp.

Trois-Rivières Ski Club ski jump, similar to Montreal jump, 1930: creaking and shifting in the wind.

It is neither esoteric nor complicated, the feeling that comes from ski jumping: it feels as if you can fly. Granted, it lasts only two or three seconds before the Earth comes rushing up to take you back in her arms. Except that those two or three seconds are forever.

One after the other, Rhoda and Rhona landed on their feet. Then they immediately cornered Edgar and told him about their first taste of flight.

"That was nothing," he replied, conscious of his brotherly duty to tempt and challenge. "You don't get to brag until you've gone over the senior jump—and are still able to speak after you hit the ground." When were the twins going to try *that*? Obviously, though older and wiser, Edgar still didn't understand his little sisters. They could resist everything except temptation—the temptation of a challenge. So they answered, simply: "Today." And as he saw his sisters climbing up to the launch area, he considered that he might be the first one called in for questioning if one of them broke a leg. Or a neck.

Now he had to stop them. "It's icy today. Not the best day to do it," he tried.

But it was much too late. "If not now, when?" the twins called back. "You afraid?"

The Côte des Neiges senior ski jump was nailed atop a rickety wooden scaffolding that creaked and shifted in the frigid wind. It was built by Aleksander Olsen, a Norwegian immigrant engineer who was six times Canadian champion in ski jumping (his son Kaare also jumped and skied; today he is a member of Rhona and Rhoda's Twinski Club). Jumpers reached the top by climbing stairs from the base. The twins clutched the railings, lugging their brothers' skis. Up top, where February blew hard, you could see the entire city spread out below. One million people at your feet, the three hills that rise in mid city dusted with powder around you. According to Quebec's greatest ski pioneer Herman "Jackrabbit" Johannsen in 1928, Montreal was "unique in being the only place on the continent where good skiing can actually be enjoyed in the heart of a great city." Despite the crushing Depression, there was a lot more to be enjoyed in the city too—if you looked closely, you could also spot more than two hundred gambling joints and a bevy of brothels on de Bullion Street. On the roads into town, streams of cars and trains brought Americans fleeing Prohibition. Going the other way across the border were bootleggers like the Bronfman family, feeding the same need. Mayor Camillien Houde, the flamboyant eccentric who was in and out of office for twenty-eight years, was trying his best to keep the city on its feet.

Photo courtesy McCord Museum

Skis and the city—on top of Mount Royal, 1930. From a "painted lantern" slide.

From the top of the ski jump too, you looked directly down on what less adventurous souls might have considered a warning: Mount Royal Cemetery, already jam-packed, but always with

Photo courtesy McCord Museum

As soon as Montrealers discovered skis, they began jumping: Mount Royal, 1905. One hundred years later, women are still banned from jumping in the Olympics.

room for one—or two—more foolhardy souls.

The twins don't remember today who went first, but it hardly mattered. Both girls landed on their feet, their heads still in the clouds. They landed in a crouching position, making sixty feet on the first try and eighty feet on the second. "It's actually easier than the junior," Rhoda told her brother. "You've got more time to prepare." Both had survived the crushing shock of landing, although Rhona says she might have busted a few ribs. Or it might have happened in the next thirty or so times they tried it in the next two weeks. Said a local paper at the time, "For a bruising, glorious fortnight the twins bumped their derrieres and scraped their knees on that ski jump, while awe-struck boy companions gazed incredulously at this feminine double-scoop."

No woman under the age of eighteen had ever flown off that jump before; few women of any age had. The *Montreal Star* later said they were "the only girls to do it in 15 years." And yet their glorious career in ski jumping came to a crashing halt one day. Someone had suggested they go off the jump together, holding hands, during the George Washington tournament. The twins had thought it a smashing idea. But someone, perhaps the Montreal Ski Club, or the newspapers, or a worried neighbour, had called their parents and let the secret out. Their father, John Stone Hunter Wurtele, was suitably impressed (he even sent a friend to record the event with a 16 mm movie camera), but Mother thought it wouldn't be a good idea for her little birds to jump out of the nest in such a spectacular fashion. "It isn't a ladylike sport," she said.

Quite the ladies: after church in Westmount, the 1940s. The twins' sister Jean, Rhona, and Rhoda.

After those heady flights, the impact of that forced landing was harder than any other.

"It isn't a ladylike sport." That kind of statement seems crazy in our modern world, more than eighty years later. Think of the spectacular feats of today's female athletes, and imagine someone claiming that *ladies* are physically and psychologically fragile beings who need to be coddled and protected from the damaging influences of the world. Imagine someone saying something like this: "Ski-jumping is like jumping down from, let's say, about two meters off the ground about a thousand times a year, which seems not to be appropriate for ladies from a medical point of view."

Incredible? In fact, that quote is from Gian Carlo Kasper, Fédération International de Ski (FIS) and International Olympic Committee (IOC) official—in February of 2006. As of this writing in 2007, ski jumping is the only sport women are still banned from in the Winter Olympics. Alissa Johnson, a young American ski jumper who had to sit on the sidelines while her brother went to jump at the Olympics in 2006, had trouble believing it too. "So far, we've been told every excuse in the book. That it's too 'dangerous' for girls. That there aren't enough of us. That we're not good enough. That it would damage our ovaries and uterus and we won't be able to have children, even though that's not true. It's so outdated, it's kind of funny in a way. And then it's not."

Côte des Neiges ski jump, Montreal 1930s.

That these kinds of limitations are still placed on women may not be surprising to anyone born before 1960. Not too long ago, girls were given the same excuses when they wanted to play Little League baseball; the women's marathon wasn't added to the Summer Olympics until 1984 because officials still believed women wouldn't be able to handle it.

Even before Rhona and Rhoda got to an age where they would encounter these limitations, they had already seen their older sister Jean held back from her passion. A natural dancer who in the 1930s performed at His Majesty's Theatre in Montreal and who at the age of eighty could still kick her leg above her head, as a girl Jean was stopped from pursuing a career in the art. "Ladies didn't do that kind of thing," says Rhona.

Jean certainly *seemed* psychologically fragile. When she was only fifteen years old she suffered a nervous breakdown. "She just came downstairs one day and wouldn't talk," says Rhona. "It was a very difficult situation because nobody really knew about these things. The neighbour told Mom that she thought Jean was doing too much, because she used to get these nosebleeds and things, and cry over her homework." Yet Jean's misfortune led to a winter-long holiday for the twins; their mother packed up all three girls and went to the family's second home at Acton Vale for the season, taking the twins out of school. (A short while later Jean would become one of the first people in North America to receive electric shock therapy when the European neurologists who developed it toured to promote the method. "It worked—to a degree," says Rhona.) Blissfully unaware of the serious problems around them, the young girls revelled in their freedom, building forts, skiing cross-country and generally getting into as much mischief as they could find.

Well, they stayed off the ski jump most of the time. Rhona flying over the jump at Côte des Neiges, with the cemetery and mountain in the background.

Looking back, the twins acknowledge they were lucky; they were privileged. Not every young girl had the chance to be a carefree child in the Depression. Back in Montreal, a third of the work force was unemployed. The majority of women, kept out of paying jobs in the best of times by their supposed frailty (even though they did hard physical work at home), now had even less chance; many made sure to take off their wedding rings lest their employers fire them so their jobs could go to men. But the twins' family was well off, and Hunter Wurtele, a breadwinner whose job was not at risk, could afford to send his wife and children away for the winter. Years later, when they were young women and their work schedule didn't jibe with their skiing schedule, it was an easy decision: quit work. Influenced by that early, invigorating taste of absolute freedom, the expectation that they could do what they wanted, when they wanted, would stay with Rhona and Rhoda forever. For they not only had freedom in their childhood to be tomboys, and freedom from financial worry, they also had the security of each other. Rhoda and Rhona, despite their penchant for wild flights, were good girls. That day when they were stopped from soaring off the ski jumps, they listened to their parents. "We haven't tried it since," Rhona says today. However, their parents had said nothing about *racing* downhill. And so began a double career that would help revolutionize women's sport in North America. In a few years, the twins would go further and faster on skis than anyone else had before, beating the best male skiers of their day. Rhona became the first Canadian skier to hold both American and Canadian national championships at the same time; the twins were the first and only women with Canada's first true Olympic ski team; Rhoda was the first North American woman to place in the top three in a European Kandahar event; they jointly won the Athlete of the Year award. "Canada's Terrific Twins" would go on to be featured in *Life* magazine, the *Saturday Evening Post*, *Time*, *Chatelaine*, *Maclean's* and the *New York Times*—they would even be drawn up in a True Picture comic book during wartime, which otherwise told stories of heroic soldiers battling Nazis. The girls would have loved to see stories about themselves as heroic fighter pilots too, but that proved to be a barrier even the twins couldn't surmount.

The two skiing pioneers had carved an easily identifiable trail for others to follow. Canadian women's skiing is directly indebted and linked to them, from Lucile Wheeler, Anne Heggtveit, and Nancy Greene, to today's World Cup championship–winning women's ski team. Even when the twins were no longer racing, their influence was felt: in 1959 Rhoda managed and assistant-coached the very first National Ski Team that Canada sent to Europe for the World Championships. It is no coincidence that Canada's wins in the Olympics and world championships have largely been in the women's division.

Today, seventy years later, Rhoda and Rhona are still propelling themselves through the air. Within the last few years they have gone heli-skiing, bobsledding, paraponting, even bungee jumping. Always ladies, however, for the most part they stay off the ski jumps.

The first page of the True Picture-Magazine comic book featuring Rhona and Rhoda and their parents, 1945.

Freedom 1922–1939

BIRTH TO SEVENTEEN YEARS OLD

A CENTURY OF PROMISE

Rhoda and Rhona hold their first swimming competitions, 1926, Drummondville, Quebec.

"Saturday, January 21, 1922. This morning at about 8 o'clock beautiful little twin daughters arrived to join our happy family. They are exactly alike and very small—only 4 ¼ lbs each—but they seem healthy and sharp."

John Stone Hunter Wurtele's diary is full of hope, and had every right to be. His wife, Edith "Colly" Douglas Fairweather, had given birth to Grace Rhona and Isabella Rhoda Wurtele at home on Birch Street in St. Lambert at only seven months. In that decade more and more parents were choosing hospital births, but "respectable women" still shied away from them out of modesty, class consciousness, and fear of puerperal fever—concerns which for Hunter and Colly apparently even overruled the further risks involved in having twins. The risk of infection in hospitals was still quite real; it was only at the turn of the century that doctors had stopped laughing at the quacks that said hand washing could help stop one of the greatest killers of women. For those that could afford it, a home birth with a doctor at hand was still preferred.

There were apparently no complications with the births, although "our sister Jean thought we were Indians because we were all red," Rhoda says. "Mother must have surmised she was going to have twins because her legs were all swollen. We heard she could hardly move." As soon as the ramifications of having two new infants and an exhausted mother in the house sank in, Hunter Wurtele leapt into action and quickly shuttled off the other three children to friends and relatives.

Hunter Wurtele in *Who's Who* in Canada.

A hydroelectric engineer when hydroelectricity was still a brand new field, Hunter Wurtele had recently become Plant Manager at the Southern Canada Power Company; with this promotion he decided he could move his family away from what he felt was the damp and unhealthy environment of Montreal's South Shore. Westmount was a brand new development then, where fox and pheasants still ran across front lawns. They settled at 756 Upper Lansdowne.

Thanks to the pioneers who came before them, the Wurtele twins were born into an era when girls and women were finally able to cut loose. This was the Jazz Age, the time of thin girls trying to cut a boyish figure, wearing make-up previously reserved for ladies of the night, smoking and drinking and dancing the shimmy and the Charleston. And while the previous generation had thrilled to the freedom of the bicycle, it was nothing like the newer, faster vehicle now at their disposal. Women didn't want to just ride along in them, they wanted to drive them too. Henry Ford's automobile was fast, and risky—like the flappers themselves.

In 1921, the year before the birth of Rhona and Rhoda, the Dominion Ski Championships in Montreal had become the most important ski competitions in Canada, although, like most skiing of the day, it featured only cross-country and ski jumping. And in nearby Ottawa that year, it looked like the world title for ski jumping was going to be challenged, by a woman. The flamboyant "Countess Alma Stang" soared off the platform and seemed ready to finally set a level playing ground—until an unfortunate wind

Rhoda doing the long jump, 1930s. Only a decade before, women weren't allowed to compete in track and field.

blew off her wig, and revealed her as a man in drag.

Still, despite the advances made during the Great War, some things returned to the way they used to be, once the men came home. While hospitals had accepted female medical students during the war, in the 1920s they were rejected on grounds of modesty. Women's wages after the war reverted to what they had been before: exactly half of men's wages.

One can only imagine the even greater obstacles the Wurtele twins would have faced had they been born a few decades earlier. The year before they were born the first "Women's Olympics," the Jeux Féminins, were held in Paris, after the International Olympic Committee had refused to let women participate in track and field. While they were infants, the Montreal Ski Club held its inaugural Ladies' Race. By the time they had their second birthday cake, the first Winter Olympic Games were held in Chamonix, France (although the only sport for women was the ladylike pursuit of Fancy Skating). The playing ground was cleared for the twins; now all they had to do was take advantage of it.

Family Roots: **Strength**

The twins' family background is a judicious mixture of Scottish and Germanic roots. Faint hope and family legend trace the Wurtele name back to 1550 and that irrepressible reformer Martin Luther. Traces of the first Wurteles in Montreal can still be found underneath a museum in the Old Port: the foundation of an inn opened by brothers Josias and Georg. Josias's son Jonathan married a Scottish girl fleeing the American Revolution, Louisa Sophia Campbell. In 1831, in Quebec City, her brother John Saxton Campbell built the first ship to cross the Atlantic under steam, the Royal William. One gets the impression that the ship might well have crossed the sea under the steam of John Campbell himself. "He was not only tall and well built, but very strong, calm and collected," said his niece Margery Durham Campbell. "My uncle John had prodigious strength, and it is told of him that when a schooner being launched stuck on the ways, he put his shoulder to her and the vessel moved off."

Jonathan Saxton Campbell Würtele (1828-1904).

Keeping Mom busy: the Wurtele kids. From left, George, Rhoda, Jean, Rhona, Edgar. Acton Vale, 1924.

THE SWEET LITTLE GIRLS

Edith "Colly" Wurtele was very busy. She was busy as only a Westmount housewife could be busy in 1927. She didn't have a job, never gave a thought to having a career. Her husband at forty-seven was just reaching his career peak, climbing to the job of Vice-President and Consulting Engineer at Southern Canada Power Corp., so she didn't have to worry about money. Colly also had five children underfoot, including her oldest teenaged boy who was into radical and extreme sports like ski jumping (Edgar), a teenaged girl who wanted to be a dancer (Jean), a pre-teen boy who followed his older brother off every jump (George), and two unstoppable identical twin girls who not only thought they might be boys, but also had an inkling that they might be all grown up too. But Colly had help.

There was a maid on Upper Lansdowne Street—in fact, there were two maids, and a nurse. The twins remember the house filled with rooms, three stories of them. But Colly also had a cleaning lady. And the kids had a whole undeveloped mountain as their playground. That year, the twins having reached the ripe age of five, their father had strapped a pair of skis on each and pushed them out the back door. Annie Long, their nursemaid, walked them all over Westmount, unsuccessfully trying to tire them out; she brought them to the Dominion Douglas Church on The Boulevard, where on Friday nights children could watch movies

Basket o' Twins, 1920s, in the daisy field at Acton Vale.

such as *The Last of the Mohicans* with Randolf Scott and Wallace Beery, or the latest Mickey Mouse, Our Gang, Felix the Cat and Rin Tin Tin adventures.

Still, Edith Douglas Fairweather Wurtele was busy. "She was in and out of the house all the time," remembers Rhona. She volunteered for all kinds of organizations, using her free time to help where she could. But her favourite way to keep busy was to entertain. The house in Westmount was the epicentre of colossal bridge parties that took over the neighbourhood, tea parties with long tables set with the best silver and petit fours, a grandiose bouquet

GRANDPA REVEREND LOUIS WURTELE **AND THE DR. JEKYLL CONNECTION**

The Reverend Louis Campbell Wurtele and wife Isabella Tracy Hunter Wurtele.

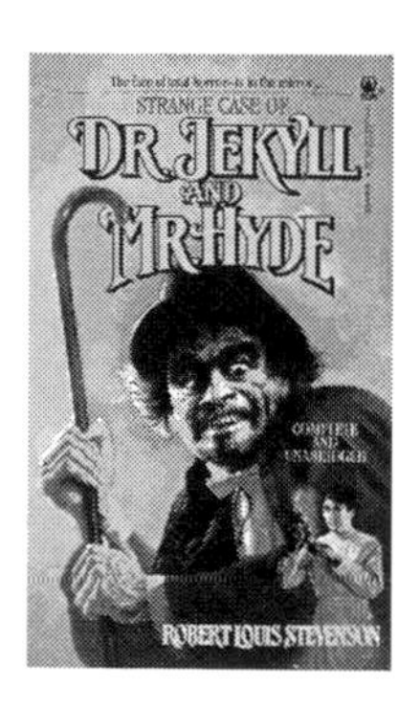

While Jonathan and Louisa Wurtele had sons who grew up to become judges and engineers and lawyers, one of their nine children aspired to treasures in heaven rather than worldly success. The twins' grandfather Louis Campbell Wurtele became an Anglican priest in 1861, then was assigned to the new mission of Acton Vale in the region of Montérégie (100 kilometres east of Montreal). It was a tiny village, but an international rail line and a rich vein of copper drew a steady hoard of rough and ready hardrock miners looking for quick money and a stiff drink. Reverend Louis also offered spiritual guidance, and was priest there for fifty-seven years, until 1917, easily outlasting the vein of copper—and the miners. Highly educated, proficient in Hebrew, Latin, and Greek, he was also a member of the American Association for the Advancement of Science. After his first wife died in childbirth, the Reverend married Isabella Tracy Hunter of Maine. She too claimed an association with science; one of her ancestors was John Hunter, the "father of modern surgery" in England in the mid 1700s, a grave-robbing dissector who brought Western medicine out of the dark ages—and whose macabre downtown London laboratory was the model for Robert Louis Stevenson's *Dr. Jekyll and Mr. Hyde*. A rubbing from the Westminster Abbey plaque dedicated to "the founder of scientific surgery" still hangs in the Wurtele house in Acton Vale.*

The Reverend's scientific interests were less chilling; he wrote a paper on the geology of the St. Francis area in the same region. After arriving at the Acton Vale mission he not only founded the church, but in 1862 had the rectory built as well; the international rail line passed in front of the driveway. And at that house Isabella bore them two sons, who would each pursue one of the dual paths of their father: the first son Arthur, who would become a priest (albeit in a place very different from the copper mines, but as desperate for salvation—Hollywood); and, in 1880, Hunter, the twins' father, who would grow up to be a well-respected hydroelectric engineer. The rectory would stay in the family all these years, and in the next century would welcome the infant twins. Today, eighty-four years later, it is their country home; and under their breath they say that it is full of ghosts. It is undoubtedly filled to the rafters with memories.

* John Hunter is the subject of a recent biography: *The Knife Man: The Extraordinary Life and Times of John Hunter, Father of Modern Surgery*, Wendy Moore, Bantam Press, 2005.

The twins at Upper Lansdowne, 1931: "We used to hide."

spilling out of its vase in the centre. Yet the main attractions at her parties were often hidden right when they were needed most. Colly just happened to have the most adorable twin girls—and you couldn't tell one from the other.

Colly's bigger problem, however, was first trying to find them. Rhona and Rhoda were inevitably chasing after boys. They didn't want to kiss them and make them cry. Well, maybe make them cry—with the agony of defeat. They chased them down in the parks on the mountain to play hockey or football or baseball or basketball or tennis. Even though there was only a handful of houses on their street, "There were tons of kids in the neighbourhood to do things with," say the twins. "We loved it, never had to call anyone up." Even the neighbours' dogs Happy and Chummy, a German Shepherd and Airedale, patiently waited for the twins to come home from school, knowing they'd get a good workout with the girls. And now this new-fangled downhill skiing thing, barrelling down gullies on seven-foot hickory slats, with steel toeplates and leather heel straps for bindings. No poles. "Poles were for sissies,"

Dress up at Ile Bigras in the 1930s: more like it.

Rhona explains. After all, they were already five years old.

It was their mother's intention to separate the girls from the boys and bring the twins home and scrub them down and dress them in sweet little dresses with sweet little bows in their hair, and bring them into the tea party to sit down at the piano and play a sweet little duet.

"We used to hide," says Rhoda.

This coddling by their mother, they felt, was going altogether too far. So they talked about it between themselves first, then one day went to their mother and told her that since they had now reached the age of five years they were old enough to care for each other now, and their nursemaid Annie Long would no longer be necessary.

Surprisingly, their mother agreed.

It could never be said of the twins that they didn't take advantage of every opportunity that came their way. Even when opportunity wasn't there, they forced its hand. At age four their mother bought them bright-yellow rain slickers, with matching hats, and rubber boots. Unfortunately, it wasn't raining that day, so the thrilled twins couldn't try out the new coats. No matter: they dressed up, trundled into the big bathroom and turned the shower on to test the outfits. It was a delight—only they had locked themselves in, and by the time their mother heard the shrieks of joy, she also saw water flowing out under the door. No one could get in to turn off the water, so the Westmount firemen were called. The window to the bathroom was at the top of the house, and the firemen had to climb their ladder from the steep driveway, pry open the narrow window, bypass the shower rack, and turn off the water. One imagines the twins as excited by the "rescue" as they were by the new slickers. "They were wonderful rain outfits," says Rhoda, "and they really worked!"

Winter held just as much adventure. Dressed up in Red River coats with red touques, a grand red tasselled sash around the waist, red pullovers and mitts, the twins might have looked charming but soon discovered the drawbacks of wool in snow. There were the traditional amusements of sleigh and toboggan rides behind the fire station, and skating on "cheese cutters" (two-bladed skates) at Roslyn School. But they also watched in fascination as the snow collectors came down their street. Drawn by two horses, the scoop collected snow along the way; then the driver would pull up the large wooden handles and dump the snow to the side, "the horses snorting and puffing hot steam from their noses." The piles of snow were perfect for digging tunnels and caves. Later on the twins would tempt fate by playing in front of a new kind of snow truck, which ate up snow on its revolving paddle wheels, then shot it to the side. Then there was brother George's homemade tandem bobsleigh, a two-by-eight-inch plank with a wooden sled attached to each end, that the twins rode down Clarke Avenue from Westmount Boulevard—into oncoming traffic.

It was when the girls were kept indoors that they began chafing at the bit. Besides the odious hair ribbons, they wore beautiful pink Angora sweaters their godmother Marg Ironside knitted them every birthday; they wore flannel skirts, white ribbed stockings held up with garter belts they detested, "and of course black patent leather shoes with a strap across the instep and a black shiny button holding them in place," Rhoda remembers. Dressed like that, they were ready to go to dancing lessons at Schlefflers on Sherbrooke Street every Saturday. Their parents took ballroom dancing once a week and went to dances often, expert at tangos, rhumbas, and fox trots, and so hoped their girls would follow. But although Rhona enjoyed the dancing, it was becoming obvious that these two were not cut out for show biz. Rhoda's most glorious memory of dancing on stage was posing as a bridesmaid on a cake; just as a photo was taken when another child popped out of the cake, the kid behind her got sick and ruined her dress.

"I don't remember how the show did," Rhoda says, "but that was the end of my ambition to become a dancer as far as I was concerned. We were missing all the games with the kids on our street."

The Vote **and the Corset**

In 1918, two years before women in the US, Canadian women won the battle to get the vote; the freedom they were beginning to explore was reflected in dress, and many women threw out

their corsets at the same time. In Quebec things moved much more slowly under the piercing eyes of the clergy. Women only got the vote twenty years later. William Weintraub notes that in 1949, 61% of *Québécoises* were still keeping the corset industry alive. By contrast, only 14% continued to lace them up in British Columbia.

The family watching the trains go by at Acton Vale, 1925: left to right, Hunter, Rhona, Colly, Rhoda, George, Jean, Edgar.

ACTON VALE AND COUNTRY LIFE

The most glorious opportunity for the young twins was the house and the land in Acton Vale, nestled in the Appalachian foothills. The seemingly magical name (Oak Valley, in old Anglo-Saxon) keeps coming up in any conversation with them. It was something only a lucky few had in those days around the Dirty Thirties—a country house, and the means to keep it. It was more than a cabin in the woods; it was a family heirloom that had just been passed to the next generation. Grandpa Reverend Louis had died in 1919, and Grandma Isabella followed him the year the twins were born. The twins' father was born in that house. It featured an outdoor toilet with three seats ("The parliament building," interjects Rhoda), a lower kitchen for summertime cooking, a mud floor, an old washing machine with a wringer, and a "hat" bathtub that hung up on the wall when not in use. It also came with its own guardian, nurse, cleaning lady, two maids, and a groundskeeper—and, Rhoda says, "Many, many ghosts."

"Dad loved that old place," says Rhona. "But Mother thought it was the end of the earth." There was no sea there, just the quiet River Renne; the quickly exhausted copper mine eventually became a rock quarry. Those two features, however, would serve the twins quite well.

There were springs all over the mountain, and the abandoned pit had filled with clear water; the girls casually dove off the cliff's edge thirty-two feet into the mine. There was a shaft too, entered through a yawning cave, which went into the earth five hundred feet. It was perfect for practicing yodelling.

"We weren't allowed to swim there for a long time," says Rhona, "because of the shaft, and people thought there would be wooden structures we'd dive into. But finally our Uncle Arthur came from Los Angeles (he was the rector of St. Thomas Episcopal Church on Hollywood Boulevard), and he said it was okay for us to swim there. No doubt we swam in there a bit before that, too."

No doubt. The twins really learned how to swim, however, with their brother George. When he had to miss classes at Lower

Diving at godparents Marg and Wemyss Ironside's home, Ile Bigras, 1931.

Women Versus **Men**

When women didn't have any other women to compete with in sports, they turned to men—and promptly got themselves banned when they started winning.

"Jackie" Mitchell with Babe Ruth and Lou Gehrig, 1931.

First Britian's Made Syers got women banned from world figure skating championships when she placed second in an all-male competition in 1902, then thirty years later in 1931, women were banned from professional baseball after "Jackie" Mitchell struck out Babe Ruth and Lou Gehrig (she was seventeen years old). The ban lasted until 1992. Female students at McGill held weekly ice hockey games in an indoor rink, but put boys "on guard" at the door. In 1910 Annette Kellerman was hauled off to the clink for showing her legs while swimming in Boston Harbor. Even in the 1940s Rhoda would encounter the same kind of stunned disbelief when she beat all women and men by twenty-four seconds at the Taschereau Cup.

FAST **TIMES**

The twins' parents, Hunter and Colly Wurtele, grew up in an era when changes in society were coming fast and hard. At the turn of the century, women were getting more freedom, represented perhaps most visibly by the new choices in dress (to escape from the confining layers of laced petticoats, padding, boned lining, corsets and bustles, Amelia Bloomer had introduced a radical tunic over trousers) and in working outside the home. The popularity of bicycles, according to suffragist Susan B. Anthony, had "done more to emancipate women than any one thing in the world."

Colly Fairweather (seated middle) and her "Middy brigade," in Rothsay, New Brunswick, circa 1900.

While Montreal got itself industrialized and women got the vote, women now hoped to go to university too—at the risk, according to sports historian Bruce Kidd, "of all kinds of diseases, even death, if they stopped having children and pursued academics." Before the twins were born, their mother had been regularly playing golf with her husband. It was only natural that Hunter and Colly would accept and even encourage their own children—their own girls—to get involved in sports as soon as they could walk.

In his youth, Hunter Wurtele had been a sportsman himself, playing with McGill University's nascent hockey club, one of the first organized hockey teams in Canada, and the first place official rules were written down. During one of the wild and woolly games, a stray puck left him deaf in one ear. "His mother didn't want him to play hockey anymore," says Rhona. "I think he was so disappointed that he wanted to make sure we did whatever we wanted to do, and he supported us."

Hunter Wurtele circa 1918. "Note the empty seat beside me," he had written to his future wife.

Canada College for a few months after being laid up with an infection, the twins were bundled off with him to their godparents, the Ironsides, Margaret (knitter of the Angora sweaters) and Wemyss (also at Southern Canada Power), at Ile Bigras in Laval. "We were eight years old, and George was fourteen, and that was where we learned to swim," says Rhoda. "Really, we spent half of our lives in the water." Earlier, at the age of five, they had trundled down to the YWCA near Windsor Station in Montreal. "We wore these weird little grey suits when we got there," says Rhona. "I remember the scary little places to change, with a multitude of doors; you could get lost in there, a very dark and scary place.

Photo courtesy Power Corporation

The Hemmings Falls power development at Drummondville, Quebec. Designed by their father Hunter Wurtele, the power station was also an early swimming hole for the twins.

This is perhaps a surprising admission from the twins, that they actually found something scary. It is even more surprising when you learn that another place they learned to swim, and one they preferred, was the Hemmings Falls power station at Drummondville, Quebec. Their father had designed it, though not with them in mind.

"While Mother played golf and Dad visited substations, we got into the powerhouse and listened to the huge engines, and looked at the sluices, and went fishing where the water came down," says Rhoda. "There was a huge raft and several diving boards. We used to jump in above where the water came in the dam. Under the water, you could hear the rumble of the turbines and the powerhouse."

Hunter and Colly: **A bright idea**

John Stone Hunter Wurtele was born around the same time as the light bulb, and by the time he was twenty-three years old Quebec had made history by installing the world's largest hydroelectricity generator near Shawinigan; Hunter promptly got a job there. Later he surveyed the Banff-Windemere Motor Road across the Canadian Rockies in 1911. After washing his clothes in a convenient hot spring, he noted it could be a wonderful place for tourists; it became Radium Hot Springs. Hunter would eventually rise to the position of Vice-President of the Southern Canada Power Company (later the Power Corporation), after designing and building dams, power plants, and distribution networks across Canada.

When he was thirty-six, Hunter met Edith "Colly" Douglas Fairweather, a New Brunswick woman with Scottish roots. Colly's father was a Commander in the Navy who claimed his ancestors came over on the Mayflower, which perhaps explains why, along with growing up on the seaside, Colly had an undying love for the sea all her life. She painted seascape oils in the house at Acton Vale, trying to recreate the sounds and smells of the sea, making up for the absence of seagulls and crashing waves. The oils still hang on the walls.

Not **the iPod**

Rhoda was watching her brother Edgar playing tennis with his friends one day when the hurdy-gurdy man came by with his hand-cranked barrel organ. Edgar paid him to stay and entertain them with songs like "That's Peggy O'Neil" during their games—"A long cry from the stereos of today," she says.

What does it say about two young girls that they found an enclosed space with walls and doors scarier than swimming at the head of a roaring dam, or flying off a 125-foot ski jump?

While visiting their cousin's farm in Farnham in the Eastern Townships, the twins cornered cows and jumped on their backs, running bovine races; then they found some green oats and fed it to the horses. "They nearly exploded," remembers Rhona, who hadn't realized the oats would swell. While their father was checking out another powerhouse he'd designed nearby, the twins were fascinated by the cement waterway that led the water, churning and frothing, to the dam. "So of course we jumped in," Rhona says. When that wasn't exciting enough, they got into the powerhouse and found a window that looked out on where the water entered the sluices. So of course they dove out that window. "It was so deep and bubbly that it didn't hurt at all," Rhona recalls. "See, that was the beginning of the idea, using bubbles where divers enter the water. Unfortunately, some people saw us and reported it to the powerhouse managers..."

The open expanses outside of the city seemed to bring out wildness in the girls. In their country house in Acton Vale they were delighted to get a horse named Phil from their parents. But if the beast thought it was in for gentle trots down country lanes, it had

Bovine rodeo at Farnham, Eastern Townships, Quebec, with Rhoda riding: the country brought out their wildness.

another think coming. The girls quickly pushed Phil to his limits, too. The horse had to navigate trails they bushwhacked through the woods, traipse up mountainsides, swim down rivers. On one excursion they crossed a swamp and the horse got stuck. The more it struggled, the deeper it sank. "We had to get branches and stick them under its stomach," says Rhoda. "We did get it out, finally."

It was that horse that brought them to another level of play, more common to boys, but which seemed a natural extension to the twins. Without hesitation, they slung their BB guns over their shoulders, hopped on Phil, and set out to explore the wild lands of cowboys and Indians. The Western movie was gaining popularity at the time, and in the 1920s and '30s great epics with little dialogue (even after the first talkie Western in 1929) and the spectacular scenery of the American West captured their imagination. In those films, life was reduced to its basic elements—so basic, in fact, that women were extremely rare except as saintly housewives or gold-hearted prostitutes. But the Westerns did feature outsiders and wild men, facing harsh mountains, trying to live up to codes of honour, and bemoaning the regrettable arrival of civilization. Those themes resonated with the young girls, and would stay with them as they faced a different kind of frontier.

The house in Acton Vale, 1970s.

In another play-acting game, the twins chose an époque even more renowned for ignoring women—the culture of Ancient Greece. "We were taking a class called Ancient History," says Rhoda. "Well, we loved it because they talked about the Olympic athletes and how they gathered together; they rode in on their chariots with olive branches on their heads, for their country." Fascinated by the Greek's sporting and warrior culture, they soon

The Montreal Ski Club

In 1911, skiers await their turn during a ski jumping championship hosted by the Montreal Ski Club on Côte des Neiges.

With a bold and apparently egalitarian motto—"Every man, woman, boy or girl in Montreal out on skis—or in their graves!"—the Montreal Ski Club aimed high. Nonetheless, after its founding in 1903 it was twenty years before the club held the first "Ladies' Race." Even the McGill downhill ski club formed in 1928, the Red Birds, didn't have women on its roster. "Given the attitude of the day, nobody so much as thought of admitting women," says Robert Stewart in his book *The Trail Breakers*.

built their own chariot to attach behind what must have been by this time an extremely patient horse. "Then we shocked the villagers of Acton Vale," says Rhoda, a mischievous grin still on her lips. It may have been the only time the inhabitants of that quiet village witnessed the triumphal entry of two young girls on a chariot; they could have had little idea the two would be true champions in a few short years.

What were they to make of the two girls swinging from tree to tree, Tarzan-like, as they tried to cross the forest without touching the ground? Or of the twins bending back saplings and launching themselves like catapult fodder into the nearest tree? Or, turning their eyes to the Appalachian foothills in the autumn, of the twins, impatient waiting for the coming snows, on their brothers' old jumping skis dug out of the Rectory closets, skiing down the slopes on leaves? And

Phil the horse gets co-opted for the Olympics again. The twins built the cart in Acton Vale from the remains of their brother George's Model T. From left, Rhona, cousin Mary Moore, cousin John, Edith Fairweather in the lap of Rhoda. 1936.

today's kids think that *they've* invented extreme sports.

When the twins weren't inventing new sports, they would try their hand at construction; one summer they built a shack under the back veranda from an old icebox. While both twins sawed and hammered, Rhoda especially enjoyed construction.

"I was always fascinated by Dad doing carpentry," says Rhoda.

"Oh, we were just having fun," the twins say, with impish grins that haven't quite worn off since childhood. "We wanted to be boys." Rhona and Rhoda display their new skis they got that Christmas. Val-Morin, 1937.

Montreal **Centre of Sport**

Since Montreal was the economic, cultural, and academic centre of Canada at the time, most firsts in Canadian sports began there. When the Montreal Curling Club was formed in 1807, it was the nation's first sporting club. Montreal also proved essential to the development of football, ice hockey, track and field, and golf. When the Montreal Amateur Athletic Association (MAAA) was formed in 1881 to provide "rational amusements and recreation for its members," it proclaimed itself a national regulatory body for sports, even though its members had trouble travelling or even communicating with the rest of the country.

The MAAA Winged Wheel.

The twins on the river at Ile Bigras, with some of the "Yak Ski Club", 1930. From left: Rhoda, Marg Ironside, unidentified skier, Rhona, Paul Marchand, Ruth Salter.

"After we got married and visited home, Rhona would go upstairs and help our babies, and I'd go downstairs and make things with Dad." She found it infinitely more preferable than sewing or knitting—although she and Rhona would eventually do that too, for the troops during the war. But Rhoda has never lost touch with the builder in her. Not too long ago she used to go do construction work for her nephew Scott, son of Edgar, at Niagara-on-the-Lake, "Whenever I'd get bored with Toronto," she says. "I'd be on duty at 7 a.m. Even operated the backhoe for awhile."

If anyone had tried to tell the young girls that what they were doing was good for their bodies, was conditioning, training for future contests, they probably would have laughed outright. What they were doing was purely for fun. There was little thought about breaking new ground, certainly no ideas about opening doors for girls and women. It was an attitude they keep to this day, and it is one often found among pioneers in sports.

"We were very fortunate having each other," says Rhoda. "There was always somebody to do things with, who was as good at the same thing."

"I WISHED I WAS A BOY"

Slowly, as the girls got older and entered the 1930s, they began to notice that the freedom they had among their family wasn't always there outside the home. The first time Rhona remarked on it was when they wanted to enter organized sports. "I always wanted to play hockey with a team," Rhona says.

Although women's hockey had been played since just after 1900, it was almost impossible to imagine an organized young girls' hockey team, even after the swinging 1920s. Among the dangers facing older girls on the ice were fights, stitches, and ridicule from the men. They were indeed rough girls that tried it, often working class, usually unafraid about what people thought. So no upper middle-class mother was going to let *her* girl enter into that fray.

The Gore Bay girl's hockey team from Manitoulin Island, Ontario, 1921. Among the dangers were fights, stitches, and ridicule from men.

"I wished I was a boy," says Rhona, "so I could play hockey." Hockey for girls would only start getting organized in the 1960s.

"All the sports we did," adds Rhoda, "we just played with the boys."

In the sports world there was a distinct lack of women heroes Rhona and Rhoda could look up to and emulate. Granted, some amazing advances had been going on in the world of sport—the 1928 Amsterdam Olympics were the first where women competed in track and field, and the Canadian Matchless Six (see Myrtle Cook sidebar) were a sensation—but these women were all in Toronto. In London, England, women competed in the 1934 British Empire Games in thirteen track-and-field events, including the storied 800-metre. But sports for women in Canada were often still reserved for moneyed families, daughters whose daddies belonged to the

WILD JOY AND TOKES **WITH PLUMMER**

A young Christopher Plummer.

With their proper upbringing and encouraging parents, Rhona and Rhoda were good girls, naïve by their own admission. When they pushed their limits, it usually meant doing as good as they could in sports. But their friends and acquaintances had their wild sides; were they drawn to Joy Thomson because she pushed her own limits too?

Perhaps Joy Thomson's parents were stricter with her, and that's why she had to rebel harder than anyone else. Her father was P. A. Thomson, the man who, with A. J. Nesbitt, had become Hunter Wurtele's boss. The pair amalgamated all the hydro companies they could find to establish Power Corporation of Canada in 1925. The name was apt. Thomson would become one of the wealthiest men in Montreal, and the company would become a multibillion-dollar financial, industrial, and communications holding company that spanned the world.

Meanwhile, little Joy was growing up, and reveling in her own power. She had a nursemaid until she was sixteen. Then, while most people were still scraping together pennies near the end of the Depression, her parents gave her a car. "Then she just went wild," says Rhoda. "She smashed it up immediately. That's when we started getting into the wine."

One day Joy decided to put on a play at the family's sprawling Westmount mansion on The Boulevard; the twins were roped into playing parts too. The *crème de la crème* of Montreal society women turned out for the amateur production in the backyard tennis court; or perhaps they too were pressed into being an audience.

"Of course Rhoda and I were anything but actors," says Rhona. "We were going to raise money for the SPCA. But when Joy's mother saw the costumes—Joy had her father's best top hat on—she nearly flipped." It would turn out to be the least of her worries. As Joy grew older, she found she couldn't shake the theatre bug.

"Joy was always into theatre," says Rhoda. "One time we got into the sauce, that actor was there, what was his name?"

"Plummer," says Rhona.

"Christopher Plummer," Rhoda says. "He was a friend of Joy's. They taught us about 'tokes'.

Which I didn't touch. Except I certainly tried it—never again in my life."

"Oh, I don't remember that," Rhona says.

Christopher Plummer had been a student at Montreal High School, and acted in his first play there. He went on to act and study with Joy Thomson, acting at the Stratford Festival, on Broadway and London's West End, and in television and films (including something called *The Sound of Music*), in 2007 he is still active in film and occasional theatre, and writing his autobiography. A one-time resident on Pine Avenue, Plummer had his own early brushes with fame: his high-school band included Oscar Peterson and Maynard Ferguson. "It was some hot school band, I'll tell you," he says.

All the tennis court's a stage: from left, Rhona, Joy Thompson, friend Alfreda Wallace, and Rhoda get the theatre bug, 1930s.

"I've written about the early Montreal days," he said in a *Globe and Mail* interview in 2002, "which I knew very well. I knew every bar—there were about 345 of them—so I have some damn good stories to tell. I want to paint Montreal as a rather fantastic city, which it was, because nobody knows today what it was like. And I'm one of the last survivors, or rapidly becoming one."

For her part, Joy, after studying at McGill, would go on to be a leading figure in the creation of English Montreal theatre, a founder of the Canadian Art Theatre, the Mountain Playhouse, and the Mount Gabriel Tent Theatre in the Laurentians. She then moved to New York and became a specialist in mime, along the way earning a far-reaching reputation. *Globe and Mail* theatre critic Herb Whittaker described her as "rich, eccentric and dynamic, so talented and gifted in many different ways."

Christopher Plummer called Joy Thomson "the only true eccentric" he knew. Shortly after her death in 1996, the National Gallery of Canada announced the creation of a $1.5-million endowment fund "in honour of Joy Thomson, philanthropist, artist and visionary."

Club. Nonetheless, in the Halifax Five Mile Swim championship in 1928, women won eight of the first eleven prizes; sixteen men had entered the race. In Toronto, amateur women's softball consistently attracted larger crowds than men's professional baseball. Paradoxically, these rough and ready girls still had to have chaperones wherever they went, as if they were debutantes at teas and socials. The first Canadian woman to have a sports column, *Toronto Daily Star* writer Alexandrine Gibb, thought calling them chaperones ridiculous in 1925. "They're really managers," she said.

"We liked tennis," says Rhoda, "we always had a partner." Rhoda middle left, Rhona middle right, with unidentified (extra) partners, 1930s.

When the Depression hit Montreal, it was no coincidence that people living on top of the mountain were above a lot of the more difficult times. There, people could still play tennis, golf, badminton—and ski. Rhona and Rhoda grew to be teenagers in that era, and their father was in no danger of losing his job. Their concerns at the time were those of young girls going to a private school. Schoolbooks were expensive, they remember; they had to share one, which led to a few minor fights. Trafalgar School for Girls, which they started attending in 1930 at the age of eight, wanted to separate them into different years; they wouldn't hear of it. "We were very even anyway," says Rhoda. "Who would they put ahead or back? We liked it that way."

Emile Allais
World Champ

Frenchman Emile Allais revolutionized ski techniques by introducing parallel skiing, called the French Method at the time. The French and Swiss kept their skis side by side and dove down the hill, unlike those using the Arlberg technique (featuring the snowplow). Allais also was the first to wear pants specifically crafted for skiing. All of these things gave him the edge. Allais won two silvers in the 1935 World Championships, two bronze medals at the 1936 Olympics, and owned the podium at the 1937 World Championships in Chamonix, taking three golds. The following year at the Worlds he took a gold and two silvers. Many racers soon chose to use Rossignol's Emile Allais ski. Yet the "father of the parallel ski" was a modest man, who would start his own school, help develop ski resorts and come in 1948 to coach a fledgling Canadian Olympic team that included two bright young women stars: Rhona and Rhoda Wurtele.

"OUR GREAT HEROES"

The twins' brother George performing some early extreme skiing, at Acton Vale copper mine, late 1930s.

Up in the hills north of Montreal in the winter of 1932–33, when the twins were ten years old and getting ready to ski jump, the rarified world of skiing began to slowly change. Two events would influence Rhona and Rhoda greatly: the creation of Foster's Folly, and the unlikely appearance of Penguins in Quebec.

Since the turn of the century, skiing in the Laurentians had been the domain of the brave or the foolish. Equipment was costly, but so was getting out to distant hills. Before the 1930s skiers often shared railcars with lumberjacks and miners, dodging spittoons and coarse language. Even more daunting to dilettantes, however, was the workout the potential skier had to go through in order to pursue the sport: first you had to climb the mountain, often with seal skins strapped to the bottom of your skis to add grip (the hooked tip on many early skis provided a place to hook the skins). Then, after walking sideways up a forested mountain in the middle of winter for three hours, you had a good fifteen minute run down, picking your way through the forest—bushwhacking, as ski pioneer Herman "Jackrabbit" Johannsen called it. There would be no one else on the slopes, save for the occasional pack of wolves. No wonder most early downhillers were looked upon as slightly mad. Until the 1930s, they'd been the equivalent of today's extreme sports thrill-seekers.

But that winter of '31, on a cold day after New Year's,

How to dress for
skiing, 1937

Movie star Gladys Swarthout models the height of fashion for the 1930s.

"Clothes for skiing have come to take a definite, if not important place in milady's wardrobe of today. There must be a certain classical perfection about her outfit. 'Practical' was the word applied two years ago, now it is still 'practical' but also 'chic'. Put a little thought and time into the selection of your costume, that it may be graceful, showing off to advantage and creating the impression that you are 'sporty' but not 'hardy.'"

— Canadian Ski Year Book, 1937

Canadian ski champion Alex Foster took a four-cylinder Dodge that he used in summer as a taxi, jacked its back wheels off the ground, and wrapped a 2,300-foot manila rope around the rear axle. The other end looped around the top of Shawbridge's Big Hill. It was the first rope tow in North America, and magically sent skiers schusshing *up* the hill with hardly any effort on their part, and in a matter of minutes. It would change skiing forever, and help make it hugely popular. For a while, any ski resort worth its salt had to boast of a rope tow, a hot dog stand, and a two-holed outhouse. At twenty-five cents for half a day, Foster's tow never made money. But the next winter, Fred Pabst of Milwaukee Brewery fame opened one a little further north in the village of St. Sauveur; he eventually owned tows all over the province, and then in New England, Wisconsin, and Minnesota. Soon, all over North America hills began to sprout rope tows and downhill ski runs. By 1936, the brand-new Sun Valley resort in Idaho installed the first chair lift, attracting the likes of Clark Gable and Gary Cooper. The lifts were modelled on Union Pacific Railway's banana lifts in Central America. To answer the new style of skiing where climbing wasn't necessary, a different kind of binding was also needed. In 1935 Kandahar bindings were introduced, which kept the heels fastened to the skis.

By the 1930s in Quebec, trains reserved exclusively for skiers, cheap and quick, brought an unending stream of people eager to party all weekend. Competitive racing kept pace: in Europe, the FIS world championships for men and women began in 1931, while the Arlberg-Kandahar championships for both had been going on since 1928.

Despite the advances, downhill skiing wasn't quite ready for prime time yet. In the midst of the worldwide Depression, the US hosted the 1932 Winter Olympics for the first time in North America, at Lake Placid, New York. Downhill and slalom skiing were still excluded, fringe sports that Jackrabbit's Norwegian countrymen regarded with distaste. But the third Winter

Olympics were a struggle at the best of times. Held in a town of fewer than four thousand people, organizers had to scrape the barrel to raise money. Only half the previous number of athletes could show up (all paid their own way), and most of them were North American.

Rhona and Rhoda were only ten years old when skiing was getting this new shot in the arm, but they kept up to date on the latest skiing trends through their brother Edgar; in fact, they idolized him and wanted to do everything he did. Women had been watching these trends for a few years now, too, but from the sidelines—and they were getting restless. They'd seen the men form skiing clubs, the Montreal Ski Club and the McGill Red Birds, which provided instruction, competition, and camaraderie. Although women had been excluded from other sports in the past, this time they weren't prepared to be out of the loop.

Edgar "Wally" skiing in 1932: the twins wanted to do everything he did.

So that year Betty Sherrard and her friends, chummy with the Red Bird men, formed the Penguin Ski Club, the first women's ski club in Canada. Skiing legends Percy Douglas and Jackrabbit Johannsen came on board as honorary founding members. In the *Canadian Ski Annual* of 1933, Sherrard wrote that the club set out to "help its members enjoy skiing to the fullest, and secondly, to advance the standard of ski proficiency amongst women."

"The Penguins were our great heroes," recalls Rhona, "the Johannsens [Peggy and Alice], and Pat Paré [see page 64]. They were the racing girls—and the Molsons had bought a clubhouse for them."

John Molson of brewing fame did indeed construct a clubhouse for the Penguins, but not until 1939, just as the Depression was waning—and Prohibition in the States shutting down. Before that happened, both the Red Birds and the Penguin Ski Club had rented rooms on Main Street in St. Sauveur, the sleepy village nestled in a valley of gently sloping hills. The rooms were cramped and cold, and the bathtub sometimes held the potato harvest during the winter. The Penguins rented two rooms in what now houses the Banque Nationale in St. Sauveur for many years, at fifty cents a bed; later they moved to a two-storey clubhouse for forty-five dollars a winter. After that, Molson's clubhouse seemed a palace.

It was the Penguins and the Red Birds who began to build the base for the St. Sauveur ski resort and, soon after, the premier resort in Quebec, Mont Tremblant. In 1932 Tremblant held the first Quebec Kandahar race, an offshoot of a race begun by the Kandahar Ski Club in Switzerland (officially open to men only). By 1938 the wild slopes of Tremblant would be well tamed, with Canada's first "aerial ski chairs," whisking skiers up the hill with no effort "at the pace of a brisk walk."

All of this skiing provided not only a unique opportunity for sport and friendship, but also, for many of the young women heading out on the ski train for the weekend, their first taste of freedom. Some of the early skiers Rhona and Rhoda heard and read about were skiing sisters: Hélène McNichols, the first winner of the Penguin Combined Championship, competed with her sisters Madeleine and Françoise, all of whom learned to ski in Chicoutimi; Pat Paré, who went on to

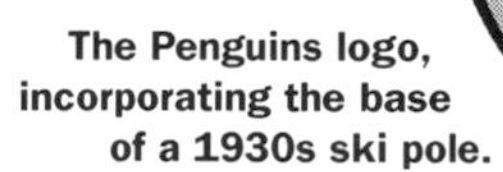

The Penguins logo, incorporating the base of a 1930s ski pole.

Jack Rabbit **Johannsen**

Not everyone was a convert to the new-fangled approach to skiing. Herman "Jackrabbit" Johannsen, who helped develop St. Sauveur and Mont Tremblant operations, returned to the back country in 1933 at the age of fifty-eight: "I've frozen enough going downhill. I'll be damned if I'll freeze going uphill, too," he mumbled.

Jackrabbit had every right to be cranky. Born in 1875, he visited Quebec frequently at the beginning of the century, and then, having fallen irrevocably in love with the Laurentians, finally moved there in 1929. Johannsen was a Norwegian who'd skied with Roald Amundsen, the first man to the South Pole, and Firdtjof Nansen, who had skied across Greenland and introduced skiing to the Alps. A lifelong proponent of ski touring, he was a true pioneer of skiing in the Laurentians, indeed, in all North America. At age 107 he was inducted into the Canadian Sports Hall of Fame. He lived to the age of 111.

Sleeping in at the new Penguin Clubhouse. Rhona and Lorna Casgrain, plus dog, spring 1942.

win numerous national races and become the first woman ski instructor in Canada, brought along her sister Alphonsine; and Peggy and Alice Johannsen were daughters of the unstoppable Jackrabbit—and wouldn't that make them the first ski bunnies?

The brand-new Penguin Ski Club got an early boost by corralling a wayward Russian nobleman to teach them skiing. How did Duke Dimitri Beauharnais of Leuchtenberg, a former Calvary Officer who summered in the Alps, come to bring his dashing figure to Hill 70 in St. Sauveur? Nobody mentioned a reason, although he may have been fleeing Bolsheviks. Perhaps having a former warrior in their midst helped morale; everyone around the world was feeling, if not the effects of the Depression, the tension growing between nations. The coming Winter Olympics were to be in Germany, which when chosen as the host country had been a democracy; suddenly it was a dictatorship under Adolf Hitler, who had recently deprived all German Jews of civil rights.

The Ski **Trains**

The Canadian Pacific Railway inaugurated weekend service from Montreal to the ski heaven of the Laurentians in 1927, a good four years before Americans figured out ski trains. In the first year they carried 11,000 passengers, but by the late 1930s, twenty-five trains were carrying 25,000 skiers each weekend.

The Canadian National Railway also ran regular ski specials to the Laurentians in the 1930s. In 1933 the CN-CPR Act was passed and by 1936, says Donald MacKay in *Train Country*, cooperative passenger services between CN and CPR were implemented.

Taking the ski train in 1940 to Ste. Agathe: From left, Rhoda, Joy Thompson, Rhona, Libby Elder.

SKIING'S GOLDEN YEARS—
BEFORE THE STORM

Once again, the twins' oldest brother and hero Edgar must have known something was up; after all, he kept himself well informed. "He used to stay up all night with his headphones on, listening to and calling all over the world on his ham radio," says Rhoda. "We were not allowed to step into his room. Except once, he called me and said, 'You gotta come here and listen to this kid sing. She's gonna be really famous.' You know who it was? Judy Garland." Aside from a talent for predicting future stars, Edgar must also have seen war coming. In 1935, when he was twenty-two, he signed up for the Royal Air Force in England.

Ski poster promoting Quebec, 1940s.

"He loved it, it was his meat," says Rhoda. He soon rose to become the youngest RAF Group Captain at the age of twenty-eight during World War II.

Meanwhile, Germany prepared for the show of the Winter Olympics at Garmisch-Partenkirchen in Bavaria. The government temporarily took down anti-Semitic signs throughout the country and allowed Jews to compete, and the Games were on—though not without their controversies.

At last, alpine skiing would make its debut in the Olympics, with categories of downhill, slalom, and combined. Medals were only given for combined results. Downhill skiing was now not only legitimate, but also playing out its golden years. With an international audience, alpine skiing was dramatic, fashionable, and glamorous. Chair lifts began making appearances across Europe and North America; the Montebello Seigniory Club held the first women's Dominion Ski Championships, something Rhona and Rhoda would come to dominate.

Germany too wanted to use the trendy sport of skiing to its advantage. Britain's ski guru Arnold Lunn wrote that Germany raced to prove that Nazism was better than democracy. "The course was closed to all competitors the day before the race. The Nazis, we subsequently learned, practiced down the course at dawn."

The Germans won the golds, but it was Frenchman Emile Allais and a Norwegian who stole the show on the slopes—although a wild group of four Ottawa women skiers also attracted a lot of attention.

Mrs. Diana Gordon-Lennox, Mrs. Lois Butler, Miss Marion Miller, and Mrs. Edward Chamier just happened to be in Europe at the time of the Olympics; three of them were wives of Canadian diplomats. The Canadian Amateur Ski Association had no instructor, no coach, and absolutely no funding for a ski team for the Olympics, so when the women called the Association to ask if they could represent Canada in skiing, "Well, sure," was all they could say. And with that, the women had passed the rigorous Olympic qualifications: they were willing to pay their own way. The American women had paid their own way, too, but at least they had training. On top of it, the Canadian women were walking wounded: Gordon-Lennox had a broken finger, Chamier had a bandaged foot, and Miller was just recovering from an illness. And yet, they made a lasting impression. Diana Gordon-Lennox became "the most popular skier in Garmisch," according to her peers; with her arm in a cast, wearing a monocle, fluent in Viennese German, and possessing a bottomless sense of humour, Mrs. Gordon-Lennox crossed the finish line dead last, managing to carry only one pole but keeping her monocle in place the whole time. She received a standing ovation, and a place in Olympic history. Canada's first skiing entry would be at the same time disappointing and inspirational.

It would also be a strong foreshadowing of the next time Canadian women would ski in the Olympics. Twelve years would pass before another Games. In the meantime, skiing would pale in importance next to the major events shaking the world.

Time **to Play**

The 1929 stock market crash and Great Depression in the 1930s hit North America like a heavyweight punch from Joe Louis. But the Depression didn't knock out sports. In fact, with fewer people working, more people had time to watch and play—and listening to the radio was free.

Yet the 1932 Olympics were almost cancelled due to lack of funds, and in the US the NFL lost a number of teams. Les Canadiens won the Stanley Cup in 1930 and '31, but Montreal couldn't support the luxury of two pro teams, and lost the Maroons.

A classic pairing of the 1920s: the Toronto Maple Leafs versus the Montreal Maroons.

Still, the new Maple Leaf Gardens opened for the 1931-32 season. Amelia Earhart started the decade off with a bang for women by flying solo across the Atlantic in 1932.

MYRTLE COOK **AND THE MATCHLESS SIX**

One of the first Canadian women to compete in the 1928 Amsterdam Olympics, and coming into it holding the world record for the 100 metres, the shy Myrtle Cook felt an unbearable pressure. After jumping the starting gun twice in a row, a disqualified Cook was stunned and devastated—the officials had to ask her to leave the track. She cried as the race was run, sobbed as her teammates tried to console her afterwards, and sat down in her white-and-red tracksuit by the canals of Amsterdam and wept.

National Archives of Canada/PA151003

The Matchless Six: Myrtle Cook, staring at the ground again, is third from the right. High jumper Ethel Catherwood towers over the others.

Later during these Olympics, she and Jane Bell, Ethel Smith, and Bobbie Rosenfeld (in 1950 named the Canadian Female Athlete of the Half-Century) handily won the gold in the 4 x 100-metre relay. Along with their teammates Jean Thompson (800 metres) and Ethel Catherwood (high jump) they became the most celebrated athletes of the Games after claiming the women's track-and-field championship. Dubbed the "Matchless Six," upon their return they were met by 300,000 hysterical fans and given a ticker-tape parade in Toronto. In the glory of the celebration, Cook decided "that wasn't the end and I was going to stay in competition as long as I could, and that when finished I would try and train other girls."

She did just that, and much more besides. In 1929 Cook moved to Montreal when the *Daily Star* offered the adored sports heroine her own column, and she soon fell in love with the city—and in love with fellow reporter Lloyd McGowan, whom she married. She continued to compete, breaking more world records in indoor and outdoor races. She tried unsuccessfully to arrange a rematch with Elizabeth Robinson, the American who won the 100-metre dash at the Olympics. In 1931 she reluctantly gave up competition and devoted herself totally to promoting women in sport.

In Montreal she opened a branch of the Canadian Ladies' Athletic Club where she coached budding track-and-field athletes. She organized the Montreal Major Ladies' Softball and Hockey leagues and was the track coach for the armed services during the war. She served on almost every British

Empire/Commonwealth Games Committee and Olympic Committee up to 1972. Her column, *In the Women's Sportlight*, ran for forty years.

She took her work as a sports journalist just as seriously. William Weintraub, reporter for the *Montreal Gazette* in the 1940s, remembers Cook: "At the time newspaper people covering the ski races in the Laurentians, plus public-relations people, photographers and various hangers-on, formed a pretty lively—or I might say rowdy—group. Myrtle was the only woman amongst us...As a former athlete, she was more serious about sport than we were. A good egg but a serious egg." Those close to her, on the other hand, described her as warm and fun-loving.

Rhoda with Clint Melville and a rare sight: Myrtle Cook on skis. Mont Tremblant, 1943.

She spotted the Wurtele twins in 1937, watched them develop and kept a special place for them in her heart. "She called us up all the time," says Rhona. "Myrtle Cook opened the door for women. She was quite wonderful." Myrtle's younger son, Don McGowan, remembers his childhood as one being "dragged all over the Laurentians."

"She called her son her 'little gold medal,'" chuckles Rhona.

Cook was inducted into Canada's Sports Hall of Fame in 1955 in recognition of her athletic achievements, and into the Laurentian Ski Hall of Fame in 1996 as a pioneer ski journalist. She died in 1985. Even though the 1928 Olympic Games were a happy memory for her, her disqualification had prevented her from proving herself. In that way, Myrtle Cook shared a similar disappointment with the twins' missed opportunity at the Olympics of 1948. "There's no question she would have liked another shot at it," says her son, "she took that to her grave."

Canada versus **Germany**

In a huge upset during the 1936 Winter Olympics, Britain beat Canada in hockey, something hitherto unimaginable (until it was learned that eleven of the England-born players lived in Canada). The frustrated Canadians then took on Germany in front of 10,000 fans that included Josef Goebbels and Hermann Goering, and delivered a punishing game of body-checks that foreshadowed more serious things to come. The German crowd reacted with howls and continuous noise, until Goebbels himself stood up and motioned for quiet. Canada won 6–2 and took home silver, the only Canadian medal of the games.

The winning "British" hockey team of the 1936 Olympics.

"TRAF"

Well, let's rephrase that: skiing would pale in importance for some. For young, fit, and active girls with little interest in world politics, sports would become very important indeed. Some might see it as bad timing, coming of age in a world gone mad. But the twins didn't see it that way. They were still on top of a mountain, figuratively and literally.

It was also the time of their first ski trip to the Laurentians. Their godparents, Marg and Wemyss Ironside, invited the teen-aged girls to share a little Québécois-style cabin at Val Morin. Thrilled, the girls took the CPR's Petit Train du Nord for the first time (it would soon become a weekly ritual); at the Val Morin station, horse-drawn sleighs and skiers were dashing off in all directions, and the Ironsides scooped up the twins and brought them to the log cabin. The next day the girls were up at dawn, creating a ski jump. Eventually the adults got moving and everyone went on a "cross-country jaunt." The end came too quickly for the girls, as they had to head back on an earlier train that Sunday. Skiing back to the station, they began to lose their way in the encroaching dusk; they thought they were on a lake, but suddenly the whistle of a train sounded a little too close. In the thick of a heavy snowfall they couldn't know if they were on the train tracks, and so quickly headed up a small hill. The glaring lights of the train bore down, then the train veered slightly and tore by them. It was a relief, even if they had missed the train. But now they knew the way to the station. "It was a ski weekend we would not soon forget," says Rhoda.

Since the age of eight, Rhona and Rhoda had attended Montreal's Trafalgar School for Girls, perched on the hillside on the corner of Dr. Penfield and Simpson streets. Funded and opened in 1887 by Scottish Lords and industrial barons, it was the first English girls' school in Montreal; in 1911 it became affili-

The Trafalgar Ski Team, 1938: Helen Levitt, Rhona, Rhoda, Nancy McKean.

"Best friends": The twins and friends on bicycles, Snowdon, Montreal 1937. Left to right: Nancy McKean, Rhona, Joy Thomson, Elizabeth "Libby" Elder, Rhoda.

ated with McGill University. Today it is the kind of young girls' school that can attract guest lecturers such as David Suzuki, Kathy Reichs, Peter Mansbridge, Marc Garneau—and Margie Gillis, Rhona's famous dancing daughter. But in their teenage years the twins gave little thought to the school's past or present or future. What they really got excited about were the important things: their friends, the latest movies, and beating the pants off everyone else at the Montreal Amateur Athletic Association and swimming competitions.

"We had a little group of girl friends. Called ourselves the POM sisters—the Pride of Montreal, after the bakery I guess," says Rhoda. In those days, girls often ganged together and wore the same colours to boast of their connection, a fashionable thing to do; they had feasts where they tried to see how much they could eat and drink ("Sixty ounces of Flirt and Jumbo," Rhona recalls). "Libby Elder always got sick," Rhoda adds. This was less fashionable.

"We weren't particularly interested in the boys, you know,"

says Rhona. "Just as friends. But we'd go to a movie, go to the MAAA and swim, go sliding down the mountain. There was a law that you couldn't get into the movie theatres before you were sixteen because there had been a big fire and all these children were killed; In 1927 the Laurier Palace Theatre caught fire during a matinee, killing 78 of the 800 people inside. The Catholic Church jumped on the opportunity to push for a ban keeping children from cinemas, which lasted till 1961. So we tried to look older. But we didn't want to lie. We'd go down and they'd say, 'Are you sixteen?,' and Rhoda would say, 'No, we're twins.'"

Their four inseparable friends were Joy Thomson, Elizabeth "Libby" Elder, Lynn Berens, and Nancy McKean. Lynn was the outsider who was always straight and kept to the rules; Joy was talented at anything she tried, from sports to the arts, but she had a blossoming wild side. The twins fell somewhere in between. They had their wild side too, but it usually manifested itself in taking up any challenge when it came to sports.

Of course, the twins being what they were, the sports weren't always ones that had been invented yet. One early spring, Libby Elder was visiting the twins in Acton Vale. As the trio wandered along the Black River, they noticed the ice was breaking up, leaving a lot of "icebergs" floating down river. First they went for a skinny dip in the icy water; then they decided it would be fun to ride an ice floe. Rhona and Libby managed to get on one and headed down river, with Rhoda running along the banks. But after they rounded a curve there was more and more water flowing faster, and they realized they were heading towards a dam and railway bridge. As the floe neared the bridge, Rhoda stood on the span yelling encouragement above. With a huge effort, Rhona and Libby reached for and managed to grab the metal rails above their heads, their feet dangling in the water. With shrieks of excitement, Libby pulled herself up. Rhona soon followed, and the three of them lay exhausted on the bridge as they watched their ice floe fly over the dam and smash into pieces.

The Politics of Sport

In grade school, the twins studied ancient history, learning of the high ideals of Greek Olympians (and learning how to build a chariot too, apparently). At the impressionable age of thirteen, they watched as the next Winter Olympics tried everything it could to avoid mixing politics with sport. It was an impossible task. Hitler had earlier declared the Olympics "an invention of Jews and freemasons," then reconsidered when he saw that it could showcase Aryan right and might. Famed filmmaker Leni Riefenstahl, who

Leni Riefenstahl, skier, actress, propaganda filmmaker.

directed the Nazi propaganda films *Triumph of the Will*, a film of the Nazi rally in 1934, and Olympia, showcasing the 1936 summer games in Berlin, had in fact originally qualified as a cross-country skier for the Olympics, and acted in German ski movies of the 1920s (the genre had already existed since 1902, when the first ski movies were made by the Edison Manufacturing Company—in Canada).

"Just being with our pals seemed to lead to silly fun times," says Rhoda. When Joy and Libby came to visit at Acton another time, they hitched a ride to Drummondville with Mrs. Wurtele, intending to ski the twenty-five miles back home. The skiing got a little boring just schussing beside the road. One thing led to another, and soon the girls were hanging on to the backs of trucks and getting a free tow. "It worked quite well," says Rhoda, "except for the occasional stones." By the time they got halfway they went to the Wickham train station and hitched a ride aboard the train, managing to get invited to the coal car and engine and to blow the whistle as they rolled into Acton Vale.

"We used to do a lot of pretending to drink, as we didn't like it." The twins enjoy a bracing glass of milk after a race.

The twins also loved to go visit their friends, particularly the Elders' country home at Nantel in the Laurentians. There they built pirate rafts, tried to be real live hermits by camping out alone (it lasted one night), and went partridge hunting. As the twins got older, they ventured into more adult territory. After being driven to Ste. Agathe to see "America's singing sweethearts" in *Rose-Marie* at the cinema (for the umpteenth time), the four friends decided to hitchhike back home—but not before making a stop at the Ste. Agathe liquor store. They were dropped off a few miles from the Elders' house, and the party continued after they had walked the rest of the way. "Well, as the party progressed," Rhoda recalls, "things got a bit out of hand and I remember finding Joy upstairs in the bathroom sitting on the floor with her arm resting against the bathroom stove. She had a bad burn, but didn't even feel it. [Libby] Elder was smart enough to know to get tea leaves and make a poultice to bind her upper arm." It was one of their first experiences with parties of that sort, and they found it not to their liking. "We were now deeply into swimming and ski competitions," says Rhoda, "and in fact we used to do a lot of pretending to drink, as we didn't like it. We weren't prudes, but that activity did not appeal."

"They've always been good girls," agrees Rhona's daughter Nancy Andersen. "They didn't drink, they were the ones waxing their skis while the others partied. They turned down invitations from dukes and princes because they knew they were going to compete the next day." Yet at the same time, Nancy says, "They're clubbers, they're gamers; all their lives they've just enjoyed being around people so much."

When pressed, the twins admit that they weren't absolutely perfect; there were fights between them. "About homework," says Rhoda. "We hated it. We had very expensive books, and there was one between us. But that was about it."

"There'd be one punch in the arm," says Rhona. "But every time we ended up hitting each other, we started laughing because it was funny."

Was it like fighting with yourself?

"Well, I don't know about that," says Rhoda. "But there was no jealousy or nastiness that I know of."

The twins' behaviour sounds like a textbook example of what happens when lenient parenting works. "We were pretty free," says Rhona, "and expected to be decent. We were never punished! Even when we broke into a house once and turned on the showers and rode the dumb waiter—but we didn't do any harm. But Joy Thomson's brother went in and wrecked the plumbing and Dad had to pay the bill. Our friends Joy and Libby got into *really* big trouble. They were sent away to Compton." It was a boarding school where troublesome girls were often sent; the twins were sometimes threatened with the school, but never seriously, they say.

Throughout their life, the twins' innocence would let them run headfirst into major figures in sports, politics, and entertainment with a kind of Forrest Gump serendipity. Soon, they would have their own taste of fame. It would never be something they ran after; they would shrug their shoulders and say all they were doing was being the best they could be.

Throughout their lives, the twins' innocence would let them run headfirst into major figures in sports, politics and entertainment with a kind of Forrest Gump serendipity.

A GAMES OF **THEIR OWN**

When women weren't allowed to compete in the Olympics, they always made their own—since the earliest games in Ancient Greece.

In the 1890s, French Baron Pierre de Coubertin, the founder of the modern Olympics, aimed to "make men" in a competition "completely egalitarian," during the 1896 Games in Athens—without any women involved.

Ancient Greek statuette showing a female athlete: "They run in the following way: their hair hangs down, a tunic reaches to a little above the knee, and they bare the right shoulder as far as the breast."

The reasons for keeping women out of the Olympics were many, but it was publicly stated that women were too fragile physically and psychologically to compete. This would have been news to the Wurtele twins, but even more surprising to women in ancient Greece. When married women were barred from even attending the ancient Olympiad in 782 BC, they simply made their own—the Heraia, named after Zeus's wife who sat beside him on Olympus. Maidens competed every four years in foot races, and were honoured by Greeks as serious athletics.

Almost 2,000 years later, a Greek woman who was barred from competition in the 1896 Games due to her sex was decided to run (and finish) the marathon on her own anyway.

Nineteen women went to the Paris Olympic Games in 1900, and by 1908, thirty-six were taking part in gymnastics, tennis, archery, and figure skating. The first woman to swim at the Games was Australian Fanny Durack, who in 1912 tied the men's winner of the 100-metre freestyle—and did so in a long woollen swimsuit, with a skirt.

But even that rubbed the Olympic founder the wrong way. "It is indecent," he said, "that the spectators should be exposed to the risk of seeing the body of a woman being smashed before their eyes. Besides, no matter how toughened a sportswoman may be, her organism is not cut out to sustain certain shocks." There would be many shocks in the coming decades; and it would more often be men who would have trouble sustaining them, not women.

Enter Alice Milliat, a French woman who founded the Fédération Sportive Féminine Internationale, and organized the first world "Jeux Olympiques Féminins" in 1922, the year the Wurtele Twins were

At the Amsterdam Olympics of 1928, Canadian Fanny Rosenfeld (left) of the "Matchless Six" comes second behind Elizabeth Robinson (middle) of the US.

born. The one-day track meet was a spectacular success, with eighteen athletes breaking world records in front of twenty thousand spectators. The Games were regular events until they finally ended in 1934 in London. When the International Amateur Athletic Federation (IAAF) saw the growing support women received, they finally gave in to Milliat's demands in 1926. The deal was that the women would drop the word "Olympic" from their games, and would abide by IAAF rules; in return, women would be given ten track-and-field events. (In fact, the IAAF reneged and only gave five events: the 100 metres, the 800 metres, the 4 × 100 metre relay, the running high jump, and the discus.)

Women finally competed in Olympic track-and-field events in the 1928 Amsterdam Games, after de Coubertin retired.This was the year Canada's Matchless Six competed to great success, among them Myrtle Cook, who wrote about the Wurtele twins early in their career. When several women lay spent on the ground after running the 800 metres (the winner had set a world record), the horrified IOC pledged to drop all female track events next time. Male competitors threatened to boycott the 1932 Games if the IOC carried out its threat. Still, the women's 800 metres was not run again until the 1960 Rome Games.

Women's fight to be given equal footing in the Olympics has been a long campaign, and it's ongoing. At the 1996 Atlanta Games, twenty-six countries sent only male athletes. Only fourteen women were on the 113-member IOC in 2000. But at the 2006 Winter Olympics in Torino, Canadian speed skater Cindy Klassen shattered all previous Olympic records for both Canadian women and men, when she won five medals in a single Olympics.

"The woman of the games": Cindy Klassen and her record five medals, from the 2006 Olympics in Turin, Italy.

Most women in the long history of breaking into the exclusive male habitat of the Olympics probably didn't have it in mind to change the world. They just enjoyed the games and wanted to compete—and ended up changing the world anyway.

There are piles of scrapbooks, all their accomplishments duly recorded, their cover stories, their fashion spreads in *Vogue*, and, during the peak of their fame, each small thing noted—the twins gave blood today, the twins had a cherry Coke today, the twins won again, first and second. "We didn't really care about all those articles in the paper," says Rhoda. "It was Dad who cut out all those things."

They always say that twins stick close together—certainly Rhona and Rhoda Wurtele lived up to this theory when they finished one and two in the 40-yard free style.

The scrapbooks are all aqua green, sixteen by twenty-two inches, the dates written in felt on the cover, bursting with yellowing clippings, photographs, advertisements; they follow the twins through the years, and by chance just happen to chart the rise and fall of fads, of nations, of hopes and dreams. They begin when the long road to recovery from the Depression is underway, even while far, far away the German Luftwaffe has bombed Guernica, Japan has invaded China, and that woman who began the decade so wonderfully, Amelia Earhart, has this year disappeared somewhere above New Guinea...

From the first page of the first scrapbook, the twins' future is clearly spelled out for those who care to notice. The girls are fifteen years old, swimming for the Montreal Amateur Athletic Association in January 1937. The first clipping is from what may be the *Montreal Star*:

> They always say that twins stick close together—certainly Rhona and Rhoda Wurtele lived up to this theory when they finished one and two in the 40 yard free style last night in the M.A.A.A. pool.

Then this, in Myrtle Cook's April 1937 *Montreal Star* column, "In the Women's Sportlight":

> Those two Wurtele girls—twins—cause the press folk headaches—still don't know which is Rhoda Isobel [sic] and which is Rhona Grace—do you? They swam on

opposite relays just to make it more complicated...After the race this reporter asked, "Whose team is that?" "Miss Wurtele's" answered the man at the desk. "Which Miss Wurtele?" insisted this corner. "Don't know—gosh, I can't tell them apart. You'll have to ask so-and-so." So-and-so didn't know either. Exit reporter.

In the same column, there's a nice little peek into life on top of the mountain in the Depression: not everyone is riding the rails, or homeless, or under attack:

> Sporting a sun tan that was the envy of the feminine portion of last night's MAAA swim gallery, Joy Thomson caught the eye...
>
> "Folks up there want to know where you got that nice tan?" enquired our volunteer reporter. "Trinidad," she replied briefly.
>
> If that is the way the sun treats one in Trinidad then it is too bad more of us can't wend our way to the West Indies. Later in a chat with Miss Thomson, she told this toiler that she had done some riding, played tennis and much swimming while in the south. Had been much in the sun. The even tan was the result.

The twins centred largely on swimming and diving. It was a natural extension of their childhood pursuit in the rivers around Acton Vale.

The *Montreal Star* even covered Trafalgar's School Meet, giving a good half page of pictures and columns to the egg-and-spoon races, sack races, and more common track-and-field events. Joy Thomson swept her intermediate class, with "Grace" and "Isabelle" Wurtele coming close behind her. It would be the last time their rightful place would be taken by Joy.

Then, in October of that year, at an MAAA "Tank Gala" at the "natatorium of the Peel St. clubhouse, crowd-pleasing features included a demonstration of scientific swimming...and the MAAA's young swimming sisters, the Wurtele twins, paced a junior relay team to a clean cut victory of the senior girls." This time in the 40 yards, Rhona came first, Rhoda second.

The first years of competition for the twins centred largely on swimming and diving. It was a natural extension of their childhood pursuit in the rivers around Acton Vale, at Ile Bigras and around their father's hydroelectric dams. Swim meets were still a hugely popular draw for crowds, perhaps still somewhat novel; since the events cost little to nothing to attend, they got capacity crowds during the Depression. The local papers got into the spirit too, and in a 1938 meet at the Nôtre Dame de Grace (NDG) Lions Boys' Club "one of the largest crowds ever to witness a local swim meet" turned out. The bright red ribbons for two Firsts and one Second are still pasted in the twins' scrapbook; by 1939, after a Trafalgar School Annual Swim Meet, they get their first headline: "Wurtele Twins Shine."

But at one point an ordinary-looking flyer appears pasted in the pages, torn, water-stained, well handled:

> Interscholastic Ski Meet
> St. Sauveur
> Under auspices of
> Red Birds Ski Club
> Penguin Ski Club
>
> ---
>
> $1,50 children for round trip
> from Montreal to St. Sauveur

On the other side of the page is a 1938 *Montreal Daily Herald* picture of the Trafalgar girls' ski team, Rhoda and Rhona in white; of course they've won first and second in downhill; in slalom, second and fourth. Trafalgar's ski team has beaten out the schools of West Hill High, Montreal High, The Study, Weston, and the delightfully named Miss Edgar and Miss Cramp's. They hold the shield John Molson had donated just the year before; the schoolgirl races would run till 1968.

After that, it is understood: at the Interscholastic Ski Meet, the twins will come first and second. In the early winter of 1940 when the twins were eighteen years old, Myrtle Cook was ready to make her predictions.

His voice sounded like a miner who had just uncovered a gold nugget.

"Just a little more polish and they'll beat the best of them." The Trafalgar ski team at the Penguin Ski House with their Interscholastic Ski Trophy, 1938. Jean Donnelly on left, Rhoda and Rhona in white, unidentified student on right, John Molson in rear. It was their first big race.

> "I've been watching Rhoda and Rhona Wurtele on the hills. Mark my words, they'll take some of the stars into camp if they decide to enter the competitions..."
>
> So, if you should be toiling up the Laurentian slopes and be passed by a couple of identical skiers, don't blame it on the sun. You are seeing "double." Rhoda and Rhona are twins, well known in swimming circles.
>
> Frank Schofield labels the twins as the most promising competitive talent he has seen this season. Frank buzzed our telephone last night. "They ski with dash and verve...just a little more polish and they will beat the best of them."

McGill's Ski Team would be lucky to get them, Cook surmised. "They did consider entering Park Toboggan and Ski Club, but their parents advised them to concentrate on their studies." It was good advice. And like the good girls they were, the twins would listen. For a little while.

PAT PARÉ: **FIRST CANADIAN WOMAN SKI STAR**

Courtesy of Joseph Graham

A young Pat Paré ready for a day of stylish skiing, 1940s.

When Quebecer and Penguin Ski Club member Pat Paré first arrived at the Canadian Ski Championships at Banff in 1938, she looked up at the mountain and thought there must be some mistake—the downhill course looked like an avalanche slope. On the way down, "I made two beautiful falls," she explained, "and can't understand how I won third prize." *The Canadian Ski Year Book* asked, "Who knows how many young girls took up skiing upon reading about her thrilling adventures?"

Well, two eighteen-year-old Wurtele twins, for starters. There was an edge to Pat Paré, and she appeared exotic to the twins because she was French. "She was naughty," Rhona says. "We heard she swore."

When Paré won the gold medal in downhill at Mont Tremblant in February of 1940, Mont Tremblant owner and visionary "Emperor" Joseph Bondurant Ryan, asked her parents if the young woman could teach pro at his new resort.

At the time, the Ski Instructors' Alliance (which had just been founded in 1938) had a strict policy that excluded women. The conflict reflected the heart of attitudes toward women at the time; Quebec women had only won the right to vote the same year. But under pressure from Joe Ryan and others, the Alliance dropped their strictures, and Paré became the first female instructor in Canada. But it wasn't the end of the lessons she herself would learn.

Upon Paré's arrival at Tremblant, Alliance head Hermann Gadner "promptly asked me if I'd like to learn to ski," Paré said. "I realized that my skiing was more nerve than sense. Thanks to Hermann Gadner, I was introduced to a lifelong vocation of teaching people to ski under control."

With the trails cleared, Rhona and Rhoda Wurtele stepped up to the Ski Instructors' Alliance and registered to take the course, too, in 1943. They became qualified instructors, like Paré before them. And decades later, they would open their own club to instruct women—Twinski, which is going strong to this day. Pat Paré died in 2004, at the age of eighty-five.

War and Fame 1940–1946

EIGHTEEN TO TWENTY-FOUR YEARS OLD

SPORTS CASUALTIES OF WAR

Advertisement for Andreef sports equipement, August 1943, in *Canadian Sport Monthly*. New skis are "most probably being worn by some United Nations Ski Trooper."

It was a dangerous time to be young and fit. It was the worst moment to begin a career in sports. And yet Rhona and Rhoda, seventeen years old when the war began, were able to advance quickly through the ranks; within two years the *Montreal Gazette* would call them the most publicized athletes in Canada. There were many reasons for that. The twins gave people something else to think about. Not only were they consistently sweeping sports events, they usually came in first and second, and they were identical, pretty twins; they were like a mobile entertainment unit, in this case entertaining the folks back home with their prowess.

Toronto's *Star Weekly* of November 1942 marvelled at how "reporters, coaches and even their mother has trouble telling them apart. Not only do the Wurteles look alike, they talk alike, dress alike, think alike. They agree on boy friends, movies, hair-dos—everything. In skiing Rhona paces Rhoda until Rhoda catches up; then Rhona paces Rhoda. In swimming they clock each other's sprints. In tennis they play the 'Wurtele championships.'"

"In fact their greatest ambition," wrote Lloyd Lockhart, "is to follow their brother Edgar overseas (RCAF) as ambulance drivers or with the Red Cross. 'That is, providing they let us go together,' they remark."

It wasn't quite true: the twins' greatest ambition at the time was to avoid office work and follow their brothers behind the joystick of a warplane. Two years later, in a *Maclean's* interview, they asked, "What good is a desk when we could be roaring through the air in a plane?"

Whatever women must do they must do twice as well as men to be thought half as good. Luckily, this is not difficult.

- Charlotte Whitton, 1896–1975, *Canadian feminist and mayor of Ottawa, first female mayor in Canada, 1951–56, 1960-64. Whitton was also the star of the women's hockey team at Queen's University, Kingston.*

Amelia Earhart had proved women were quite capable of flying, although she disappeared mysteriously above the Pacific in 1937. Women from the Soviet Union were already flying in combat. But this part of the world wasn't ready for that. In 1943, the *Gazette* reported that the twins were "finding it tough to learn to pilot a plane in Canada in wartime." Nobody would teach them, and they were looking to the United States for schools. Though they had learned to fly through the air (albeit on skis) at a young age, becoming flying aces in Canada was still a long shot. Canadian women weren't allowed to fly military planes, but a handful managed to go overseas to the British Air Transport Auxiliary, joining the 166 other women delivering Hurricanes, Mosquitoes, and Spitfires throughout the British Isles. Among them were Marion Orr, who opened her own flying school in 1949, and Violet Milstead, who became the first female bush pilot in Canada. Hopeful pilots had to log at least 350 flying hours before the Auxiliary—or, later, the Women's Airforce Service Pilots (WASPs) in America—would take them on.

"If they let us fly we're joining up," a still hopeful Rhona told Myrtle Cook in 1944. But the closest Rhona got to piloting was working as a stenographer for the RAF Ferry Command in Montreal, the North American equivalent of Britain's Air Transport (and for whom she competed in swimming in November 1942). For most of the other women working there, it must have been a heady thrill; dashing young pilots from all over the world converged on Montreal before flying their planes to Newfoundland and then taking what the RAF had at first thought a "suicidal" flight over the Atlantic to England. But for Rhona, working in an office instead of being in the action was torture.

"I hated it," she says. "Nobody had anything in common with me; we couldn't talk about skiing or anything. The girls would talk about the boys and that was it. I didn't want to work, I wanted to play."

Canadian society was adjusting to more than the idea of women flying; on the ground every day, parents were coping with the fact of their children going overseas to uncertain futures. The Wurteles already had two boys in the Air Force, Edgar with the RAF in Europe and George with the RCAF in Asia, and their daughter Jean was in England with the Red Cross. It was no surprise that their two youngest wanted to follow them—just as they had followed their brothers off the senior ski jump at Côte des Neiges.

It was Edgar, with the RAF in England since 1935, who set the pace for the family. During the earlier part of the war he flew with the Mediterranean Fleet, thrilling the girls with stories of taking off in Fairey Swordfish or Hawker Fury planes from early aircraft carriers HMS *Furious* and HMS *Glorious* (and landing on them in rough seas, without arrestor hooks to help stop the plane). There were stories of forced landings in London schoolyards, getting lost in the desert, and being made member "of various fancy clubs, especially in Malta." By 1941 he became the youngest Group Captain in the RAF, heading the First Canadian Torpedo Bomber Squad at the age of twenty-eight. Two years later, Edgar, better known now among the fly boys as "Wally" ("His pals in the RAF felt that 'Wally' Wurtele went with a swing," reported the *Montreal Standard Magazine* in December of 1941), met and married a beautiful English milkmaid (she delivered milk for the war effort), Lorna Scott. The way he met her proved to the twins they should avoid too much "girly" behaviour. "Edgar met her when he was dating her sister," says Rhoda, "while her sister was busy fussing around getting ready upstairs." Later, while commanding

The ferry command

The stork insignia for the Ferry Command that delivered planes from North America to Europe during WWII.

Before 1939, there had been fewer than one hundred successful flights across the Atlantic. With a luxurious salary of a thousand dollars a month and an exotic job, Ferry Command pilots became the envy of men and the object of desire for many women. They delivered almost 10,000 planes to Europe, South America, Africa, and Asia. The Command used temporary wooden buildings at Dorval during the war, William Weintraub writes in *City Unique*, and after the war Montreal was chosen to be the headquarters of the International Civil Aviation Organization. The pilots and their rare passengers braved the cold, often flying over the Arctic with broken or no heaters, and just as frequently with broken instruments and radios. It was their work that established the first transatlantic passenger flights after the war.

The woman **at Fairchild**

Canadian Elsie MacGill, the first woman with an electrical engineering degree in Canada, and the first woman aircraft designer in the world, had worked at the same plant, Fairchild Aircraft, as the twins' brother George. Later she oversaw the design and production of 1,500 Hawker Hurricane fighter planes.

The Maple Leaf II trainer, designed by Elsie MacGill.

Elsie MacGill, 1905 - 1980.

officer of the RCAF station at Lachine, Edgar searched out the Norwegian airmen stationed nearby, coaxing them to ski jump with him in Quebec and Lake Placid. He would stay with the air force all his life, moving around to various bases in Canada and eventually ending up with Air Force Intelligence in Ottawa until his untimely death from a brain tumour in 1960. The family still remembers him flying over the house in Acton Vale in the 1950s in a yellow Harvard and waggling his wings.

Following in the wake of Edgar, George turned out to be no less an adventurer. When he was ten, he had to be rescued by the police after playing Santa Claus too well: he got stuck in the chimney of a house being built down the street. He skied and jumped for Lower Canada College like his brother, but when he tried his first game for the football team it resulted in a broken nose. "He was a peacemaker," says Rhoda, "and we thought he'd become a minister." When war broke out he was working thirteen-hour days for Fairchild Aircraft on Montreal's South Shore, a plant that eventually had seven thousand employees working during wartime. George was ready to fly too, and immediately went to McGill to enlist. After an interminable two-and-a-half-hour wait for an interview, he made it to the desk, then keeled over in a faint. That, the family thought, was the end of his flying. Instead, he registered for the Radio Locator Division and went overseas to England. But soon he sent a photo back home, and the family noticed a white slash on his wedge hat—he had managed to muster into the air force after all. After coming back to Canada to train, he returned overseas to fly DC-3s. George Wurtele's most dangerous mission was "flying over the Hump," the mountain pass between India and China. More than fifteen hundred aviators lost their lives on the route; at one point, half of all planes flying were lost each month. Miraculously, George survived without incident, and returned to Canada after the war to fly for Canadian Pacific Airlines.

The twins' older sister Jean, meanwhile, wasn't looking for

Twins' brother George Wurtele at Fairchild Aircraft factory with a training plane, 1941. Soon after, he was "flying over the hump."

Flying over **the hump**

In 1942, Japan had invaded and occupied Burma, making overland deliveries from India to China impossible. The US agreed to keep China supplied with everything from bombs to medicines, and began flying what became the largest air bridge in the world. The flights were extremely dangerous. Not only did crews have to avoid Japanese attack, but the "Camel's Hump" of the Himalayan mountains attacked them too with violent turbulence and weather. Transport planes like the kind George Wurtele flew did as many as three 800-kilometre round trips a day; due to the scarcity of parts and supplies, crews often ventured into the foothills to gather debris from previous crashes to repair their planes.

that kind of grand adventure; she was the sensitive artist of the family, having studied classical dance, but also fashion design and, later, art under Arthur Lismer of the Group of Seven (later the Jean-gene would most famously transmit to Rhona's two dancing children). But Jean was disappointed when the only work she could get was drawing pots and pans for catalogues. So when the war came, Jean, well enough recovered from her early depression, signed up as a Voluntary Nurse's Aide and joined the Red Cross in England.

The twins' sister Jean Wurtele ready for service with the Red Cross, 1943.

"She was a bit naive," says Rhona. "All the bombing and devastation didn't seem to bother her. She didn't talk about how terrible it was. She was the kind of person who could get the big Buick started in the middle of winter when nobody else could. Or when she was working with the blood clinic in Montreal, and she drove the truck full of blood under an overpass and took the top off, but nothing happened to her. I don't how many things happened like that; it was like she had a guardian angel."

That angel was apparently working overtime when Jean prepared to leave for England, one of 641 women in the Red Cross Overseas Detachment. She had boarded the HMS *Rangatikki* in New York, where the passengers had to observe blackouts and sleep in their clothes; two days out there was engine trouble—"Or was it the threat of a submarine?" wonders Rhoda—and the boat returned to New York. Back in the city, as she was walking down the street with some of the other nurses, a taxi pulled up in front of them. "Isn't that your brother?" a nurse asked Jean. It was Edgar, coming back from the front to take command at Lachine Air Base in Montreal. Jean hadn't seen him for years, but her nursing friend had a photo of him (and must have been keeping an eye on all the young pilots) and recognized him immediately. Edgar generously gave his sister some money, since the girls only had a few dollars between them, and the brother and sister caught up after all those years. Six weeks later, Jean had finally crossed the Atlantic, winding through the Azores to avoid the enemy. She served three years there, working some of the time in a tuberculosis hospital. When Jean returned from overseas she worked in the Children's Ward of Westmount General Hospital. And she always kept her love of performing, dancing like Gene Kelly with an umbrella in *Singin' in the Rain* for meetings of the Red Cross Overseas group, and at the senior's home Fulford Residence in her later years. "Even," Rhoda says, "throwing in her high kick, which she could still do after she was eighty years of age."

They run in **the family**

Like his brother, George married an English woman, Margaret Noble, a nurse; in 2005, their daughter Suzanne (Wurtele) DeMartin had identical twin girls of her own. George's eldest son, Glenn Wurtele, also followed in the family's tradition: for seven years (1984–1991) he was the head coach of the Canadian National Alpine Ski Team; he's been called "the greatest-ever Canadian-born ski coach" by *Ski* magazine.

The twin's nephew, Glenn Wurtele.

LIFE DURING **WARTIME**

If the first casualty of war is truth, sports must be among the walking wounded. In light of what World War II destroyed, of course, sports could not be greatly mourned. Fighting left millions dead, and even more homeless. Lives everywhere were uprooted. Cities and countryside were devastated. Some thought sports a frivolous pursuit while so many were dying. Yet sport became important for two reasons—training young men to fight, and distracting men and women from the horrors at the front. Sports clubs at home did what they could and organized benefits for servicemen.

At its beginning in Canada, the war for most may as well have been taking place in a galaxy far, far away; even though a Montreal ship had been torpedoed just three days into the war, it took a while for the repercussions to reach North America. Canada had joined the war almost immediately, but only enforced conscription years later. Those still maintaining strong connections to the United Kingdom, symbolically or realistically, were often sooner affected: Edgar Wurtele had been training for this moment for years. All too soon, however, the war would affect most Canadians in some way, whether through death or restrictions on their own lives.

Montrealers were prepared for air raids and staged trial blackouts; they suffered through the rationing of tea, coffee, butter and meat and even their beloved maple syrup; the rationing of sugar meant cooks didn't ice their cakes or put sugar dust on their cookies. Men's suits went without cuffs, patch pockets, or vests, and women's skirts were shorter due to necessity, not fashion. The famous Zoot suit riots of Montreal during the 1940s came about partly because people thought the excess use of cloth in the baggy suit was unpatriotic. Still, it wasn't all bad. Brunch at the Ritz was $1.85 plus tip, and Trans-Canada Airlines had begun a Montreal–Toronto route, with three crew and room for ten passengers.

The Zoot suit.

THE TWINS GO TO WAR

With all those exploits going on in the family, it's no wonder Rhona and Rhoda wanted to join the armed forces; like many women of the time, they were eager to take part. The Canadian Women's Auxiliary Air Force division of the RCAF had 17,000 women in World War II; the Canadian Women's Army Corps had 22,000, and the Women's Royal Canadian Naval Service, 7,000. While none had combat roles, they were all volunteers, and many did jobs normally reserved for men.

American wartime poster promoting women at work, 1941-1945.

That said, there was still opposition to women joining the forces in any way. A 1943 survey that asked "How can women best serve Canada's war effort?" found that 26 percent chose "maintaining home life," 23 percent chose "doing work in factories," and only 7 percent chose "joining the armed forces." Generally, women who stayed in Montreal took nursing classes, were air-raid wardens, helped at blood donor clinics or information centres for the many troops stationed in the city, put on theatrical benefits, or packed food parcels for prisoners of war; the Civilian Protection Committee also enlisted women to help police and firemen in emergencies. The biggest contribution from women was replacing men in factories as riveters, welders, and workers dealing with high explosives—the latter work described at the time as "actually safer than working in your own home." Yet the equalization of women in the work force would turn out to be a temporary measure.

So, besides the social pressures, there was also the resistance the twins got from their own family. Hunter and Colly were loath to see their sweet young twins (now grown-up young ladies) fly off towards a thrill that wasn't just hijinks and pranks, but life-threatening. "We wanted to fly, very much so," says Rhona, "but we had three people in our family overseas, so our parents weren't too keen. There weren't any courses open at the time and of course we liked to do things right away."

Then too, their brothers were seeing firsthand the kind of reception women got in the air force. "Our brothers said, 'Don't let the twins join,'" says Rhona. "They were aware what the boys were like."

"We had signed up to do a course fixing cars and trucks for the war effort," says Rhoda. Unfortunately, they got the idea between the times when the course was offered, and so fell into a more traditionally female volunteer role: taking care of children. "We took a play therapy course," says Rhona. "There were all these children sent over from England [as orphans or for protection from the war], and Jean was involved with that and told us about it. We already had an English girl staying with us that Mom had 'adopted.' Mom had thought Anne Collins was a little girl, about five years old; when she arrived she was thirteen months old. Now Mom and Dad had a new daughter, until well after the war, for eight years in fact. Quite an undertaking for Mom, when her own family was all grown up. But Anne was one of the family. Eventually Anne rejoined her parents, who were both majors in the British Army, and ended up in South Africa. Then we had two others for the summers." Their volunteer work might not have been flying planes, but in true Wurtele fashion, they brought all their enthusiasm to their new role.

Of course, what perhaps affected them the most, without their giving it much thought, was their social position. In his book *City Unique*, author William Weintraub (who was a contemporary of the twins and had reported on them in the *Montreal Gazette*), said, "The most active volunteers were usually women from affluent families, daughters who didn't have to work for a living and wives who had maids to do the housework." That described the Wurtele women.

Even so, their father believed in preparing them for any eventuality. They began by training at the Motherhouse, a business school on Sherbrooke and Atwater, where they studied Pitman

Working **Women**

As men returned from the war and women were bundled back to the domestic theatre, their experience of essential war work and acquiring of technical know-how were now only needed for operating the "new and improved" appliances in the kitchens and laundry rooms of the nation. In 1945, Saskatchewan CCF MP Gladys Strum announced in Parliament that "no one has ever objected to women working. The only thing they have ever objected to is paying women for working."

General Electric advertisement, 1950.

shorthand and typed to music with their hands covered by sheets of paper. "We actually rather excelled at this, as it was a sort of competition. The twins won pins for doing 135 words a minute—but they hated the accounting," Rhoda says, referring to herself and her sister in the third person as she often does..

The *Montreal Gazette* was already closely following the twins' athletic prowess, and with it, their personal lives. "Both graduated from business college in June," the paper reported in 1941, "and both are on the prowl for jobs, although Rhona admits they are not looking too strenuously. There is one hitch in this job hunting, though, for as they were always with each other in sports, they insist on being together in their work, so that their eventual employer will have to hire both."

Typing classes, 1940s. "We rather excelled at this, as it was a sort of competition."

They insisted, but the business world wasn't quite as dedicated to keeping them together. They did end up working: "We were secretaries or some damn thing," says Rhona. They both got jobs at the Royal Bank, but Rhoda was at the Westmount branch on Victoria Avenue, Rhona at Bleury and St. Catherine.

"Clock watchers," Rhona says derisively. "I would walk down to the cafeteria and pay a quarter for a three-course dinner; they thought their employees should eat well and keep healthy and produce well. We'd take weekends off and race, and get in some swimming too."

The banks quickly took advantage of their photogenic employees; *Banking* magazine, the journal of the American Bankers Association, featured them in a March 1942 issue, after the Royal Bank's own newsletter called them "Twin ski wonders." *Banking* said, "Last winter saw Montreal's famed Wurtele twins, Rhoda and Rhona, attractive young employees of the Royal Bank of Canada, reach new peaks in their star-studded careers." With a photo of them in natty ski outfits—tight pants, button shirts, ties with pins, and not a glove, hat, or coat to be seen—their employers crowed about them winning nearly every downhill event they entered that season.

WAR

CANADA'S GREATEST INDUSTRY

Starting from scratch—without factories, without trained personnel, without blue-prints — Canada's scant twelve million people have built a tremendous armament industry.

Guns, tanks, motorized vehicles, planes, ships, small arms, explosives—equipment of every kind—are today in mass production. We have created a navy of 400 ships. We have equipped fighting forces of 450,000 men. We have played the major role in the British Commonwealth Air Training Plan, one of the greatest schools for fighting airmen the world has ever seen.

Such in broad outline is Canada's proud record. Much more remains to be done. Still greater effort, still greater self-denial must be the solemn pledge of all till victory is won.

This advertisement is published as a contribution to the general knowledge of our country's war effort and as an inspiration through the days ahead. For reasons of security complete figures are not available. The facts presented, however, are impressive evidence of the growing might of Canada's war machine.

THE ROYAL BANK OF CANADA

Royal Bank ad from the Dominion Swim Champs program.

One such weekend the inevitable happened: work conflicted with sports, and it ended in a knockout. In July of 1942, the Dominion Swimming Championships were to be held at the Ste. Adele Lodge and Country Club, on a Saturday. Rhoda asked for the Saturday off but was refused. The next day she went in to see the manager and handed in her resignation. Rhona followed suit. In their scrapbooks, there are hand-written scribbles beside the programme from the competition: "Twins quit the Banks for this meet! (No Sats off) After 3 months training! Who needs the $40 a month!"

They had the luxury to make that decision. The twins had been winning everything that year, and maybe they were feeling a little cocky; they had been training hard in swimming, and "we didn't have to worry" about having an income, says Rhona. "Which was fortunate for us. We didn't give it too much thought—first things first." Most young women working as stenographers on St. James (now St. Jacques) worked hard for sixty dollars a month; half of that could go towards renting a small room in a building where the bathroom down the hall was shared and the washing was hung on the radiator. Burgeoning Montreal was feeling the housing crunch already. Many women, too, chose to stay at home; Rhona was shocked to learn that some of the girls they worked with gave their whole paycheque to their parents.

"Of course we were fortunate," says Rhoda. "We were able to go skiing and the family took an interest and we just took it for granted; nobody discussed it. But we didn't ski half as much as people thought we did, we just skied weekends. We'd run for the train and practically lie on the floor of the train out of breath until we got to Piedmont. Then to save the quarter we wouldn't take the snowmobile thing they had, we'd hike it all the way to the hill and then climb all the way up the hill and train ourselves, then race the next day."

"We didn't ask for money though," says Rhona. "We were scatterbrains, we had our minds on twenty things all the time. So yeah, we were privileged, we took it for granted. But we appreciated it."

The girls obviously knew what they were doing. That weekend, Rhona took second in the 100-yard freestyle; Rhoda took second in the 100-yard backstroke.

Rhona and Rhoda exercising for *The Standard* magazine of Montreal, 1943. Work conflicted with sports, and it ended in a knockout.

"IF YOU ENJOY IT, YOU WORK HARD"

Rhona and Rhoda might not have liked working in an office, but the energy, time, and commitment they put into the hard work of training and sports competition seemed like play. That is evident even today when Rhoda talks about anyone who makes the choice to go into a sports career: "If you enjoy it, you work hard. If you don't care, forget about it."

A look at the 1941 *Gazette*'s recapping of their early years before their first major competition makes clear just how busy they were:

> Rhoda perhaps has a slight advantage over her sister. She gives way to her twin in the swimming, but is a shade faster on the cinder path, a little better on skis, and a mite superior in tennis, although in all those sports they have to fight it out to see who emerges the winner each time. In basketball, they are about on a par.
>
> Both were on the first line of the Trafalgar basketball squad, from 1938 to 1940, and in the final year Rhona was the team captain. But just to show her, twin Rhoda was the aggregation's leading scorer. But when it comes to speed swimming, Rhona stars.
>
> During the winter the twins spend their spare time skiing, for that is admittedly their favorite sport. And they do quite well, too. Top women's ski club around the Laurentian Zone is the Penguins, to which they not only belong, but represent very prominently in a good many of the Zone races. Rhoda is the Penguin club champion, having beaten out Peggy Austin for the title, while Rhona came third in the same competition.
>
> They were both on the Trafalgar ski teams which did so well in 1938, '39, and '40. In 1940, Rhona was captain,

> and twin Rhoda took top spot in both the downhill *and* slalom...
>
> Rhoda was kept inactive in a skiing way for the greater part of last winter, for she had her appendix removed in November, and was under doctor's order not to don skis before March at the earliest. However, although not racing, she was schussing around the Laurentians on every occasion. She finally was able to show her stuff in the ladies' Provincial meet at St. Adele, where she tied Yvonne Godmer for second place in the slalom, and came fifth in the downhill. And all this in her first year of racing outside of schoolgirl meets, as well as being her first full season using downpull harness.
>
> In Rhona's first excursion into big-time skiing, she tied Dorothy Michaels, former Canadian champion, for third place in the open standing of the twin slalom meet...and placed first in Class C. In her first run, she beat the highly-touted Eleanor Boyle, from Lake Louise, by over 16 seconds.
>
> And they play tennis too. Rhoda was junior net champion at school, while both were on the tennis team... Together in every sport, they spend practically all their remaining time together too.

Together in every sport, they spend practically all their remaining time together too.

One of the few sports they didn't continue in was basketball, a sport Myrtle Cook tried to interest them in. The twins voice a rare complaint about the women's teams. "We played women's rules in school, where you had to stand when you got the ball—but when we tried out for another team after Trafalgar, they played men's rules where you just keep running all over the place. And because they were used to playing together, they didn't pass the ball to us. We were mad as heck."

It's not only obvious the girls were busy, it is equally obvious they were extraordinary in their pursuits: nobody beats anybody by

With required hats: from left, Rhona, Joy Thomson, Rhoda, Libby Elder, all about 16 years old in 1938.

sixteen seconds in skiing anymore. Sixteen hundredths of one second, maybe. And all of this activity came in their first year of racing outside of school. Apparently, the only way to keep them back was to put one out of commission. While Rhoda was in the hospital for her appendix operation, wrote Lloyd Lockhart in the *Montreal Star Weekly*, her twin Rhona "languished about—did a little skiing—didn't win anything—didn't care." It was the longest period they endured without each other's company, "ten long, dreary days." Always being together, of course, was part of their secret powers, something they had long ago learned as young children. Together, they could surmount anything, conquer anyone; separately, and without the other's constant encouragement, they felt lost. They would live seven more years like that; then, after a spectacular double wedding, pursue their separate lives on opposite coasts of the continent. They would never again be so close.

"They were a force to be reckoned with—as a duo," says Rhona's daughter, Margie Gillis. "They bounced off each other. They sheltered each other from the storm. And they would immediately drop something if it didn't work. The fun stuff was where you could go the furthest."

For now, Rhona and Rhoda still found time to rejoice in just being girls. Asked what else they did for the war effort at the time, Rhona sighs and says, "Well, we did make sandwiches and dance with the boys," as if this role was a bit of a sacrifice. After all, "During the war just the dregs were left [at home], and we weren't really interested in these pimply-faced boys."

Perhaps it was all for the better. The girls wouldn't have had the time or inclination for all that dating and courtship, not when there were races to be won, training to do—and girlfriends to hang out with. In 1940s Montreal, William Weintraub points out, "Almost all middle-class teenage girls were determinedly virginal," even if they did "happily join in the raunchy singsongs that featured ditties like 'Roll me over, lay me down and do it again.'" At their business school, the girls were strictly instructed to always wear hats and "dress properly." One day they forgot their hats and were sent home to get them; instead they stopped by their friend Libby Elder's and borrowed some hats from her mom, then "paraded back to class." On weekends the girls kept going to the MAAA for swimming (with the "Aquabelles" team), badminton, squash, and other sports. At a 1942 swim meet, after the twins won a senior relay and Rhona her 50-yard freestyle event, not only did the press report that "both these beautiful mermaids can be classed as the pick of the swimmers in the Dominion," but also that Rhona was voted "the most likeable and popular" member of her Quebec squad. Between training, the twins usually took a quick lunch at the Honey Dew or Murray's Lunch Counter with Libby Elder and Joy Thomson, "our greatest pals."

Not a lot of time for dating—not when there were races to be won and girlfriends to hang out with. From left, Libby Elder, Rhona, Nancy McKean and Joy Thompson, Mont Tremblant, 1941.

The twins were also great fans of the movies; when they went, they usually sat through two viewings. *Mutiny on the Bounty* with Clark Gable was one of their favourites (it had won Best Picture at the 1935 Oscars), but the tops would always be Jeanette MacDonald and Nelson Eddy in *Rose-Marie*—after all, the picture began with MacDonald singing opera in Montreal, and the killing of a Canadian Mountie, and featured beautiful shots of the Canadian wilderness—perhaps the girls' first close-up view of the Rockies. It wouldn't be their last.

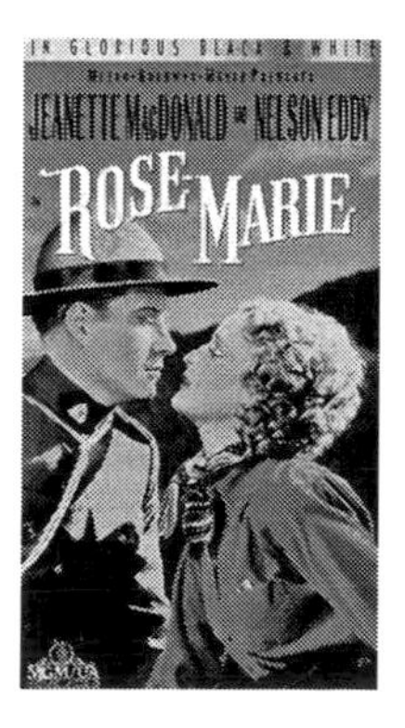

***Rose-Marie* featured Mounties, Canadian wilderness—and potential ski territory in the Rockies.**

"DURING THE WAR IT WAS PRETTY CRUMMY"

Despite all that activity, it was no coincidence that the twins and their peers were kept sweet and pure—the Roman Catholic Church that ruled Quebec, with the approval of Premier Duplessis, censored every movie that came into the province. Audiences never heard the word divorce, or saw scenes with a man and woman together in bed. Even libraries were censored, and the government was loath to fund them. The Catholic Index of Prohibited Books still held. Not one Western philosopher was to be found in the libraries of the province, nor were Robinson Crusoe, Madame Bovary, or Zorba the Greek anywhere to be seen; Adolf Hitler's *Mein Kampf*, however, was readily available.

The strength of Catholicism in the day, was no match for the traditions of the moneyed and Presbyterian Scots on the mountain, looking down on the rest of Montreal. At the end of every November, a simple ritual turned into an extravagant display at the St. Andrew's Ball: the "coming out" of the city's most eligible debutantes. Since 1835, Scottish money had pulled out all the stops for the Ball, which became one of the most outstanding events of the Montreal social calendar. For weeks leading up to it, the *Gazette* and *Star* featured photos and profiles of the debutantes in its society pages while the girls and their parents fussed over details and teas; afterwards, two full pages were devoted to the event, largely a listing of what every woman wore. The debutantes were paraded in by pipers through a cordon of Black Watch officers, and so was the haggis (only the haggis got stabbed at the end); Drambuie, champagne, and Scotland's "mountain dew" were the drinks of choice, while a massive curtain featuring the red lion of Scotland was draped behind the orchestra, along with various tartans and shields of the clans. In 1941, like most years, the Governor General was in attendance; during the war it was Sir Alexander Augustus Frederick William Alfred George

The twins Rhoda and Rhona at the 1941 St. Andrew's Ball: "Very stiff beautiful gowns..."

Cambridge, Prince Alexander of Teck, also known as Major General The Earl of Athlone. His wife, Princess Alice, was there too; she was the granddaughter of Queen Victoria. In a few years, the Earl would host Mackenzie King, Churchill, and Roosevelt at the Citadelle in Quebec for strategy meetings, but for now the effects of hostilities were slight. The *Gazette* reported that even the two women who presented the debutantes set a fine, peaceful example: "Mrs. Wallis wore a tartan sash of the MacDonalds of Glengarry and Mrs. Molson a sash of the Campbells of Argyle. It is interesting to note that these two rival Scottish clans who for centuries have had a death feud, met on common ground at the presentation of young Montreal ladies." Despite the lack of battles by men in kilts in the halls of the Windsor Hotel, there was still fun to be had dancing and supping after midnight, and once the debutantes were presented before the Governor General, they were officially ready to marry. It was an event like no other, and in 1941, the twins were there, both wearing "a frock of white point d'esprit trimmed with Alencon lace, and carrying an old-fashioned nosegay of sweetheart roses."

"During the war it was pretty crummy." It was just the infirm, the too young, or the too old boys left at home.

"Oh cripes," says Rhoda of the event today, "that was pretty dumb. We weren't ready. During the war it was pretty crummy." It was just the infirm, the too young, or the too old boys left at home.

"The whole deb thing wasn't exactly our cup of tea," Rhona agrees. "They always had deb teas before, you know. Very boring."

The girls felt they'd been roped in to the thing; at the time, nineteen-year-old Rhoda was doing work for Millie Hutchinson, the National Commandant of the Red Cross Nursing Corps (and later an OBE recipient). Millie appeared a strange bird to Rhoda. In the morning Rhoda would walk down the street to her house to get her directions for the day, and Millie would command the whole of the nursing corps from her bed, checking off a long list of things for Rhoda to accomplish. But Millie was also the Chair of the Ladies' Committee of the St. Andrew's Society, her husband, Major Keith Hutchinson, the President—and she insisted the twins simply *must* be debutantes this year. Rhoda became a secretary for the Society. "I'd go to all these meetings and they'd all be drinking. Those lovely luncheons where they'd drink all afternoon."

They went to the ball, and of course among sixty debutantes and fourteen hundred guests, including royalty and the head of the RAF Ferry Command, everyone snapped their pictures—they were adorable, identical, *famous*. "Anyway, it was a big to-do," recalls Rhoda, "and us in these very stiff beautiful gowns, coming home at about eight in the morning, and the son of the Hutchinsons leading the way up the street with his bagpipes going..."

On the same page as the endless listing of gowns and accessories, another headline jumps out: "2,500,000 Poles torn from homes in Nazi drive to wipe out race." There was another reality intruding on Montreal, so it would be the last Ball of wartime—only to be revived even more extravagantly in 1946, where the twins would once again steal the show. The Ball would continue through the years, changing venues from the storied Windsor Hotel to the Queen Elizabeth, even earning the distinction of being the only major gala held in Montreal during the 1970 FLQ crisis ("although held under trying conditions," says the Society's records), and continuing the traditions of debutantes, reels, and haggis to this day.

It wasn't only society balls that the war was interfering with, however. While the busy twins had turned down an offer to be ski instructors, the *Gazette* reported that "they want to go to Europe after the war and visit Norway, Switzerland and the

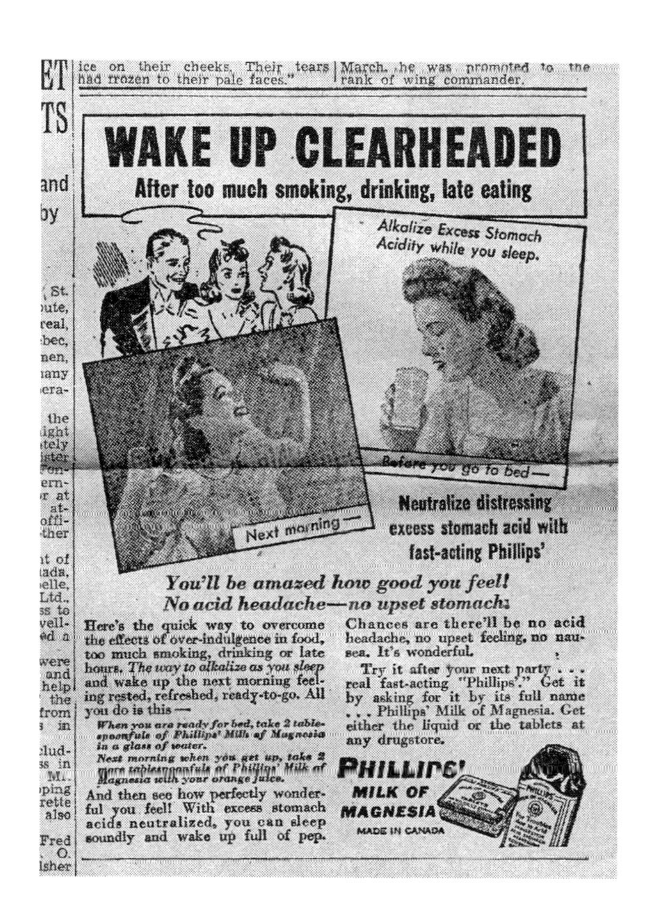

On the same page as the listing of what each debutante wore, in the November 1941 *Gazette*, was this timely advertisement for hangovers.

An ad for a state-of-the-art leather ski boot, in *Ski Magazine*, November 1948.

Austrian Tyrol—to go over there and compete in some of the big championship events." The girls were already getting restless, after having found they had soared beyond most competition in Quebec. But it would be a long wait.

Sports in Quebec began to feel the crunch of a long war by 1942, when transportation by train became more difficult, when fuel like coal became harder to come by, and when more and more people made the dangerous journey overseas. Even before World War II began, the 1940 Olympics, scheduled for Sapporo, Japan, had been cancelled due to Japan's invasion of China. Neutral Switzerland offered her Alps, but bickering among the Olympic Committee about allowing ski instructors to race stalled that. Then Garmisch-Partenkirchen in Germany was asked to repeat their 1936 hosting, but Hitler's invasion of Poland cancelled the Games once and for all. In 1944, that year's Olympics were cancelled because of the continued fighting: the host was to have been Cortina d'Ampezzo in Italy's Dolomites.

"We had to wait eight years for the Olympics," says Rhona, "because of the war—we really missed out. And the races, too, you had to wait another four years for another big race. There weren't any weekend races or World Cup or National races at the time, or National Teams—you had to do it on your own."

Racing in the Laurentians was also reduced drastically; the Quebec Kandahar, the most important race in the region and held at Mont Tremblant, continued from 1940 to 1942, but then was cancelled till 1945; the clubhouse the Penguin Ski Club members were so happy to finally see was now being used temporarily by refugee families. Women interested in sport at first saw their opportunities open up as men went off to service; arenas and gymnasiums were empty for them, but the spaces were quickly commandeered by the armed forces for training. Then women, too, began to be recruited into military service.

War continued apace. By February of 1943, Roosevelt pronounced the only way to end the war was with unconditional German surrender; the Nazis had just suffered their first large defeat at Stalingrad. Every activity was now subject to scrutiny, the better to put all resources toward stopping Hitler. In that same month *Montreal Star* sports columnist Myrtle Cook felt she had to defend Rhona and Rhoda.

“We had to wait eight years for the Olympics, because of the war—we really missed out.”

> Ten Canadian girls went to Lake Placid today to compete against American stars. It is not an official Canadian team; each skier is going down there on an express invitation from the host club. It is their privilege as free citizens to accept, provided the requirements of passport, visa, etc, are fulfilled.
>
> Yet, there are bench critics who claim they should have stayed at home. Most of the girls are doing wartime work or are at college and are entitled to use their week-ends for healthful recreation, or competition, as it is in this instance.
>
> In some quarters the idea is to criticize the girls and boys in sport who are trying to carry on in limited fashion, their recreation of peacetime. Yet, very little criticism is directed at other pleasures indulged in by citizens and which mean a great deal more outlay in expense and transportation...
>
> Canada has nothing to lose by their Lake Placid

This was the safest way to ski in 1948: both American and Canadian Olympic teams used these bindings. From *Ski Magazine*, 1948.

invasion but plenty to gain in keeping up the good will and friendly ski engagements.

Know what the girl skiers did on the way home from the intercity meet last week-end? Sing the now familiar ski songs? Sure. But, their fingers were busy shaping out scarfs, socks and caps for members of Canada's armed forces. Did not see a skier idle.

Rhoda and Rhona Wurtele each had a huge scarf in the making for the Merchant Navy men; Margaret Turner-Bone was knitting navy socks; just to mention a few.

Later, a soldier wrote in reply to Myrtle Cook: "Definitely in all spheres the girls are doing their part—in more ways than we can set down—service clubs, knitting, entertainment, thousands in uniform. By all means, let them carry on their sport. Ask any man in uniform, to see them on the ski trails, in basketball, gives us a big kick. They deserve what little recreation they can get!"

The twins certainly seemed patriotic, especially compared to their fellow Montrealer, Mayor Camillien Houde. By 1940 he was in a conscription camp, perhaps knitting socks, after having urged Montrealers to refuse to register for possible war service—the first step, he claimed, towards the French-Canadian horror of conscription. He was arrested at City Hall, and without trial served four years in camps, where he was inevitably elected mayor of his hut. When he got out he said, "It was the only holiday I ever had." The colourful Houde was re-elected with a majority at the next election.

LOVE IT OR LEAVE IT

Amid all the action of wartime, skiing was having a difficult time. Still a young sport wobbly on its legs in the 1940s (there were ongoing controversies over who was a pro and who an amateur, and over exactly which method one should use to ski), it was also difficult for anyone but the independently wealthy to pursue racing. All expenses were paid by the racers—or their parents.

"It was a great sport with great inconveniences," said Morten Lund in *Skiing Heritage, A Ski History Quarterly* in 1996. "The 1940s skier had to love it or leave it, and many left." Rhoda and Rhona, however, had been trained to never give up; they hung in with a vengeance.

To better understand those great inconveniences, imagine yourself suiting up for a ski outing with Rhona and Rhoda in the 1940s. First, you'd dress yourself in as many layers as you could, using clothes normally made for hunting or hiking, because there is little or no clothing available that is specifically designed and made for skiing. You start with some wool long johns, some wool hiking pants, a wool sweater and wool scarf—in other words, anything that collects snow really well and then doesn't breathe and is slow to dry. Now, you take your maple or hickory skis out of the clamps that keep them bent just right, to make sure they aren't too warped and splintered to use. Then you get your bamboo poles out, if they hadn't broken the last time you used them. Next, you lace up as best you can your leather ski boots, which have stretched considerably since you bought them for twenty bucks. Finally, with all the force you can muster, you laboriously fasten the buckles on your bindings by hand, somewhat imperfect bindings that will only release if you force them or have a spectacular fall (at which time the ski itself will stay well attached to your leg due to the "safety" strap, perhaps slashing you a few times in the process; should this strap break, your ski will go hurtling down the hill like a shot from

An ad for French ski star Georgette Thiolières' ski clothing line, from *Ski Magazine*, 1948.

a loose cannon).

At this time the Anglican minister Canon Horace Baugh has begun the Blessing of the Skis at St. Francis of the Birds, a local chapel in the Laurentians, and Catholics can go to St. Sauveur for their blessing. And it's a good thing, too, with that kind of equipment and ski slopes.

Blessed and dressed, you are now properly prepared to actually go down the hill. But first you have to get up. Luckily, things have come a long way since the days of climbing the hills with sealskin under your skis, and you have all the modern conveniences of tow ropes and even some chair lifts. Of course, with the lifts inching their way up, a good one- to two-hour wait in line is not uncommon; you're doing well if your wait is under thirty minutes.

"We had to prepare our own skis," says Rhoda. "Boy, did we know how to wax, we spent so much time doing it".

Now, none of this says you'll do well do on the course. A lot of that will have to do with your wax—which, sorry, you'll have to prepare yourself. It isn't just a question of sliding a little stick under the skis. Wooden skis have to be waxed after every few runs. And underneath your wax, says the *Canadian Ski Yearbook* of 1935, should be a base of "tar klister, kare or pine tar. Don't attempt this until you have the time to make a good job of it. Apply your base...and heat it as hot as the hand can stand, using a blow torch or a stove (you can't beat a fireplace). Heat and rub, heat and rub, until the surface is fairly dry when hot."

Waxes themselves at this time are secret recipes, each individual or team coming up with its own formula.

"We had to prepare our own skis," says Rhoda. "Boy, did we know how to wax, we spent so much time doing it. Hermann Gadner, the twins' first instructor and mentor, used to make his own wax for us. After he died, we never had success duplicating what he had done. It never worked for us."

Rhona's future father-in-law (Gene Gillis's father) had been instrumental in starting skiing in the Western US; in those days he made his own wax too. He was making a terrible stink in the basement, so his wife told him to go somewhere else and make it. He and his friends set up a shack in the woods—and soon got a visit from the sheriff, who thought they were making hooch. Back in the Laurentians, Jackrabbit Johannsen's son Bob was a scientist, and concocted a very good wax. "But then there was a scandal, because he sold his de-icing formula to the Germans during wartime. But we're not supposed to talk about that," says Rhoda. "He was a beautiful jumper and skier..."

The pungent smell of bubbling waxes and waterlogged wool would permeate ski lodges for years to come. Skis themselves would finally take a great leap by the end of the 1940s, when technologies researched during wartime leaked into civilian life. First skis appeared with metal edges, then aluminum skis appeared, then aluminum ones with plywood cores; and finally ski entrepreneur Howard Head came out with plastic-bottomed skis that did away with the constant waxing. Bob Lange created plastic boots only in the late 1950s, and bamboo poles survived until 1958. That decade too saw the first clothing designed for skiing—made by Bogner, a European family whose name would intertwine with the twins and their families for decades.

Photo courtesy la société d'histoire de l'église St-Francis of the Birds

The Anglican chapel of St. Francis of the Birds in St. Sauveur offered annual blessings for skiers. The chapel still stands but is threatened with demolition.

If simply going skiing was so complicated, *racing* down a hill

Photo courtesy CPR

Man waxing skis, Laurentians, 1940s.

called for even more patience. For timing a race, wires had to be strung from the top of the mountain to the bottom; these could be conveniently laid by the men with snowshoes who were packing the whole mountainside. Sometimes the twins and other racers would test the course beforehand, and risked having shovels thrown at them as they cut up the snow. Or the packers would sit on their shovels and slide down; later on they developed a log on a barrel stave, with a little seat for the ride down. "We were packing a course once, sidestepping up a whole hill," Rhona remembers, "when the Swiss team came up beside us going straight up. They had skins on their skis, sealskins, with the fur going against the hill."

Once the course was packed, poles were needed to mark the slalom course. "Years ago," Rhona says, "they didn't even bend—we just bashed them down. We cut Jack pines down 'cause they were straight and long. Of course they'd knock you out if you banged into them."

There was little in the way of protection: no helmets, shields, goggles, or shin pads to protect legs when hitting the slalom gates. But that was no concern to the twins at the time: "We liked racing, and just wanted to get to the bottom. Now, of course, racers *have* to win, there's so much time and money invested in them. But we just wanted to do the best we could. We took it seriously in that we waxed our skis carefully."

At a Laurentian Zone International Meet at Mount Baldy in 1944, Rhona, captain of the Canadian team, fractured her wrist the day before the race. It made headlines in the *New York Times*. Myrtle Cook in her sports column said, "Shortly after the doctor put her wrist in a plaster cast, Rhona was out on Baldy again, coming down with one arm in a sling and using one pole. She

Rhona watches Rhoda waxing for the Taschereau—using Hermann Gadner's secret recipe, 1945.

"Going to Tremblant for Big Meet," 1940. Riding from train station in truck to international races vs. US Left to right: Ethel Beauvais, Joey Abbey, "M" Burden, Joan Tyler lying down, Rhona, Ebie Snively (Toronto), Peggy Pugsley, Gaby Pleau. Picture taken by Rhoda.

wanted to race but Zone officials refused permission."

Of course, with one twin out, the other went down, too. Rhoda fell in the downhill and came an unheard of eleventh, and fourth in the slalom. Some reports had Rhoda falling at the exact same spot where her sister fell the day before, but it seems apocryphal. In the twins' scrapbook, another note explains the reason: "Hit high in tree practicing late, dark out." It was the twins taking their ski practice as late as they possibly could, long before the days of lit slopes and night skiing. Rhona, unable to compete but impossible to keep off the slopes, continued, undaunted. While men complained of riding the tow rope on slush and grass, she glided up the hill holding on with one hand.

In those racing days, competitors had to keep the same pair of skis for the whole meet, no matter what kind of race they were running. Rhoda recalls the stencils put on the skis so there would be no substitutions; they used long 212-centimetre skis for downhill and slalom.

That strange rule led to many worries and late-night repairs. "Well, Irving of Montreal was the big deal for ski clothes at the time, and we got suits from them," says Rhoda. "So I was going down the hill wearing this jacket with a hood lined with sharkskin. I came down the downhill course and through a narrow spot on a short turn, and the damn hood came down on my eyes. So of course I brushed it back up and skidded out and broke my darling ski. I managed to finish, but it was all bent up." Luckily there was a kid from out west ("who was very fond of Rhoda," adds Rhona) who had brought the Denver ski team out east so he could meet the twins again. "And he stayed up all hours to get me into the damn skis." With the skis repaired, she ended up fourth in the combined totals.

It seemed an arbitrary and useless rule, of course. "But we didn't question the people in charge," says Rhoda. "We don't know why they had the rule. The trouble was, the Canadian Ski Association was really backward. When we went to Europe we weren't allowed to race before the Olympics! That was asinine."

The trouble was, the Canadian Ski Association was really backward. When we went to Europe we weren't allowed to race before the Olympics! That was asinine.

"And one pair of skis!" adds Rhona. "I put them in the oven—and burnt them." The only choice she had was to scrape off the charred remains and continue on.

And yet, for all that—despite fragile equipment, hours of waxing, dysfunctional clothing, cryptic rules, and little safety—when Rhoda is asked how she felt before a race she replies, "You're nervous of course. But excited, really excited. I don't think we were scared of it. You have to ski above and beyond to pay off at that point; just go for it. The ones that win are at their peak at the right time; the ones that make it to the bottom standing. There's a lot of luck involved too."

"AS GOOD AS MEN"

There were, despite the hardships, three major benefits that something as disruptive as war brought to skiing. A later benefit when the war ended was the large number of former soldiers now trained in skiing. And the skis and equipment they had used—large, heavy, and metal-framed skis, tough khaki rucksacks, and bulky canvas parkas—were a cheap if roughshod way into the sport for many post-war families. In America, too, thousands of 10th Mountain Division survivors took to the hills after the war; two thousand of those soldiers trained for fighting on skis became ski instructors.

A more immediate benefit to North America was seen even before Hitler's *Anschluss* of 1938: a small but highly influential wave of talented and experienced Austrian skiers came to North America for refuge, first because of Nazi threats, then from troops marching into Vienna. As soon as they entered Austria the Nazis had imprisoned Hannes Schneider, a pioneer of Austrian ski teaching who developed the stem christie in 1910, later the basis for the Arlberg technique (named after the pass in the Alps where he was raised). His book *The Wonder of Skiing* sold 100,000 copies in 1925, helping to make his technique and teaching formula the worldwide standard by 1930. Schneider had also helped begin the first international alpine combined meet, when his Ski Club Arlberg met with British skier Arnold Lunn's slalom at the Kandahar Ski Club; the Arlberg-Kandahar was first raced in 1928. None of this was enough for the Nazis to fear him, although he had trained hundreds of soldiers in skiing during World War I. What did him in, he told friends, was bad-mouthing Hitler to his co-star in the early ski film *White Ecstasy* who had gone on to befriend Adolf. That co-star, Leni Riefenstahl, began as a skier but went on to direct the most spectacular propaganda films of the twentieth century, glorifying the Nazis.

Schneider's quick arrest was enough to push more instructors out, and many came first to the New England states. Among them was the town of St. Anton's best young racer, Rudi Matt, who escaped to Mount Cranmore; racer/instructor Friedl Pfeifer went to Sun Valley and began the first comprehensive lift system in the US, then later helped plan the resort at Aspen, Colorado; Otto Lang began ski schools in the American Northwest at Mount Rainier, Mount Baker, and Mount Hood; Luggi Foeger went to Badger Pass; Benno Rybizka had been at Mount Cranmore in New Hampshire since 1936. Eventually, Rybizka and Foeger would move north to Mont Tremblant—but only after Hannes Schneider had been released when a moneyed American twisted enough arms, and the Austrian hero took over the school at Mount Cranmore in New Hampshire in February 1939.

Hannes Schneider's *Das Wunder des Schneeschuhs* (The Wonder of Skiing), 1925.

"And with that, the center of gravity in the ski world had shifted to America," says *Skiing Heritage Quarterly*, with typical American understatement. What in fact happened was that skiing took a huge leap in North America with Austrian teachers, coaches, and equipment. Skiing in Canada, while not as widespread, was as advanced technically as skiing in the US, and often more advanced.

Rhona and Rhoda felt the influence of the Austrian gurus directly, through the person of Hermann Gadner. A man of Teutonic habits, he never smoked nor drank, but rose early and went to bed early, spending all the time he could outside. "The wind and sun tanned his face to leather-brownness and he was amazingly strong," William Weintraub later wrote in the *Gazette*. At five foot eight, "He had a wiry build, but could on occasion lift an injured skier to his shoulder and ski down three miles of Mont Tremblant trails to a first aid post." The Austrian ski instructor, in early pictures never seen on the slopes without a perky little hat and natty suit, had come with the rest of the Austrian invasion in 1938; he had recently opened a ski school and become head instructor at Gray Rocks, near Tremblant. Gadner, teaching the

Hermann Gadner's Snow Eagle Ski School at Gray Rock's 1945: "The greatest fun thing for us."

Arlberg technique of Schneider, fast became one of the most respected instructors in the Laurentians, and the twins' father heard about him; Gadner also wrote about skiing in the *Gazette*. Hunter immediately called him to help the twins.

So in the early 1940s, the twins began attending Hermann Gadner's courses. "In early December we attended the Canadian Ski Instructors Alliance course," Rhoda says. "This would give us a chance to train and ski first thing in the winter, and we thought it a great idea to get an early start and understand the Arlberg method of ski teaching." Gadner also led a slalom school. "It was the greatest fun thing for us," says Rhona (Gray Rocks was filled with young single men and women, too).

Naturally fearless, the twins excelled at propelling themselves as fast as they could on the downhill slope, but the needed finesse for slalom was still giving them trouble. Gadner was a perfect fit: a great racer, an even better instructor. With Gadner's training, the twins won Mont Tremblant Gold Pins for their racing skills; the only other woman to win them had been Pat Paré, the first woman instructor in Canada. "Hermann gave us many coaching hints for the next few years," says Rhoda, "and we tried to live up to his teaching." Hermann's influence would really take effect in the coming years, and be felt for decades beyond, as the twins themselves took up ski instructing.

Actively training for sports was still a pursuit practiced by only a few. The results of dedicated training took the twins by surprise. During a swim meet, Rhona had watched as the visiting Americans walloped the Canadians. Her father sent her with her mother to New York to learn about swimming freestyle, to meet with, and possibly hire, a trainer. "So the guy told me to do ten lengths," says Rhona, "then I got out and he said, Okay, do ten more, and this time keep your feet higher. I just about drowned, I was so tired. That was a real eye-opener. These were people who actually *trained*. You got better, you actually trained." Rhona didn't join the American club, but she learned her lesson well.

Ski School at Mont Tremblant, 1941: now all they had to do was climb to the top of the hill. Rhona on the left, Rhoda second from the right.

Gadner was as captivated by the twins' potential as they were impressed with his skill. "Why, they don't even wait until they have finished their apple pie and ice cream before they are back on the slopes," he said to Myrtle Cook. "That's why they are so good." Gadner would be the biggest influence on the girls in their early ski years, but he would also be gone before the war's end. Later, the twins would meet Hannes Schneider when he came to visit Canada; Fritz Loosli, Hans Falkner, Benno Rybizka, and Luggi Foeger would also directly influence them.

Now with a taste of training, the twins' capacity to sweep away the competition in a race was becoming glaringly obvious. By March of 1942, *Time* magazine found it much easier to report that they *didn't* win. The international magazine also still had to explain skiing to the masses. On the cover is a daunting image of General Yamashita, Japanese bane of the Allies' existence. Inside, women's skiing comes under the spotlight.

> Probably the only international sport event that will be held in the U.S. this year took place last week at Lake

Placid, N.Y., between ten lady *Kanonen* representing the U.S. and Canada.

A *kanone* is an expert skier, and skiing is one of the few sports at which women become expert. Discouraged from jumping (too dangerous) and cross-country running (too tiring), women have adopted the most becoming ski sport: downhill racing. Even so, whooshing down a mountainside at 40 m.p.h. requires steel nerves, stamina, split-second thinking...

Last week thousands of U.S. ski fans crammed the sidelines at Lake Placid's Rim Rock run. Like most downhill meets, the races were divided into two sections: the straight-down (popularly called the downhill) and the *slalom*, a zigzag course defined by pairs of flags which skiers must thread (from the Norwegian words slad, steep terrain, and lom, track).

Few weeks ago, when practically the same U.S. and Canadian *Kanonen* met in a tournament at Mont Tremblant in the Laurentians, the Canadian girls lost the slalom but streaked off with the downhill race. In last week's return engagement, Canada's dashing Wurtele twins, Rhona and Rhoda, who have finished one-two in every downhill race they have entered this year, failed to lead their side to victory...

Despite all the problems skiing and sports in general had, in typical fashion Rhona and Rhoda plowed ahead with no regard for obstacles.

It was hardly a coincidence that the only international sport event that year was exclusively female. That was the third effect of wartime that directly benefitted women: they took the sports spotlight from men.

Despite all the problems skiing and sports in general had, in typical fashion Rhona and Rhoda plowed ahead with no regard for obstacles. The all-women's Penguin Ski Club was having tough times and having to battle a more formidable McGill women's ski team; when the twins finished high school and joined the Penguins in 1942 to grab the spotlight away from the McGill team, they "not only reversed Penguin fortunes at home, they put the club on the map internationally," says the Club history. At races, the twins were coming in first and second again; they were beating standing champions like Peggy Austin, Yvonne Godmer, and Gertrude Mann. They raced at Pico Peak, Tremblant, Mont Gabriel and Ste. Marguerite, and of course Lake Placid. Suddenly, the future of women in skiing didn't look so grim—at least for Quebec.

The first major race was the 1942 Canadian Team Trials at Tremblant, their first time down those slopes. Their MAAA Aquabelle swimming team members had sent them a telegram before the first meet: "Do as well in skiing as in swimming—that's tops." They would do better.

"We just bashed down as straight as possible," said Rhoda, "and—wow—we were first and second in both downhill and third and fourth in slalom." It was an apt description of their style. Bashing down was fine for the downhill—the *Globe and Mail* called them "brilliant in the downhill and average in the slalom" at the time—but finesse was called for in the slalom, and as they climbed higher they would need training.

Interestingly, another sister act, Dorothy and Ethel Beauvais ("the dark-eyed beauty of the Laurentians"), also did very well in races. In fact there were a number of sisters skiing, including the McNichols, Hélène, Françoise and Madeleine; Barbara and Pamela Kemp, and Jacqueline and Simone Boucher, among others.

Having handily made the team, the next week the twins and their teammates raced the Eastern US Ladies' Ski Team in an international meet at Mont Tremblant. The team included some of the top skiers in Canada, including the pioneer woman who had raced in the 1936 Olympics, Mrs. Gordon-Lennox of Ottawa (she of the monocle). The twins were "newcomers," but Myrtle Cook's column said that "Rhona and Rhoda, the two amazing Montreal twins, who have put the name of Wurtele to the fore in tennis, swimming and skiing, are favored highly in this international struggle."

In a heavy blizzard, the Americans didn't know what hit them. The twins were in their element, and Rhoda came exploding out of the powder to take first in the downhill; Rhona was nine seconds behind for second place.

IN A LEAGUE **OF THEIR OWN**

The Rockford Peaches, 1944, the model for the team in the film "A League of Their Own."

They were a sports publicist's dream: athletic, pretty, and identical. No wonder Philip Wrigley's scouts approached Rhoda and Rhona in the 1940s about playing on the Chicago Colleens—the latest team to join the All-American Girls Baseball League.

That's the same one that Madonna and Geena Davis made famous again in the 1992 film *A League of Their Own*.

The Girls' League already had 10 percent of their players from Canada; half of those were from Saskatchewan.

After watching a game in Montreal, the twins were shocked. "They're so rude and coarse," they told the scouts, "and they swear!" The Rockford Peaches, the Kalamazoo Lassies, or the Grand Rapids Chicks could only be worse.

A women's baseball league was still a radical idea, even though more and more women were playing sports. Women's hockey had been popular after 1900, but fighting, stitches, and male ridicule meant respectable girls avoided it. Women had played softball for ten years, but that was rough too. Only catchers and first base used mitts, resulting in plenty of broken fingers. The girls were seen as too masculine, freaks, or lesbians. So when Wrigley started the league, he made sure it would stay away from the short-hair, pants, spitting and swearing that was obviously still common when the twins saw a game. His league would have "the highest ideals of womanhood," where the audience would see "nothing but healthy wholesome 'All-American' girls."

Had the twins known this, they might have been more interested. Despite all their wildness, their fearlessness and pioneering, they were at heart ladies, and by their own admission, terribly shy. "Well, we were intimidated by everything. People used to think we were mad at them or stuck up. We were very shy."

To maintain the image of all-American girls, the league had strict rules: the girls must wear lipstick, but must not wear slacks or shorts in public, or their skirts higher than six inches above the knee. They could not smoke or drink in public or drive their cars outside city limits without the special permission of the manager. All of their social engagements had to be approved by a chaperone, and, to keep the proper competitive spirit, there was to be no fraternizing with other teams.

In addition, players had to maintain a high degree of femininity—attending Helena Rubenstein's Beauty Salon was as important a facet of spring training as shagging balls. The players received a beauty kit, and were given advice on beauty routines and clothing suggestions.

They might have been models of propriety, but they were also outstanding athletes. Wrigley had studied his audience well. The mixture of hardball, softball, and pretty girls worked well (although injured legs from sliding home in a skirt were common). Attendance was good, usually 2,000 to 3,000 per game; at its peak in 1948, the league had almost a million fans at games.

The girls—some as young as fifteen—were paid well, too. When Rhona and Rhoda were making $60 a month as stenographers, the ball players made $45 to $85 a week. They often made more then their parents.

The All-American Girls Baseball League had worked so well because during the war, and for a short time after, people were used to seeing women in non-traditional roles. Ironically, when peace came the advances women had made fell apart. The men came back from the war and women got laid off from jobs. Sports felt the same effect. From 1949 to 1951 the league dwindled down to nothing, finally petering out in 1954. In that decade, CCM stopped making hockey skates and baseball gloves for women.

And yet the pioneers of women's sport had left their mark, and left a step for another generation to build on. Like the twins, though, the ball players didn't think of themselves as pioneers. "We were just kids then," said one player, "and all we wanted to do was play baseball."

Laurentian Ladies' team at Tremblant Int'l, February 1942, from the *Montreal Gazette*. Front row: Eleanor Boyle, Dorothy Michaels, Ethel Beauvais. Second row: Dorothy Beauvais, Mrs. Diana Gordon-Lennox, Yvonne Godmer, Mrs. Lorna Casgrain. Back row, the Wurtele twins, Rhoda and Rhona.

On the first day, in a heavy blizzard, the Americans didn't know what hit them. The twins were in their element, and Rhoda came exploding out of the powder to take first in the downhill; Rhona was nine seconds behind for second place. The closest American was 16 seconds behind Rhoda; the Penguin team captain, 23 seconds behind. Still, it was the slalom where they lost ground again. The next day the Americans came back as they said they would, easily taking the top five positions in the slalom. Rhoda was tenth; Rhona missed flags and was disqualified. Although Rhoda was fifth in the combined results and the top Canadian, the Americans easily swept the combined title. The Americans had training, and it was becoming obvious that if the twins wanted to really win internationally, they would have to get professional help. In fact, they would not get formal coaching until just weeks before the 1948 Olympics. For now, however, their win was more than the Penguins had hoped for; it merited a mention in the *New York Times* and got them top spots on the Penguin team.

The next big race was the Seigniory Club Inter-City Trophy, with entries from Quebec, Toronto, Ottawa, and Montreal. The McGill club had won in previous years, but the Wurteles easily led the Penguins to victory. It seemed they liked difficult conditions: the event saw "the most bitter blizzard ever encountered in the nine-year history of the race." They were first and second in the downhill again (Rhona first this time), less successful in the slalom. Later that February, they also took the top two positions at the Taschereau Downhill at Mont Tremblant; the next race was the Lake Placid Invitational with their surprising loss. Despite the disappointment of the results, the twins' irrepressible optimism turned it into a lark—and they got to meet the famous radio singer Kate Smith. "Great fun with the team," Rhoda wrote, "and such a lovely place at the Lake Placid Club. The Kate Smith Trophy was at stake and she was present but she didn't sing 'When the moon comes over the mountain.' She was as big as she was famous, and great fun."

That year, to no one's surprise, Rhoda ended the season by winning the Penguin's Combined Ski Championship at St. Sauveur, taking first in both the downhill and slalom events; Rhona came a close second.

The frenzied activity of 1942 and their almost perfect downhill record catapulted the twins into the limelight. Besides *Time* magazine, *The Montrealer* magazine featured them in a photo essay on the "Beauty and the Barrel Stave," and *Canadian Skier* magazine, "the official organ of the Canadian Ski Instructors Alliance," put "The Flying Wurtele Twins" on the cover.

"There has always been considerable debate about the most interesting kind of ski meet," the *Canadian Skier* reporter writes, "that is, from a spectator's point of view...There is a rich measure of spectator interest in an all-feminine event like the girls' annual inter-city meet held for the ninth time at the Seigniory Club in February. Watching the girls taking the last schuss of the downhill run, for instance, had all the emotional and theatrical elements: thrills, suspense, tragedy, comedy, pathos. Some of them flashed down, cannonlike at a terrific speed that would terrify many men... It was Rhona Wurtele of the Penguins who flew the fastest..."

It was indicative of the times that all the articles and features on the twins still reflected the need to justify their interest in women's sports; *Time* magazine explains downhill racing as the "most becoming" sport; *The Montrealer* focuses on pulchritude, not skill; and even *Canadian Skier* seems slightly bemused by the fact of a women's race. Yet things were slowly changing, and women were beginning to earn some respect in sports. Newspapers began to list what the girls did when not skiing: "Captain Dorothy Houghton is employed in an insurance company in Montreal—Elizabeth Snively is a student at U of T—Frances McLeod is a laboratory technician at Royal Victoria Hospital—Rhoda and Rhona Wurtele work in a bank in Montreal..."

Working women **go Hollywood**

Hollywood was fascinated by the phenomenon of women's changing roles. The same issue of The *Montrealer* featuring the twins also reviewed *Woman of the Year,* starring Katharine Hepburn and Spencer Tracy. The actors burned up the screen. Hepburn plays a columnist who writes that baseball should be abolished until World War II ends; Tracy plays a sportswriter who battles with her in the same newspaper. They meet, sparks fly, and they marry; and then things really begin to get complicated. Hepburn's character is radical for the day: a prototypical feminist, she is trying to figure out how to balance

Woman of the Year, *1942, Spencer Tracy and Katharine Hepburn.*

marriage and career decades before most women confronted the dilemma. An original ending had Hepburn's character learning to love baseball; but at test screenings women felt threatened by Hepburn managing to be everything at once. A new ending was shot, where she screws up cooking a breakfast for her man, and test audiences cheered with relief.

The Lou Marsh **Trophy**

Joe Krol, CFL quarterback and winner of five Grey Cups, took the Lou Marsh Trophy in 1946; before and after him another name that would steal the twins' limelight took the trophy three times: Barbara Ann Scott. Other notable women skiers would take the trophy in the future, including Lucile Wheeler, Anne Heggtveit, and Nancy Greene.

Olympic champion, Nancy Greene.

THE CLASS STRUGGLE

There were battles all over the place in that decade—in the theatre of war, on the silver screen between Spencer and Tracy, and on the ski slopes. The first big fight for Rhona and Rhoda was nothing other than a class struggle.

Columnist Myrtle Cook was always on the lookout for women in sport; she had taken part in the 1928 Olympics when it was still a male bastion, and dedicated her career to making it easier for women who came after her. In 1941, she spotted a discrepancy in class divisions in skiing: "Standing out like a red cherry on a green salad is this fact," she wrote. "Laurentian Zone Ratings Committee has some chores to do...graduate some of the girl skiers to their rightful division. Accomplished skiers like Rhoda Wurtele and twin sister Rhona belong in the higher bracket, not in Class C. They literally walked off with this division on the Esterel slopes yesterday. Their splendid record of last season plus yesterday's undoubted proof of ability certainly merits a lift to Class B."

Like all beginners, when the twins began racing for the Penguins they started in the lowest skill category, Class C. By the time of their first big ski meet in January of 1942 (on Mount Venus, natch) they had easily proven themselves, often finishing in a tie or beating women in the next class above them. Rhoda, already called "one of Montreal's best all-round athletes" by the *Star*, won the Class C division and received the Silver Cup. She and Rhona were already chasing the older girls in Class B, such as Yvonne Godmer and Gaby Pleau.

That January, Cook reported that her needling had the desired effect. "Laurentian Zone ratings committee got around to those chores we mentioned the other day...they have graduated skiers Rhoda and Rhona Wurtele to Class B. The twins were much too fast for the Class C company in which they raced last weekend. Graduation of the twins will make some of the current Class B

Rhona and Rhoda with their Rose Bowl win: "Canada's most outstanding athlete." Make that two... *MAAA Magazine*, August 1945.

favorites hustle to keep their topflight places in both downhill and slalom."

Then with some puzzlement, Cook fixed her eyes on the next mountain: "Apparently there are no Class A girl skiers listed although several of those in Class B have enjoyed both Provincial and Dominion championship titles. Some of them have beaten the boys too in open events and if that does not merit them Class A rating—what does? It does seem strange that a skier who is a Dominion champion is listed Class B, doesn't it?"

That's how it was with the associations. We were in the *Dominion* Championships, not the Canadian; we were in the *Ladies'* Division, not the Women's.

Yes, it did seem strange. The Montreal Ski Club had been around some forty years already; the McGill downhill ski club, the Red Birds, had raced for fourteen years. Yet skiing was still in its infancy, and clubs and associations were making things up as they went along. Apparently nobody had counted on women racing so well. Nobody had counted on the Wurtele twins keeping pace with—or bettering—male skiers. Myrtle Cook accepted the responsibility of getting the Laurentian Zone to accept reality, and would wage her campaign well into the winter of 1946–47 before it was acknowledged that women could become Class A skiers.

Outside of the Laurentians, things were just as backwards. The twins knew of the US Nationals being held in Franconia, New Hampshire, in 1945, and says Rhoda "we thought we would just get in touch with the president of the Canadian Amateur Ski Association—we had to get permission to go race. We also discovered we were Class B racers because we were *ladies*; they didn't have a Class A. And this is racing in the U.S. So we went down with the Ottawa boys and beat them all.

"That's how it was with the associations," says Rhoda. "We were in the *Dominion* Championships, not the Canadian; we were in the *Ladies'* Division, not the Women's. And the President of the Swimming Association had even said to us, 'When are you girls going to quit competing in this?' Can you imagine? God. The other girls had to have something to reach for. Imagine him saying that."

Rhoda, seated, and Rhona in their increasingly cramped trophy room at Upper Lansdowne. 1940s.

With no Class A ratings for women across all of North America, the twins did what they had always done: they raced with the boys and men. And when they beat them, the repercussions were felt for months.

To say it was about time for the twins to get Class A ratings is an understatement. Between them the twins had won the Taschereau Downhill at Mont Tremblant five times; been on the international ski team for Lake Placid seven times and won the Kate Smith Trophy three times; took the US National Championships at Franconia in 1945, and the US Nationals in Utah the next year; took the Dominion Championship at Mont Tremblant in the combined in 1947; and took the Rose Bowl and shared the the Women's Amateur Athletic Federation's Outstanding Woman Athlete award in 1944. In 1946 they shared the runner-up spot for the Lou Marsh Trophy for Best Canadian Athlete overall.

"She was as big as she was famous, and great fun:" celebrity singer Kate Smith was always involved in sports somehow; here she presents a bobsledding trophy.

Rhona in particular turned in remarkable performances when women finally did get an A rating. She took the Kate Smith Trophy for the third time, the Alberta Cup, honours at the Ontario Championships at Collingwood, and won the US National Slalom and Combined Championship. Rhoda did no less. That year she handily won the Taschereau Downhill for the third time. She was the Laurentian Zone Champion, then won the Silver Belt Trophy at Sugar Bowl, California, and was the runner-up to the Alta Cup.

Despite the mix-ups with the class struggle, something else separated the men from the girls. A few years earlier, at a Seigniory Club Inter-City meet held in February of 1943, the Penguins had beaten the Toronto team. Rhona had taken the downhill this time; Rhoda had had a fall and finished twenty-first. Myrtle Cook took a look at how the girls handled it and remarked, "One delightful feature of the women's ski races is the fact that the girls can take a tumble and laugh and joke about it later. There is no gloom of 'what might have been' ... it is simply wiped off the slate as 'one of those things.'" Later at the meet, as if to prove it, Rhoda came back to win the slalom, with Rhona in third place behind her.

"A MERE SLIP OF A GIRL"

When men were involved, as Myrtle Cook observed, there was a lot of "what might have been." In February of 1943, Rhoda having already won the downhill at the Laurentian Zone Championships, and the downhill and combined at the International Ladies Ski Meet at Tremblant, and the twins having just returned from victories at Lake Placid (Rhona taking first that time), the girls got ready for what may have seemed like just another race. It was the Taschereau Cup at Mont Tremblant.

As soon as the twins arrived they knew this was going to be a race like no other. A huge storm blew in with a dastardly combination of high winds and a bitter cold of –36 degrees. Snowdrifts soon blocked all roads, shutting down trains and buses and eventually even ski lifts. Skiing soldiers, unable to get back to their barracks, went AWOL. Other skiers, most with little money, were left to find a place to stay for the night. Rhoda sent a message home: "Snowbound...at last!"

It was exactly the kind of conditions the twins seemed to excel in. There was nothing they liked better than to be stuck on a snowy mountain with no hope of getting back to their secretarial desks. And as it turned out, according to *Montreal Star* reporter Lloyd Lockhart, "It was an amazing ski race with a thousand amazing aftermaths."

There were ninety-three skiers ready to race that day, including the top pros of Quebec and area: the fabulous Johnny Fripp, plus Rolph Endre, Punch Bott, Roger Trottier, Pierre Cochand. The women were out too, though they were still regulated to Class B. So Rhoda approached the course with her usual aplomb, ready to "blast a course wide open no matter what the opposition," according to Myrtle Cook. She wore number 120 in the race, putting her later in the day after the snowy course had been scraped down to the fast ice.

RCAF airman Johnny Fripp, the favourite, had already had a spectacular ride. He clipped a tree on the way down and tore his leather harness after the S-curves flattened out; after trying a quick fix he gave up on the harness and skied the rest of the way down with one ski, using his free foot as a rudder. Though nowhere near a win, he skied so well most of the crowd didn't even realize he had lost a ski until he was at the bottom. He even passed an earlier competitor on his way down.

The weather, the cold, the blowing snow, *something* must have been off-kilter for a "mere slip of a girl" to win.

As Rhoda streaked down the ice, she took a spill too. But it was *before* the steep and icy S-curve, and she quickly righted herself and kept her speed up. When her time was counted at the bottom, it was four minutes and seven seconds. That made her the winner of the whole field—the nearest threat was Roger Trottier, a full twenty-four seconds behind her. Rhoda had decimated all competition, including the professional Class A men.

All of a sudden, said Myrtle Cook, "The bench quarter-backs, observers, some competitors, in fact a good number of the ski fraternity [were] wearing that 'we can't believe it' look since Monday morning news broke of Rhoda's triumph.'"

The first grumblings were about the timing—certainly the weather, the cold, the blowing snow, *something* must have been off-kilter for a "mere slip of a girl" to flatten a whole team of rough and ready RCAF pilots. Reporter John Walsh said, "The Penguin star's victory caused a lot of head-shaking among ski veterans, however, despite the fact that Zone and St. Jovite Ski Club officials formally crowned her the winner." Another article in the *Star* featuring sport headliners (Joe DiMaggio is drafted, the Watson-Hextall-Patrick line of the New York Rangers come to threaten the Canadiens) said, "Rhoda beat some of the best Eastern Canada men skiers in the Taschereau and there are reactions, repercussions and seething discussions in the wake of that great performance."

Lloyd Lockhart in the *Star* was perhaps the most skeptical of those in print. "The only person who seems to think Rhoda [was] faster is Hermann Gadner. And Hermann Gadner is Rhoda's coach." For him, the extreme weather was the story; "The results, they aren't very important," the reporter said flippantly. "Through some witch-craft, fastest time belonged to Rhoda Wurtele." Luckily, true skiing experts readily squashed that kind of attitude, some of whom analysed the race turn by turn to prove that Rhoda could indeed win in that time.

"So let's dry the tears boys," Myrtle Cook recommended.

Out of that controversy, however, an even clearer fact emerged: Rhoda had won (and Rhona came ninth of all men and women) because she and her twin were ready for the race. And the reason they were ready was because that funny-hat–wearing Austrian Hermann Gadner had taken them under his wing and taught them the value of training and practice.

"The results, they aren't very important," the reporter said flippantly. "Through some witch-craft, fastest time belonged to Rhoda Wurtele."

"There is one thing that most persons don't take into consideration," respected Laurentian skier George Jacobsen said, "and that is that Hermann Gadner, reputed to be one of the best instructors in Eastern Canada, has a very soft spot in his heart for the Wurteles, and gives them the benefit of every word of experience he has picked up in years of skiing."

Gadner had taken them aside at the top of the hill, Jacobsen explained, and told them to keep to the centre of the trail, avoiding skidding through the turns and losing time. That, he felt, was why Rhoda won—and why every student skier should listen to "the advice of the men who did so much to perfect ski technique in this district."

(Jacobsen seems an ideal diplomat. He gave Rhoda full marks for her performance, noting the twins took their training seriously, but also appeased the male ego by stressing it was masculine wisdom that pushed her to victory.)

In fact, Hermann Gadner was responsible for getting the Wurtele twins ready for prime time. And he did have a soft spot for the twins—who wouldn't? Jacobsen painted an enchanting picture of the three of them together.

"It was getting dark over Mont Tremblant last week-end and

the famous Flying Mile was deserted. That is, almost deserted, but if you strained your eyes up past the lower level you would find three lonely figures up there—two of them on skis and the other just watching. The three were Rhoda, Rhona and Gadner—and what they were doing was practising their slalom style through flags. Ridiculous for the Wurteles to practise, you say. Well, that's where you're are wrong, because in skiing—or most any other sport for that matter—constant practice is the only solution. That's one of the reasons why the twins are tops in their field today."

Hermann Gadner instructs Rhona, Gaby Pleau and Rhoda. Gray Rocks, 1945.

Gadner for his part remained relatively silent; he was humble about himself, but the twins' strongest supporter. He had not one doubt about their abilities. "In style and racing technique the Wurteles are as good as men," he said in a *Maclean's* interview in February of 1944. "On any course of moderate length they could probably hold their own against anyone."

Through their career, many people fell under the spell of the Wurtele twins. Their energy and enthusiasm were and remain infectious. The same *Maclean's* reporter was smitten: "What are they like, these sisters of the skis? First of all, they are good-looking girls. When they sit together on a chesterfield under a standing lamp in the living room of their home, you notice they have the kind of healthy, bright hair that looks as though it has been slightly bleached from long hours in the sun. They have clear skins, good color and merry brown eyes. They are not Amazons; neither are they will-o'-the-wisps."

A *Sport* magazine article from 1947 agrees. "Rhona and Rhoda may be the greatest all-around woman athletes in Canadian annals," writes a reporter, "but unlike certain muscle-molls in sports, the well built girls are extremely attractive. These winsome sisters stand five feet six inches, and weigh 138 pounds. Each wears her chestnut-gold, wavy blond hair in a long schoolgirl bob. Fresh and wholesome they looked in their periwinkle blue cotton print dresses (it was a hot September day in Montreal) as they thumbed through their skiing scrapbooks, pausing at every page to make pertinent comments. No self-consciousness, no silly giggle stuff, about the Wurtele girls. Unlike so many woman athletes, Rhona and Rhoda know what to say and how to say it."

They knew how to talk to men, certainly. And Hermann Gadner was as much a man as any on the slopes. Anybody else could see his soft spot for the twins. "He had written me a letter," Rhona admits, "and wanted me to marry him. *Marry* him?" She laughs at the memory. But she didn't laugh at Gadner. "I very carefully wrote a letter and said that I cared very much for him as a brother and that we'd always be good friends. But after that I got to notice him more and...well, he had nice blue eyes..."

But really, that wasn't a consideration yet for the girls. Sure, they'd had a few boyfriends here and there, but right now they had other, more important pursuits. And, anyway, most men found it difficult to keep up with them.

The *Montreal Standard* imagined how it was for Rhoda.

> The Zone has not taken official action on the matter but there is an underground movement to have an armed motorcycle escort proceed Rhoda Wurtele down Mount Baldy tomorrow, when boys and girls mingle in the giant slalom at St. Margaret's.
>
> Two weeks ago Miss Wurtele, by legerdemain, accomplished the greatest feminine triumph since the Reform Bill of 1928. Getting the vote was nothing compared to this 21-year-old Penguin beating 100 males in the Taschereau by 25 seconds.
>
> Well, there has been pro and con about La Wurtele

The first ski classes in **North America**

Emile Cochand, a Swiss immigrant to Canada, was the first North American pro to teach classes, in 1911. The classes were set up eighteen years before any US operation. He later set up his own resort in the Laurentians, the Chalet Cochand. Later, Canada would start the first Ski Instructors Alliance in the Laurentians, in 1938. The US didn't get around to starting one until 1960.

Postcard of Chalet Cochand circa 1935.

> and her ski wax ever since, and certain it is that tomorrow eyes will peer at her all along the trail. Whatever magic formula she possesses will remain private no longer. The secret will out.
>
> Where does the armed motorcycle escort come in? That springs from malice. The boys argue that if Rhoda came down the Taschereau in four minutes and seven seconds—when they needed five—she should cover Baldy in nothing decimal eight.
>
> And anybody traveling that fast should have an armed escort.

The next week at a Mount Baldy Giant Slalom, Johnny Fripp redeemed himself. He beat everyone, including Rhoda. But she came in first among the women, and was faster than twenty-six of the men. Scribbled above the scrapbook pasting about that event in her handwriting is just one comment: "Nuts!"

By then the CBC had picked up the story, calling it "one of the greatest upsets in Canadian skiing competition." Neither Rhoda nor Rhona ever again laid waste to both male and female competition with the same effect. But the next month, Rhoda handily won the St. Adele women's downhill and slalom; among the men and women she came in third in the slalom, sixth in downhill.

"Yet there is no howl this brisk Monday morning that the watches were off," Myrtle Cook writes. "Are the lads convinced at last that Rhoda can race with any and all of them? Ethel Beauvais, another feminine speedster, was ahead of some of the slalom boys too. So was twin Rhona Wurtele. And so the boy vs. girl battle goes on."

But by the beginning of summer, feelings still weren't sorted out. When *Canadian Sport Monthly* wrapped up the main events of the season, they talked about the Taschereau race, the terrible blizzard, the problems with timing—but pointedly failed to mention who won the race.

And Rhoda herself?

"They wouldn't admit it," she says of her win. "Actually, I didn't even think about it. I raced as fast as I could and the results were that I won and I just accepted them."

Sometimes, the people involved in dramatic events are the last to realize the importance of their outcomes. Columbus didn't set out to find a new world, either. Certainly the twins were not using sports to further the cause of women's rights. They were racing because they loved to go fast.

Today, when pressed about how they felt being women in sport when they were pioneers no matter what they did, they shrug it off. "Oh, we were just having fun," they say. Rhona's daughter Margie Gillis, herself a pioneer for women in the field of dance, agrees that regarding the difficulties of women, "the things they talked about, even now too, was that there were just not that many opportunities for women. They never talk about more than that."

Yet the hoo-ha over Rhoda's win that bone-chilling day on Mont Tremblant may have been one of the pushes they felt to go further afield. There was less and less for them in the circle of Quebec racers. Not only were they crushing their competition, the men were whining about it. They began to look to the US Rockies for races. The Americans: they had good training, and money to spend. If they truly wanted to get better—if they wanted to keep challenged—they had to hit the Western US races where the Swiss and French came. "The French actually came back and raced here in Tremblant," says Rhona, "and we beat them again. So we had tremendous competitions and had a lot of fun, but we went out on our own, you know, and paid our own way."

They had to hit the Western US races where the Swiss and French came.

It was always that way. That taste of absolute freedom, the expectation that they could do what they wanted, when they wanted, would stay with Rhona and Rhoda forever. They always had the security of each other.

NO MAGIC: JUST TRAINING

The Taschereau race had made clear to those interested in skiing that training was important; to the twins it became imperative. Compared to the regimes of those who came after them—Lucile Wheeler, Anne Heggtveit, Nancy Greene, Kathy Kreiner, and Kerrin Lee-Gartner—the training regime of Rhona and Rhoda might seem hopelessly inadequate. Usually they only skied on weekends, unless they were attending annual instructors' courses or slalom schools at Gray Rocks. They worked with what they had, making what they achieved even more astounding.

By December of 1943, the twins were already giving Hermann Gadner all the credit for their progress in ski competition. "We asked them," a *Gazette* reporter said, "what kind of magic he taught them, anyway. ' No magic at all,' they said. 'He just started us all over on the fundamentals. But this time we learned them correctly.'"

The Canadian Ski Instructors Alliance (CSIA) began in 1938 when Bart Morgan brought Heinz von Allmen to introduce proper ski teaching to Canadians; Quebecer Louis Cochand was also instrumental, serving as one of the first presidents and writing the instructors' manual (in 1948 he would also be the manager of the Olympic Ski Team). For eight years, the Laurentian school was the only one in all of Canada. Women, however, were not allowed to even take the course, never mind become instructors. It took Pat Paré's spectacular downhill win at Tremblant in 1940 to break the barrier; Joe Ryan asked her to teach, and with him behind her they got the Alliance to join the twentieth century.

After two courses and two years as an assistant instructor, members were eligible to be tested for full-fledged instructors. The twins began taking the courses in 1943, and continued every year. The next logical step, and one that many good racers followed, was to become instructors themselves. It was an excellent way for ski

Longtime swimming coach for the twins Jimmy Rose shows Rhona the proper form for swim races while Rhoda looks on. Montreal, 1943, in the *Montreal Standard*.

lovers to make some money while keeping up their skills—but it also ended any hope of a racing career, since strict amateur rules applied in almost all races. The twins both passed their exams to be instructors, but it didn't take long for them to decide not to go pro—they had always wanted to race in Europe and compete in the big championship events, but the farthest they had gone so far was to New England. They would stay amateurs until into the 1950s. However, they would deal with the stubbornness of CSIA officials for decades to come. As late as the 1960s, when the twins were running ski schools, Rhona and Rhoda confronted sexism in the organization. When they took another instructors' course to get the highest level of training, Level 4, a CSIA official called them over when they were going to give out the pins for passing their training. "And they said, 'Well, girls, we know you did really well,'" remembers Rhoda, "'but there's no way this pin is ever going to be given to a woman.' That was a fact."

Say **What?**

A *gelandesprung* was a jump from a crouching position using both poles. Its direct translation is an "open field jump," since one didn't need a jumping platform in order to perform it.

Obviously, the person had no idea who he was talking to. They got their Level 3 pins soon enough.

Despite the obstacles in the 1940s, Rhona and Rhoda continued taking the ski instructor courses and attending Hermann Gadner's slalom school. They had precious few other options for training. Gadner's course attracted skiers from a wide area, among them Paula Kann, the Austrian-born sensation living in New Hampshire. She met the twins at such a course, and would cross paths with them more than once in the future as she raced for the Americans.

The lack of a real training program for the twins—for any athlete, in fact—became more obvious the higher they climbed. The year before the Olympics, columnist Myrtle Cook was concerned; they didn't seem to have any regime in the summer. An experienced Olympian herself, she knew the value of training. Oh sure, as soon as the snow melted the twins were off swimming again. And of course Rhona in particular won everything she entered: relays with the Aquabelles, 50-yard freestyles, the Dominion Championships (the one they had quit the bank for), Provincial Championships, and racing for the Ferry Command. The "twins of many wins" were named the quickest starters in swimming by Andy Forker, the official starter for Quebec meets, and he added, "Both these beautiful mermaids can be classed as the pick of swimmers in the Dominion." There were also the Aqua-Ganza shows, comic and musical numbers in the pool that were the forerunners of synchronized swimming, but then mostly used as fundraisers for the Navy—to send the poor boys overseas some cigarettes.

But while swimming was good exercise, it wasn't really training for skiing. "The two sports don't mix," Rhoda said later in a 1947 interview. "Any kind of sport helps to keep you in form for skiing but to train for swimming you have to swim." Rhona agreed. "Yes, at least a mile, perhaps two a day," she added. There was more to it too: swimming didn't have the excitement and risk of skiing. "With skiing there is the added interest of varying snow condi-

Rhona and Rhoda ready to do their laps at the Dominion Championships, Montreal, 1943.

tions and different slopes. In swimming it's just length after length of pool and when training we are not even allowed to dive."

So in the summer of 1947 Myrtle Cook invited them to join the Mercury Athletic Club, a club started to get disadvantaged kids involved in sports. They could come train with the kids, Cook suggested, not only to inspire the youngsters, but also to keep themselves fit. Rhoda had had appendix problems earlier; now it was Rhona's turn to have appendix trouble; she was kept out of commission for a few weeks with a series of attacks; but Rhoda leapt right in, in her usual style.

"I threw this javelin," she mentions. "I went to three meetings with this girl who showed me how to throw this thing (and the shot put too, and the discus). Anyway, I broke all the records in the damn thing."

It seemed that if the twins really wanted to, they could probably become Olympic track stars as well. In Rhoda's first track competition since a young girl in Trafalgar, she won the Shamrock Trophy for the Aggregate Club Championship, having clobbered all comers in the baseball throw, the previously mentioned javelin, the high jump, and the running broad jump. She was also the key member of the winning 440-yard relay team. With the javelin she had not only beaten the Provincial record, but tossed "the damn thing" farther than the last winner of the Dominion Championship.

"With some new sprinters it takes quite a time to get them to use the proper arm action," wrote the *Montreal Daily Star* that September. "With Rhoda and Rhona, it seemed to come naturally...With this attitude of paying strict attention to what a coach has to say, of following instructions and co-operating which has made them the champions they are to-day...Hermann Gadner, their ski instructor, used to tell us what co-operative pupils the Wurtele twins had been since their first session under his guidance."

It may have been this brief flirtation with the club that started the twins coaching schoolgirls around the same time—or it may simply have been the legacy of the Penguin Ski Club, which had supported the twins when they were youngsters too. At any rate, as early as the winter of 1943–44 the twins were already leading young girls down Murray Hill where they had skied as children, a taste of their future as full-time instructors. The importance of practice and training sunk in deep, and to this day they still love to pass on what they've learned.

But when they raced in those days, says Rhoda, "We liked it and wanted to get to the bottom." That was about all it took.

But when they raced in those days, says Rhoda, "We liked it and wanted to get to the bottom." That was about all it took.

"Now of course the racers have to win, there's so much time and money invested in them," she says. "Look at these top-notch people: they have their trainers, their nutritionists, their diets, their psychologists. It's such a kick the money they have in it now."

Rhoda, Hermann Gadner and Rhona performing a *gelandesprung* at Gray Rocks, circa 1943: fascinating to the boys.

COMIC BOOK HEROES

January of 1945 started out with promise. Overseas, in the seven months since D-Day, the Allies had made great progress pushing back the Nazis. At home on the slopes, Rhona and Rhoda, "two of the very few amateurs accepted," had completed Gadner's ski instructors course. Then they went on to his "Snow Eagle Ski School" at Gray Rocks. The cover of the January issue of *Canadian Sport Monthly* featured a wonderful photo of Rhona, Hermann Gadner, and Rhoda leaping over a jump—the twins beaming, Gadner serious and spiffy in sweater and tie. A *gelandesprung*, they called it. Not in the picture was Canadian war ace Buzz Buerling, who stayed at the lodge for a few days with a friend. "Rhona liked the friend," Rhoda says, "but I found Buzz fascinating."

"They'll be back!" Advertisement telling skiers all equipment going to war effort: from the *Saturday Evening Post*, Dec. 11, 1943.

The twins must have been no less fascinating to the boys. There were photos of the girls in newspapers every week, magazine articles across the continent, and newsreels playing in cinemas featuring the Flying Wurteles. Even their making the news made the news. *Canadian Sport Monthly* said they got "the biggest combined magazine publicity 'blast' ever accorded two Canadian athletes": *Maclean's*, the *Saturday Evening Post*, *Life*, Paramount newsreels, plus every local media, including CBC radio—and of course Father's Southern Canada Power Company newsletter. The upcoming piece in the *Saturday Evening Post* on "The Wondrous Wurtele Twins" was advertised by advance posters plastered all over Montreal. Coverage of the war filled every page in the magazine, each ad either trumpeting a company's involvement in helping the war effort or assuring clients their product would soon be back on shelves—including skis, racquets, and golf balls. The small feature on the twins stands out as a brief breath of fresh air that has nothing to do with war. "In all its years as a skiing stronghold," the magazine says, "Canada has never seen anything quite like Rhona and Rhoda Wurtele. When these twin sisters enter a women's race, it generally reduces things to a question of which of the pair will win."

Perhaps the most surprising media coverage they received in those heady years was in a 1944 *True Picture Magazine*—a comic book that included the story of "Canada's Terrific Twins" from their young days to their current triumphs. Full of inconsistencies, errors of fact, and just plain lack of knowledge (the famed Taschereau race where Rhoda beat all men and women shows the whole group of skiers coming down at one time, and the girls flashing across the finish line just ahead of Johnny Fripp), the comic is nevertheless a joyful romp in a comic book otherwise filled with war, killing, and deceit. Alongside the story of young skiing girls were "Giant Killers," the story of cruisers bringing down battleships; "Fearless Funmaker," the story of gunners in the air; "Carlson's Marine Raiders," and "Special Agent of the FBI."

The twins had already done more than attract and compete with the attention of war heroes; a few years before at the Laurentian Zone Championships, Rhoda and Rhona had placed first and second respectively in all three scores: downhill, slalom, and combined, which got them a mention in the *New York Times*. But even visiting royalty was put in their place when it came to skiing. Prince Bernhard of the Netherlands was one of a few royals spending wartime in Canada; when he invited the twins to join him for dinner (Princess Juliana was in Montreal having a baby), they said that would be impossible—they had to wax their skis and get to sleep early for the next day's events.

The front cover page and an inside page of ***True Picture-Magazine*** **featuring "Canada's Terrific Twins."**

That kind of discipline had already paid off. In 1945, the twins were honoured with the Rose Bowl, the annual award given by the Women's Amateur Athletic Federation to the outstanding woman athlete of the year. The award was created by Alexandrine Gibb, an early proponent of women in sport in Toronto (and a contemporary of Myrtle Cook). It was the first time Quebecers were given the award; it was also the first time skiers had won it, and the only time twins shared it.

Accolades came from men swept off their feet, from women respectful of their accomplishments, even from men they beat on the slopes. "Those girls used to do a lot of jumping on the hills," said Johnny Fripp, ski instructor, racer, RCAF—and loser to Rhoda in the '43 Taschereau. "To jump, you must have speed. They became accustomed to speed, lots of it. Now when they go into competition speed has no terrors for them."

Fame caught Rhona and Rhoda, put them under a microscope, and analysed the results. They couldn't have cared less. It was like when they were newborn infants and their mother fielded calls about what they were eating that day. Except now the papers covered it when they donated blood for the war effort, and magazines put them in winter fashion spreads. There was even a slight weariness for reporters used to fighting for juicy news, since twin wins were inevitable, and they seemingly could do no wrong, even off the hill. They got more press than a young hockey player for Les Canadiens who had just started in 1944, who the papers were already saying was destined to be one of the greats. They called him "Rocket" Richard. But the real rockets were double-barrelled and shooting down an icy slope.

When Rhona cracked a wrist practising on Mount Baldy, it made headlines in the *New York Times*. Rhona had surprised a lot of people since taking Gadner's courses. She was finally beginning to out-ski her twin. In 1944, the Laurentian Ski Zone committee voted Rhona "Woman of the Year"; she had won six out of eight major Laurentian ski events that year. Rhoda won the two races Rhona had lost, of course.

In 1944, the Laurentian Ski Zone committee voted Rhona "Woman of the Year"; she had won six out of eight Laurentian ski events.

Rhona's coping with the wrist injury that year illustrated the spirit of the girls. Both had been out practising the day before the Mount Baldy international race. In the days before lit slopes and night skiing, the girls pushed their training as far as they could, into the dangerous shadows of dusk. An injury was almost inevitable, but luckily it wasn't more serious. Rhona didn't think it was serious at all. With one arm in plaster and a sling and holding on to just one pole, she told the officials she was ready to race. Unfortunately for her, ski regulations had come a ways since the 1936 Olympics, when the first Canadian woman's team happily raced with broken fingers, bandaged feet, and monocles. Officials didn't give Rhona permission to race, though she skied that day. Some of the men racing at Baldy complained of going up the tow rope on slush and grass. They obviously hadn't seen Rhona going up. With one hand.

But with Rhona out, it was now up to Rhoda to win over the Americans at Mount Baldy. She could easily have done it too, were it not for one thing: that seemingly mysterious connection between twins. Their mother knew the phenomenon well: when one had an injury, the other soon followed, sometimes with the same kind of injury. Like when they were younger: Rhona was hit on the forehead with an oar while she was out boating and it

"Prince Bernhard of the Netherlands congratulates Rhoda after winning the Laurentian Zone Championship at Mont Tremblant, 1943." Apparently, the Prince wasn't too offended at being snubbed.

left a scar. Others thought it would finally solve the problem of identifying them. A few weeks later, however, Rhoda fell out of a tree—and got a scar in the same spot.

Rhoda rocketed out of the Mount Baldy start and looked good going down, but took a mighty fall in the downhill. Fortunately, there was no injury, but she came in an unheard of eleventh place, and only fourth in the slalom. Said the *Montreal Standard*, "As the Wurteles go so do Laurentian skiers, has been the old cry of experts, and it proved correct more than ever this afternoon." The Americans, led by Rebecca Fraser, cleaned up. Later the papers claimed that Rhoda had wiped out at exactly the same place Rhona had, but that was perhaps wishful reporting; Rhona had veered off too close to the trees in the nighttime, while Rhoda had fallen on the course. But it sure made for a good story.

But with the Wurteles out of the picture, as George Jacobsen reported in *Canadian Sport Monthly*, "The difference between [the Wurteles] and the rest of the Canadian team lies not so much in their undoubted ski talent, but [that] as athletes they know that to [be] 'tops' in any sport means hard work and continuous learning. They are the only ones who take continuous lessons from Hermann Gadner, who is an outstanding coach and skier. They therefore know their fundamentals."

In 1944, Rhona and Rhoda were back in form at Lake Placid, with Rhona taking the Kate Smith Trophy for the second year in a row (this time Cook didn't have to defend their travelling to race). The *New York Herald Tribune* had the temerity to publish a photo of the "American women skiers who competed at Lake Placid." Underneath the clipping in the twins' scrapbook is a handwritten note: "They competed—we won!"

"It can be truthfully set down," the MAAA magazine wrote, "that Rhoda and Rhona stand alone today as Canada's greatest contribution to women's skiing at home and across the line... as competitors, as instructors and as an inspiration to those coming after them." While that was only 1944, it would be a prescient summation of their contribution to a long line of skiers stretching into the future, and a reflection on Canada's Olympic hopes for decades to come.

Then, in March of 1944, fledgling reporter William Weintraub reported that Utah had invited the Wurteles to come ski the Rockies. A letter that "came all the way from Utah's snow country" asked them to compete in the famed Alta Cup in mid April, with a week to practise in the mountains under the snowcapped Twin Peaks. For the twins, it seemed made to order.

"It's the kind of thing we've always dreamed of," Rhona said at the time. She wasn't exaggerating. Competition had almost completely dried up for them in Canada; Paula Kann from New Hampshire was their nearest threat. And America, as in so many other areas, seemed to have more money for sports, better

The 1943 Canadian Team at Lake Placid, New York, competing for the Kate Smith Trophy. From left, former Olympic skier Diana Gordon-Lennox, Joan Staniforth, Margaret Burden, Rhoda, Gaby Pleau, Peggy Johannsen, Dorothy Beauvais, Rhona, Ethel Beauvais, Ebie Snively, Jackie Tracy.

programs, more ski areas, fewer officials stuck in the mud. But Rhona had broken her wrist only two weeks earlier, and the doctor was emphatic that the cast could not come off for another month. "Thus the biggest thrill of the Wurteles' career came and vanished in a flash," wrote Weintraub.

Perhaps that's why 1945 seemed like it would be an even better year. They were winning everything, and even when they lost an early race—Gaby Pleau beat Rhoda by a fraction of a second at Mont Gabriel—they rejoiced with the winner. Gaby, a Huron from the Lorette Reserve, was becoming a very good friend by this point. She was also shaping up to be a top racer. Red Bird George Jost, the first North American to win an international race in Europe, wrote about her in a newspaper column. "Gaby has more style, is very graceful and uses caution," Jost said, "while the twins are rugged skiers, strong and powerful and certainly daring."

There was another young girl and future friend of the twins starting to make her appearance on the slopes. At the Mont Tremblant races in March, Rhoda had finally bested her sister by ten seconds. But *Canadian Sport Monthly* noted, "Though the Wurteles won the race, the sweetheart of the day came in eighth.

This was Lucile Wheeler who celebrated her tenth birthday by entering her first major competition. Ten years old and she took Tremblant from the top in five minutes and some seconds. Just a few more years of practice and a few more pounds and we will have another winner in our midst." They were absolutely right. Eleven years later, the daughter of Gray Rocks Inn owner Harry Wheeler would go on to become the first ever Canadian to win an Olympic medal in skiing—a bronze in downhill at the 1956 Games in Italy.

Lucile Wheeler

But that was still a long way away, and for now the twins truly had no threats for miles around. Rhona continued her domination of the slopes, taking the race at Collingwood, Ontario, the Taschereau, St. Sauveur, and Gray Rocks slalom (on the twins' birthday). She also took the Mount Orford race with Rhoda right behind. Rhoda won the Tremblant Double Downhill, but then both of them faltered at the Kate Smith international event at Pico Peak, allowing teammate Margaret Burden a win. But that voyage led to greater things. On their way home, the twins stopped at Stowe, Vermont, for a few runs, and bumped into Betty Woolsey. Captain of the US women's Olympic ski team in 1936, the managing editor of *Ski Illustrated*, and considered one of the ten best women skiers in the world at the time, Betty had heard they had missed out on Utah last year—would they like to come this year, and stay at her ranch nearby? Of course they would, but they'd have to wait and see if it worked out. Meanwhile, the twins more than made up for relinquishing the Kate Smith trophy in 1945. Rhona won the Mount Baldy slalom, while Rhoda took fourth. Then the US girls came over the border for their turn. The Ste. Marguerite's international race was one of the hot events of the season, according to Myrtle Cook.

> This is one week-end the ski-boys ride the rumble seat—it is strictly a women's show and well worth a trip to the Baldy slopes. There is more fun watching girls

Rhona, Gaby Pleau, and Rhoda, Lake Placid, 1945. On the slopes, Gaby was "graceful and cautious," while the twins were "rugged and daring."

compete in skiing than the men. Why? Because the ladies are less grim about it and their colorful racing togs add to the mountain scene. No doubt about their speed being close (sometimes better) than the men's—shades of last year's Taschereau for instance!

It was a delight to watch Pat Paré and Peggy Johannsen tear around a downhill course in the past—it is just as much pleasure now eyeing the Wurteles, Gaby Pleau, Margaret Burden, or those great Americans, run the course. The girls get plenty of laughs out of their competitive skiing.

But although the event attracted the largest crowd of the season, the weather didn't cooperate. A driving rain came down

"The girls get plenty of laughs out of their competitive skiing"—even Laurentian Zone president Fred Urquhart, middle in coat, laughs this time. Rhoda giggling on the right, at Lake Placid with the International Team, 1943.

that February weekend, temperatures soared, "and the peak of Mount Baldy was lost in low mists," the *New York Times* reported. At the top of the trail, racers could barely see past the tips of their wooden skis.

Rhona and Rhoda, of course, were in their element. "As identical as a pair of skis," the *Times* said, "the 23-year-old twins crossed the line in one-two fashion with Rhona first." Not only that, but Rhona had set an all-time women's record for speed on "Canada's most celebrated downhill," at 1 minute 2.2 seconds; Rhoda was two-tenths of a second behind her. Although Paula Kann took the combined scores eventually for the Americans (with Rhona and Rhoda just behind her), the Canadian team won on totals.

THE GREAT SKI TECHNIQUE DEBATE

The twins had attributed the win to a "secret weapon." Twenty minutes before the race they applied some "HG" to their hickories, a special wax concocted by Hermann Gadner. And now it was Gadner's turn to be in the spotlight, a place he was never very comfortable in. Gadner was all over the place. Being one of the few ski instructors in Canada, his basics—snow plows, stem Christianias, and parallel Christianias—were featured in full photo spreads in magazines.

The early days of skiing saw only a handful of ski instructors in Canada, Harvey Clifford wrote in a retrospective of the CSIA in the 1958 *Canadian Skiing Annual*. "But there was also a handful of different techniques to further complicate the first course."

Those techniques—and instructors—kept coming from the birthplace of skiing, Europe. It was a stormy time, Clifford writes, each year bringing in a new "latest thing." Among those who contributed were the now familiar names of Hermann Gadner, Hannes Schneider, Benno Rybizka, Luggi Foeger, Mario Gabriel, Hans Falkner, and Emile Allais.

First the Swiss methods of exaggerated movements were followed, then the wide-stemming steered turn of Schneider's Arlberg system. Gadner brought in his own reverse shoulder-drop system, then Gabriel brought a reverse Swiss system; Foeger had his "Drift versus Lift" system. Finally Frenchman and World Championship winner Emile Allais eliminated Austrian movements and the snowplow, bringing his skis parallel and diving forward, and bringing in rotation with an exaggerated shoulder swing. This "Parallel" skiing was dismissed as yet another fad.

If the list seems confusing to most skiers today, imagine the skiers confronted with a new technique every year. And such a dry listing doesn't do justice either to the raging debates that swelled each year, to the arguments and fights over the relative merits

Anyone, including the Wurtele twins, who raced at the Parallel Ski Club at Domaine d'Estérel would lose their Zone card.

of the different techniques—that even led to threats of banning skiers if they used new styles. In early 1945, the Beauvais sisters, Dorothy and dark-eyed Ethel, declared that they would no longer race in the Laurentians if Fred Urquhart continued as president of the Zone. They claimed he had said anyone, including the Wurtele twins, who raced at the Parallel Ski Club at Domaine d'Estérel (a resort in the Laurentians) would lose their Zone card. The ski instructor there happened to be Maurice Beauvais, Dorothy and Ethel's brother.

Maurice in turn called Urquhart a "dictator"—strong language while Hitler was still around—but Urquhart excused himself by saying, "I strongly advised the Wurtele twins not to go to Estérel because they may be influenced by the Parallel System that you are teaching."

As the twins kept getting better and better thanks to Hermann Gadner's instruction (and the women and men around them were forced to improve too), their teacher found himself in the centre of one of the most public battles of skiing styles. The hardest fought battles were between Gadner's Snow Eagle Ski School with his modified Arlberg technique—he preferred to call it "Alpine," or Canadian Ski School—and Fritz Loosli's Ski Hawk Ski School, the major proponent of the parallel technique, in Quebec City.

By February of 1945, the editors of *Canadian Sport Monthly* had heard enough: "During the past four winters, skiers of this continent have heard a good deal about the Arlberg and Parallel ski teaching. Most readers know the story of both pretty well by this time." Gadner's techniques, they summed up, dwelt on fundamentals good for any snow conditions, using time-honoured Austrian techniques. Loosli had got a lot of publicity for his methods, particularly since CP Rail backed him as a Hotel Frontenac (today Le Château Frontenac) instructor; he had also become popular through a book he had written on the method, and the shouting of his critics hadn't hurt either. Loosli now claimed he could train anyone to ski in three days; the Canadian Ski School thought

Dorothy and Ethel Beauvais, skiing sisters of Estérel, with Rhona and Rhoda at Lake Placid, 1944.

his methods a "poor imitation" of France's great FIS Champion, Emile Allais.

A few years down the road, the great Emile Allais himself would come to Quebec, taking up the post of pro at the parallel-friendly Valcartier Ski Lodge near Quebec City. On a visit to the American West, *Western Skiing* magazine encapsulated his method: "Emile Allais is here and all you Arlberg technicians beware. Allais' French Ski Method keeps your skis constantly parallel and no longer does your ski act as a steering wheel but the shifting of the body weight from one ski to another, while both skis remain parallel, is the answer to all your problems."

Image courtesy CP Hotels

Cover from Chateau Frontenac menu, CP Hotels, 1947. Publicity battles to win over skiers were fierce.

"*Canadian Sport Monthly* (like a lot of people) is still mildly curious," the editors wrote, "but a little tired of the whole squabble which should have run its course by now. To clear it up, once and for all, this magazine throws out a challenge to the two champions of these respective views...as a side inducement *Canadian Sport Monthly* will post a cheque for $250...to the winner of the race between Gadner and Loosli down Mont Tremblant."

It was a huge amount of money, said at the time to be the highest ever offered for a ski race between two people. It was more than a soldier was paid in a month, and could get you 250 good dinners in a swell restaurant. But Fritz Loosli initially turned down the offer; he called the offer "bad ski etiquette."

The whole thing was more of a publicity stunt than anything, perhaps; after all, the "Scribes' Derby," a ski race of newspaper reporters, was coming up that week. So the invitation was reworked to get both advocates to come to the Derby and simply demonstrate their styles. Hermann Gadner took it seriously enough to delay a trip to the Canadian Rockies for a few days, but Loosli claimed to get sick and didn't show. He sent his assistant Jack Miller in his stead. In a room full of reporters, Miller "found himself waving a wildcat by the tail in the person of aggressive Hermann Gadner." Each shoved the other to prove their stance was no good, "and for a moment the air was charged with potential fisticuffs," but Gadner

While the Chateau Frontenac may have used Gaby Pleau as a model to advertise their skiing, Canadian Pacific bought the rights to the famous photo of the Wurtele twins jumping and used it to advertise Canadian skiing. Somewhere along the line, the girls became redheads and not identical twins. From 1947.

The *Gazette*, March 1945. Gadner, centre left, and Miller, centre right. When Gadner shoved Miller to show his balance was not secure in the parallel stance, Miller shoved back, "and for a moment the air was charged with potential fisticuffs."

diffused arguments by bringing along dark-eyed Ethel Beauvais and child prodigy Lucile Wheeler to show their stuff on the slopes; he was apparently not averse to publicity stunts himself.

"Nothing decided at all," the *Gazette* reported, "but the hottest debate session on the sport's highly controversial 'parallel system' provided the winter's heartiest laughter for Laurentian experts and news writers alike..." Everyone turned out to be good sports after all. Eventually, the result of the controversy was that "the stuffed shirt attitude held by so many ski officials in the past is to be abandoned in favor of a more elastic policy."

The debate about how to ski had been going on for a long time. "How to ski" diagram, 1912.

The Wurtele twins had come to the event as celebrity time-keepers for the Scribes' Derby, but they had more important things on their minds than debating skiing techniques. As usual, they just wanted to race, and win; in one month Utah's Alta Cup would take place, and they were still weighing their chances about getting there. Gadner had invited them to come skiing with him at Banff and around the Canadian Rockies, too, but things were less set up for racing there, and they couldn't afford to go on both trips. At any rate, their mother Colly said she didn't have a good feeling about them going to Banff; she urged them to go to Utah instead. "She seemed clairvoyant about these kinds of things," Rhona says.

Hermann Gadner at Gray Rocks in 1944. He had just been laughing at the silliness.

GADNER

The twins bided their time; a month seemed an interminably long wait, but in the meantime they raced Mont Tremblant and Pico Peak with success. Then, on March 26, Rhoda was at work and got a telephone call from Myrtle Cook—not an unusual occurrence, reporters called her all the time. But this time Myrtle had news for her: Hermann Gadner, the twins' mentor, had been killed in an avalanche.

It was a sobering shock. Hadn't he just been laughing it up in the silliness of the Great Ski Debate the week before?

I guess if anything, his death made us more determined to do well and prove his coaching.

The details were conflicting in the first days after his death, but it was sure that at five o'clock on a clear warm day, halfway between Temple and Skokie lodges in the Lake Louise district, Gadner had been buried in the crushing weight of a snowslide. It was exactly in that area where he had spent his first two years in Canada after leaving Austria and the Nazis. He was a man who knew more about avalanches than anyone else in the country. "Two hours later," said *Canadian Sport Monthly*, "under eight feet of white they took Hermann, smothered and frozen—this man of the snows who only recently smiled and said to us, 'Ah, spring snow avalanche? Don't bother to struggle in one, because you're dead anyway.'"

Rhona and Rhoda were grief-stricken; they were twenty-three-year-olds who had been relatively sheltered from the horrors of war, but this death occurred so close to home; it could have been them. It was the first loss of innocence. "That was a very great hurt," says Rhona. "He was very dearly loved by the twins."

Hermann's body was brought back to the Laurentians, and his funeral was at the little church in St. Jovite. A group of ski instructors carried his coffin up the street to a little cemetery by a river.

"Hermann had been an inspiration to us all in our skiing," says Rhoda. "He had encouraged and cared and it was a huge blow to lose him. What memories we had of the fun times at Gray Rocks, the wonderful slalom schools we had attended, and his special wax. He had invented and experimented with it, and he taught us all the tricks that we guarded and used. After he died, we never had success duplicating what he had done. It never worked for us. I guess if anything, his death made us more determined to do well and prove his coaching."

Eventually more details came out about how such an expert skier got caught. He was giving a demonstration down a steep slope, with others watching him at the bottom of the hill. They couldn't tell whether he had started the slide or was skiing away from it, but he shot into the bowl at the foot of the hill and was covered. Two spectators at the bottom were covered too, but not so much that they couldn't be quickly dug out. The twins heard another story: he was leading a party of eight across the sharp descent. He went across first, told them not to make any sudden moves—he knew the area was ripe for avalanches. Then one of the last across, a younger kid, did a jump to turn at the end. That started the avalanche.

After eight years as the Head Examiner of the Canadian Ski School, Hermann Gadner's enthusiasm and commitment to the sport had touched almost everyone who'd been up to the hills. "Hermann Gadner had become almost a legendary figure in the Laurentians," said *Canadian Sport Monthly*. "All skidom mourned the maestro, as he was known."

He possessed an uncanny ability at picking out promising material; his favorite pupils were the Wurtele sisters.

"Born and raised in the avalanche region of the Austrian Tyrol," wrote the *Daily Star*, "he was more thoroughly familiar with avalanche conditions than perhaps any Canadian skier. He possessed an uncanny ability at picking out promising material and his favorite pupils the Wurtele sisters are today considered the best women competitors in the country."

Among the many mourners at his funeral were the Wurteles, Benno Rybizka, George Jacobsen, Gaby Pleau, and Fritz Loosli. Frank Scofield, President of the CSIA, said that Gadner had influenced Canadian skiing more than any one man. Tom Wheeler, for whom Gadner had worked for the past years, said, "It felt as a family loss."

Gadner, who had escaped Nazi control of Austria in 1938, never lived to see the end of the Nazis, just months away. Later it was discovered that he had died on his thirty-fifth birthday. Now, say the twins, "His ghost is out there [in the Rockies] in a little shack."

NEW BEGINNINGS

Ironically the death of Hermann Gadner, who was the cornerstone of Canadian skiing, also meant the beginning of a whole new era for the sport. It was then—in fact, beginning only a month after Gadner's death—that the twins began to spread their wings. From their new heights they could see much further, even to the hitherto unthinkable peak of Olympia.

Of course, there was another event that would completely change the world around them. On May 8 of 1945, the Axis powers admitted defeat, and in Europe World War II finally came to an end. Popular imagery shows people dancing in the streets, ticker tape parades for returning soldiers, tears of joy and relief. In fact, for many the war ended as it had begun—subtly, over a long period of time. Not all returning soldiers were hailed as conquering heroes. At a meeting of the Canadian Amateur Ski Association in January of 1946, Myrtle Cook reported, "It took the LCC [Lower Canada College] Club's Mr. Christie to remind the meeting that several of the boys were back from overseas and merited a warm welcome. That should have been the first item on the agenda—a welcome back for the overseas lads!"

Perhaps people were relieved that the war was finally over, and that they could get back to their regular lives; perhaps they had heard too much about it. In Rhona and Rhoda's scrapbooks and writings, too, there is no direct mention of the end of the war. Their brother George had come back to Canada, and a newspaper clipping announced his return. But for the twins, more immediate and personal victories took precedence, for this was when they began their own version of How the West Was Won.

They weren't alone. When they were racing in the Alta Cup in Utah weeks before the end of the war, the headline that crossed the top of the front page in the *Deseret News* of Salt Lake City screamed "MCLEAN AND KIDDER WIN IN ALTA CUP

GIANT SLALOM." Both were American skiers; Rhona had come in third, Rhoda fourth. The second headline underneath mentioned almost as an afterthought, "Russ 7 Miles From Berlin."

Neither of the twins had ever been the kind to trumpet their triumphs or display their emotions for everyone to see; Myrtle Cook, when talking about the twins' new triumphs, says, "You know them as not preferring to bask in the limelight." The Americans were unused to that attitude. Utah papers called Rhoda "quiet, remote Rhoda Wurtele, from Canada." Yet at the Alta race, just a month after Gadner's death, reporters found that "the feelings which the Wurtele twins showed for Gadner were in themselves a fine tribute to him and in taking second and third place in the meet, they did him an honor to which no one at Alta was insensible."

With the end of war, skiing took a great leap forward—and so did the twins. Here Rhoda (in goggles and hat) leaps with Mary Pitt at North Hatley in the Eastern Townships, Quebec, 1955.

So much of the story of the twins' rise to the peak of the skiing world—they were crowned "the Queens of North American Skiing"—was tied in to the spirit of the times. The post-war years became ones of optimism and hope, and the very real scientific advances spurred by the needs of war not only changed peacetime households and workplaces, but immediately began to affect skiing and sports too.

One of the first changes noticeable was in ski instruction. The December after the war, the twins took the instructors' course again, passing their exams with ease while many men didn't make it into the graduating class. They were still adamant about remaining amateurs, though: "It is almost a sure thing they will try out for the Olympic team," said Cook.

In that same year, applications to the Canadian Ski School, which had been quietly operating in the Laurentians for eight years, suddenly tripled; the soldiers were back from war, they were in shape, and many were familiar with skiing. The Laurentians school was still the only official avenue for instructors across the whole of Canada—skiers came from Ontario, even from the Rockies. The call quickly went out that new schools should be added. The idea was tossed around about starting a travelling ski school, since the only qualified teachers were in the East; they would take the school through Ontario, the Prairie provinces, into British Columbia. While large-scale ski resorts were popping up all over the Rockies in the US, in Canada it was still too expensive a proposition to open up the mountains. The Banff area was reserved for truly dedicated skiers, until the 1950s. They would spend a day taking an old Model T, then a horse, and then snowshoes or skis up to Skoki Lodge. The Trans-Canada highway into Banff was only completed in 1960.

The Laurentians school was still the only official avenue for instructors across the whole of Canada.

Instructors themselves were changing, too. Luggi Foeger had replaced Hermann Gadner in the Ski Alliance instructors' course; as Hannes Schneider's chief assistant in the Austrian Tyrol, he was more than qualified. Ski schools for amateurs were all over the place, of course. But the biggest news after the war was that Mont Tremblant, in February of 1946, would become the first of the big winter resorts to have a "home-grown product heading its ski school." Benno Rybizka had left. The lucky man was none other than Johnny Fripp, recently released from the RCAF and landing in the plum job. It meant the end of his racing career, but photos of a beaming Fripp at the time betray his happiness at beating others to it. Tremblant was still the primary ski station along the East coast.

Even ski racing in Canada began to feel the effects of peacetime. At the Laurentian Zone Downhill Championships in February of 1946 (Rhoda came first in all events, Rhona second, and the Burden sisters behind them), the *Gazette* reported that "there was a touch of the future about today's meet, for it was the first time in

Laurentian history that a ski race was radio-controlled. A walkie-talkie set, on loan from the army, was located at the top of the mountain, with another three-quarters of a mile away at the finish line at the bottom." The signal to start came from the radio at the bottom, almost instantaneously given by the official at the top as they came over the headphones. Running wires up and down the course for each race would soon become a thing of the past. Presumably, the next time Rhoda beat all the men and women in a race the grumblers couldn't lay the blame on faulty timing.

Skiing among amateurs had never been so popular. "The season was short, but not dull," William Weintraub said in his 1945 season wrap-up. "A mushrooming ski population made it a profitable one...with standing room only on the trains." That popularity was reflected in magazines of the time—and not just ski magazines. Women's fashion magazines, like *Mayfair*, featured skiers in ski fashion layouts, including Germaine Prefontaine, Dorothy Beauvais, and Rhoda—who was so famous by this time that the magazine didn't even mention her name, taking for granted everyone would know her.

Flier advertising Mont Tremblant, 1944. After the war, amateur skiing had never been so popular.

And yet it was exactly the growing popularity of skiing and racing that prompted Rhona and Rhoda to look beyond the Laurentians.

"We considered that the best racing and the way to improve," says Rhoda, "was to have more competition—and it was more exciting through the States and in the West." The twins won virtually everything they entered, from Utah to Tremblant to Lake Placid to Sugar Bowl in California. One headline from the time reads, "Rhona Wurtele beats Rhoda," pretty well summing up the era.

There were some sour grapes from those who stayed behind, apparently. "There's quite a lot of books written about Tremblant, and they should have covered us a lot," says Rhoda. "But they didn't because we just took off. We didn't want to race around here anymore. When we did come back we cleaned up in Tremblant."

The Dominion Championships (later the National

Championships) still hadn't been reinstated after the war's end; the twins would have easily become the tops in Canada, had there been such a competition. So instead they looked to the West and the Harriman Cup, the Silver Dollar Race in Nevada, the American Nationals—and not only got to race the Americans, but the Swiss and French who came out for those races. "And we beat them too," Rhoda says.

At a race in Mount Hood the twins and other Canadians with them didn't have the money to splurge on a big hotel. "So we went in a summer cabin in the national park. There was no heating, and we put newspapers on the bed; one person kept the fire going in the middle of the room. Back at the fancy lodge they had lovely rooms, and the Swiss team came to see us. They found a whole bunch of us in one little room, our washing hanging everywhere. And they had these lovely little outfits, and gifts for us." Meanwhile, the Canadians had to go and pocket sandwiches from hospitality tables.

Before all that, however, came the very first big race out West: the 1945 Alta Cup in Utah. Rhona and Rhoda thought they were going out West just to have better competition, more fun, and see the world. "We really didn't know too much about it," Rhoda says. "We didn't visualize ourselves as Olympians. We just liked it and wanted to beat everybody. It was just fun."

In the same way as they were blithely unaware of what they had done and would do for women in sport, neither were they conscious that they were taking pioneering steps to put Canadian skiers on the world map. Others were putting much more importance on this venture. Newspapers called it the first real test for Canadian skiers after the war. There would be "fluffy powder that sometimes reached the competitors' knees," high altitudes, and international-calibre competition: the races would be an indication of how Canucks could hold up internationally.

For all that expectation and national pride, however, it was neither the Canadian nor the Québécois government sending out

A whole new world: Leaving for Alta, Utah—and parts unknown—March 1945, at the Montreal train station. They were going to their first races out west. "We didn't really know too much about it."

its best team; there were no sponsors. In some ways, not much had changed since the wives of diplomats decided to become the Canadian ski team in 1936. Those who had the time and money could get out to Utah. Pierre Jalbert of Quebec City hopped the train, accompanied by parallel-skiing enthusiast Fritz Loosli; the twins raised their own funds, and Germaine Prefontaine (whose father had once been mayor of Montreal) was also able to come with them.

In fact, in their own home hills, after having won everything and having become fully qualified to be ski instructors, the twins were still locked in Class B—much to Myrtle Cook's consternation. She wrote in February of 1946,

> Not only have the Wurteles slalomed all opposition into the snow, at times these flying twins have beaten their male rivals. They are already labeled as Olympic prospects...If it's a matter of pride that the gentlemen who run our ski business don't want the women on an equal classification basis, then there is a remedy. Let the women run their own show as they do (and quite well) in other sports.

As an added gripe, Cook reminded Quebecers that Ontario was well into raising money to send a summer Olympic team overseas. "And what has Quebec got?" Almost nothing, was the answer. A month later Cook was furious—and embarrassed.

> Now? Or do we have to wait until Rhona Wurtele wins an Olympic crown before the Laurentian Zone will boost her into the deserved grade "A" division? She is just back from the U.S. with the National Women's Championship! Skiers from 18 states competed against our Westmount Wurteles. If the Zone is slow to acknowledge their preferred rating here, they are not backward

> with the typewriter ribbon bouquets over there. For instance the *Herald Tribune* comments Rhona "far outstripped her field" at Franconia...they add "had she been competing in the men's field of approximately 80 contenders, she would have finished in 11th place..." The *New York Times*, rarely given to overstatements, points out that Rhona was "brilliant in her technique and in interpretation of the 'gates' as she sped down the steep run. Her courageous run was loudly cheered, for her time was better than that of many in the men's division." How about it, Freddy [Urquhart]?

Her courageous run was loudly cheered, for her time was better than that of many in the men's division.

Perhaps it was best the twins went into the races naively; perhaps if they had known the expectations that would be placed on them, much beyond their class rating, they would have been more nervous. As it was, the trip west became one long hootenanny. The newspaper articles from Salt Lake City spell out one story: who won, and how. But in June of 1945, the Southern Canada Power News (their father at the helm, of course) devoted almost their entire newsletter to the twins' recollections of their trip, and told the story behind the news: "Out West With Two Famous Skiers." It was still a rare enough occasion to travel across the West, apparently; the article is full of joyful discovery, and the girls went much further than just Utah. They discovered Colorado rivers, real cowboys in Wyoming, actors in Hollywood, and the ocean in California.

April 9, 1945, would long stay in their memories, since that was the day they "started to realize one of our greatest ambitions, to ski the West and with America's top-flight skiers."

On the train trip, the twins delighted as much in their being oddities, top skiers heading out to new lands, as they delighted in the new things they saw. "Often those entering the Ladies' compartment were seen beating a hasty retreat, because of the very strange people within, bobbing up and down and doing strange

How to dress for skiing, 1940s style: wool pants, wool sweater (the twins had each knitted theirs), leather boots, wooden skis, bamboo poles—and the latest craze, sunglasses. Note the fresh-cut slalom gates. Rhona at Atla, Utah, 1947.

exercises...just Rhona and I trying to keep our muscles in condition, our skiing having been completely over for 3 weeks before we left..."

When they finally arrived in Salt Lake City, they found their skiing friends Harvey Clifford and Johnny Fripp already there. Then, "We proceeded to the Temple where a Deacon preached to us and it is interesting to note that the Mormons are now nearly all content with one spouse and always look on the optimistic side of life."

The twins' religion, however, was closer to the heavens. For the first time, the twins drove up to the Rockies, through twenty-five miles of cliffs and gorges, past avalanches like the one that had taken their mentor, through tunnels, and finally up to the ski lodge at 8,060 feet. The highest they'd been until then was in Vermont, at 4,000 feet. Immediately they started having severe headaches. "We used to blame everything that went wrong on the altitude," writes Rhoda.

The ski resort of Alta, the second major high-altitude resort after Sun Valley in the US, had been the vision of Dick Durrance, an American who went to grade school in Austria and became America's only internationally ranked male racer. It was unlike anything the twins had seen before. When they first got there, they heard two news items: one, President Roosevelt had died of a cerebral hemorrhage; and two, it had been snowing for ten straight days and there were eighteen inches of fresh powder on the slopes. Both of the news items were shocking, but the latter would affect them more profoundly.

The twins wondered at first if their techniques would work in this new "champagne powder".

With that amount of snow, most of the slopes were closed due to the danger of avalanches. But the minute Rustler's Mountain opened up, the twins were the first on its back. "It is so steep when you stand on it and put your elbow out you touch the side," they wrote. "We could hardly stop from singing with delight as we soared down, snow flying above the waist...this is the life!"

On top of Mount Baldy—the 11,000-foot Utah version—the American skiers crowded around the famous twins, anxious to see if their ski techniques were different. "The westerners are very keen skiers," they wrote, "and we had to do the best to keep up the standard of our technique, which we incidentally know to be the best. Hermann Gadner's Alpine technique which he developed is infallible, in any kind of snow." Actually, the twins wondered at first if their techniques would work in this new "champagne powder"—but with the westerners gathered at the top of the hill, they discovered "with immense satisfaction" that Gadner's method worked just as well in the deep snow.

There were new things to discover with fashions, too. Although the twins had something new of their own for this trip—mittens with their names on them so officials could distinguish them—the Americans looked mighty funny on the hills. Spending whole days in the sun at that altitude had given the girls sunburns before they even started racing. The Westerners combatted the sun by smearing zinc oxide on their arms and faces, making them "look most peculiar," Rhoda said, "like ghosts." They also wore a new look that would soon become a major fashion statement: sunglasses. The glasses, developed to protect pilots from high altitude glare, were another innovation that came to civilians through war technology.

There were less welcome surprises for the girls: they discovered the Americans betting on the races. That was upsetting, "as skiing has always been such a clean sport, but even the officials took part," Rhoda wrote at the time. "Big bucks were bet and offered to racers, which it would not surprise me to know some received Under the Table [as] gifts," Rhoda wrote later. In another race when Rhoda won the Harriman Cup, "I was given a beautiful orchid by a man who won a bundle." The twins dealt with this new aspect of the sport the best way they knew how: they left to go wax their skis for three hours.

There were a lot of things the Americans did differently; they were astonished to learn, for instance, that Rhona and Rhoda were weekend skiers. With high-altitude mountains and money behind them, the American racers skied every day from October to July. Barbara Kidder, the nineteen-year-old Denver skier and their major competition, was attending college on a skiing scholarship—something utterly unheard of in Canada.

There were a lot of things the Americans did differently; they were astonished to learn, for instance, that Rhona and Rhoda were weekend skiers.

Yet for all their advantages, the American skiers were not that far ahead of the "back country" twins. While Rhona and Rhoda were encountering for the first time the conditions they might find in Europe and at the Olympics, their first race, the Giant Slalom, was also run in a blinding snowstorm—usually a good omen for the Wurteles. With the course more open and longer than they were used to, they used more caution in case parts were icy. They "weren't unhappy" with third- and fourth-place finishes, behind Kidder and Kann.

They knew the downhill was their strength, though. The twins had checked out the course thoroughly, knew its sharp turns, icy patches, its drifts like jumps—three full miles of speed. "We had toiled up that trail many more times than the rest of the competitors, as we wanted to be sure our legs would hold up on such a tough course." The day of the race the snow was still coming down heavy. Everybody was up early, too: there were no ski tows to the top of the course. But in the downhill Rhoda came in fourth, Rhona a distant tenth; because neither Kidder nor Kann had beaten her, however, Rhoda led the combined at the end of the second event.

By the third day the twins were getting well acquainted with the conditions, and Rhona won the slalom, with Kidder second and Rhoda third. It looked like a very tight race for the combined totals. At the banquet when the winner was announced, Kidder came out on top—by 33/100ths of a second. Rhoda took second and Rhona third for the tournament. It was a most successful first foray into the high reaches of ski competition, and Rhoda said with her usual modesty, "Barbara [Kidder] is a charming girl of 19, who skis beautifully, and we could not have lost to a more worthy competitor." The men's side hadn't done badly either. Pierre Jalbert, Fritz Loosli's exponent of parallel skiing, came in third in combined points.

After ten days in Utah and all the skiing in deep powder they could fit in, the twins rushed off with Germaine Prefontaine to catch the train for Los Angeles where they would see their uncle Reverend Arthur. He picked them up at the train station, and piled the three girls, their luggage, ski equipment, and seven pairs of skis in his car. With skis poking out all windows, he apologized to the girls that he had to rush off to an important engagement—a funeral at Forest Lawn Cemetery, final resting place of the stars—so the sunburned girls and their skis went with him to the funeral, winding through the hot April sun and palm trees. It was a classic Los Angeles moment.

Arthur himself was a rare bird to the twins. His church was located in the epicentre of la-la land, on Sunset Boulevard, and in the St. Thomas Episcopal Church, "he wore a hat and had fancy incense and rang little bells at the service because the people of California prefer more thrills." His wife was even more exotic—a "strange artist," she entertained the girls with her poems and oil paintings. But even in these unusual surroundings rested a reminder of home. Arthur had taken the baptismal font from the family church at Acton Vale and installed it in Hollywood. It was a whirlwind visit for the girls, but they managed to see Grauman's Chinese Theatre, some of the studios, and the Hollywood Bowl, and to wade at the beaches. Rhona was thrilled to tour Walt Disney Studios, since she had caught some of her mother's interest in the visual arts and always thought she could be a cartoonist. The famous twins were given special treatment, led through the hallowed halls by Walt's brother.

Then it was back on the train to head for Montreal—except, as would often happen in the future, the twins had received another invitation and thought they might make another little side trip. Betty Woolsey, who had invited them to Utah, now extended the invitation to come to Jackson Hole, and the first Teton Spring Ski Derby. Who could turn that down? So they jumped off the train, delaying their trip home, and caught a bus for cattle country, competing for space with cowboys, crates of chickens, bags of mail, beehives—and their seven pairs of skis.

For the race, skiers had to walk up Teton Pass; the run was so steep, and the snow so hard, that when Rhoda dropped a mitten and a pair of glasses, and another person dropped a camera lens shade, the items —as they later discovered—shot down the run, finally lining up at the bottom at the edge of the highway. This time in the Giant Slalom race Paula Kann had the fastest time, with Rhona, then Rhoda, close behind. Betty Woolsey took fourth place, but with both twins in the top three the Canadian team won the Derby.

The gang of nine skiers (among them Paula Kann, Betty Woolsey, and Jerry Hiatt, who was beginning to take a shine to

Rhoda and Germaine Prefontaine at Jackson Hole, 1945: "We could hardly stop from singing with delight...this is the life!"

Rhoda by this point) wanted to hang around the Teton mountains a little longer, though there wasn't much snow left for skiing. Instead, they went for a four-day trip into the mountains, skiing in for nine miles to the National Forest Lodge. They got in more sunbathing than skiing, "watching the avalanches peel off the mountains, about every five or ten minutes...first there is a great roar, like thunder, then you look up at a peak and watch the wet spring snow sliding down, like a waterfall, gathering in depth and speed, sweeping everything down in its wake." There must have been many thoughts of Hermann Gadner's fate on that trip.

Their appetites for skiing now only matched by their appetite for food, "It was with great relish that we sat down to our $2.50 steak dinners." To add to their delight, sitting at the table next to them at the lodge was Wallace Beery, the noted actor of *Treasure Island* and *Grand Hotel*, hits from the twins' girlhood, and the first of the many husbands of the inimitable Gloria Swanson. When they started singing their Quebec chansons, the hard-drinking actor stumbled off into the night.

It was finally time to get back on the train, but—surprise!—they purposely missed it again, and instead opted to drive down with their friends to Aspen, Colorado, to get in some more skiing. Along the way they passed herds of cattle, horses, and sheep winding along the highways, with cowboys and covered wagons bringing up the rear. It was like going back in time, or having their childhood games and favourite movies come to life. But the people of Aspen—up till now a forgotten silver-mining town—were just as thrilled to see them. The newspapers reported that "the best skiers in Canada" had come to stay a few days exploring the area. And explore they did. After collecting ration points for enough food for a week (the war was still on), the gang first had to ski a mile and a half along the road to get to the base; then they put their sealskins on the skis and began climbing at 4:00 a.m. Four hours later, now above the treeline, and with the coyotes howling around them, they got some downhilling in, as well as some trout fishing. The next day they rose at four again, and got to the 13,000-foot-high peak of Mount Hayden.

"It was a lot of climbing," Rhoda understated, "rather exhausting, but the trick was to keep going at a steady pace with never more than a five-minute rest...wide expanses of the most perfect skiing imaginable. Every one of us was so happy...we fairly screamed with joy as we soared down on the most ideal snow conditions...on and on we went...and still we were way up the mountain side so another push off soaring anywhere you pleased. This is the time you realize skiing isn't a sport, it is a 'Way of Life.'"

Galena main street, Aspen circa 1940.

Still they weren't finished. "That night we retired at 8 p.m. and arose at 2 a.m. ..." They walked to the base of another mountain, about seven miles, then climbed up Monte Zooma, to 14,000 feet. "Our stay there was one of the happiest holidays we have ever had and we really felt sad about leaving this wonderful wild country," they enthused. Little was developed for skiing in Aspen in those days, although it had once held the National Championships in 1941; the plan that year was to open up the area, the first lodges, bars, and restaurants to be built the next year. The twins got back to the town by hitching a ride with miners, stopping to visit the mine along the way. But just one more stop—that afternoon they climbed to the top of Roch Run, the most expert trail in the US, a two-mile downhill course that was crossed by three different roads. Racers had to leap at least thirty feet into the air at each road, descending onto a steep schuss and down the road into the village of Aspen. They completed the run and—finally—the twins got on the train in Denver and went home.

Not that coming home was so bad—at the end of the season they received their Rose Bowl Cup and silver plates, honouring them as the top women athletes in all of Canada. And they would be back to Utah the next year, continuing their shenanigans, prolonging their trip by missing trains, even taking off for Mexico and causing their father to call the police in the belief that they'd been kidnapped. That next year, boyfriends would start figuring in the picture, too. What would they get into next?

Canadian Sport Monthly asked the same question.

> How about the future, and what may we expect from these modern girls?
>
> In Europe, the year before the war, it was an accepted fact that there was but a few seconds between the leading downhill men and the best of the women...while it is impossible to get a direct time comparison, as the women in Europe always race down a shorter course than the men, the great authority, Arnold Lunn, emphasizes more than once, the steady improvement in women's racing and how in slalom particularly they are about equal to the best of the men...it would not surprise me to see Rhoda's outstanding feat [at Taschereau] repeated in the future. After all, it is courage and nerve that win in the modern downhill race, and any girl who will take the chance and risk to save precious seconds, and has the technique, experience and conditioning of the Wurteles and their "will to win" is going to be hard to beat.

It was a good prediction, because Rhona and Rhoda would only continue to rise in the ranks of skiers in Canada, the US, and Europe. And in a very short time, that will to win was going to face its toughest test in the ultimate competition: the Olympics.

Reality 1947–1959

TWENTY-FIVE TO THIRTY-SEVEN YEARS OLD

THE FLYING WURTELES

"Those Norwegian sweaters..." By war's end the twins had knit so many sweaters for the troops that they easily knit these for themselves, and wore them for good luck. With some Elizabeth Arden Stop Red lipstick for good measure, they were like "a fashion model unleashed." The photo was originally published in *Chatelaine* magazine in January 1948.

Ski jumping wasn't a ladylike sport, and it was too dangerous. Cross-country skiing was too tiring. During the war *Time* magazine had called downhill skiing "one of the few sports at which women become expert." It was also "the most becoming." Right. So how do we reconcile these images:

The most becoming: Rhoda tearing down the hill at the US Nationals in 1946 at Franconia, New Hampshire, wearing Irving of Montreal's grey ski suit with a hood lined in sharkskin, looking for all the world like a fashion model unleashed, until, at a sharp right turn, that lovely hood slips over her brow and eyes—and in the moment she tries to pull it up, she loses the track, crashes into the woods, then seconds later re-emerges with a broken ski and plows through the finish line, branches still dangling from her suit.

Not a tiring sport: Rhona at the top of the Alta, Utah, downhill, her first time in a race down a real mountain, looking down the steep slopes she hasn't been able to judge earlier because the threat of avalanches had kept it closed, the other women terrified to go down, trying to talk the others out of it. And Rhona, while they are worrying, rushing back to the lodge and changing her wax. "Never seen anything like it," she confesses, and, "Never so nervous before." Visibility is so bad skiers have to feel their way down. They head down a giant slalom course where "any dopester was bound to be thrown for a good eggbeater," according to Louise Gerdts in the colourful Utah press. Racers there "pushed off from the top of the Peruvian and snake-hipped their way through 30 gates down the face of Collins to the bottom of the hill, dropping vertically 1,800 feet in about a mile. Many a seasoned racer crossed the finish line on spaghetti legs, and a good portion of the girls pooped out completely on the 'Face' gates." Not Rhona—she took the giant and "put 30 men to shame" at the same time.

There was the downhill, "laid out as neatly as a maid in her coffin."

Then there was the downhill, "laid out as neatly as a maid in her coffin." The race was late in starting. Why? The racers were still getting the course ready, tramping it down with their skis. The conditions? Gerdts continued:

> Friday's photogenic clouds had joined hands and became one solid mass of unsympathetic indifference, making it difficult to tell where the terrain began and the sky ended. Shortly after one a shot of tapioca peppered the mountain and sped up the already terrifically fast course. However, it was only the forerunner for a gusty blizzard which set in for the duration of the race shortly thereafter...It was coming down so hard that even we standees needed windshield wipers on our goggles just to watch the racers go by. And as they swooshed past in the smothering white dust, they were either frantically wiping off their glasses, tearing them off in despair and tossing them to the winds, or cussing their waxes. Friedl Pfeiffer was muttering something about 'Where's the course?' as he came slithering by.

Who could do anything in that? Rhona, who else, taking down Denver's Rocky Mountain–raised Barbara Kidder and her own twin sister in the process.

Later in Nevada, Rhona catches an edge near a flat and is

thrown down the side of a hill, then gamely limps back up the last cliff carrying her seven-foot skis and poles on a sprained ankle, earning her the Sierra Sue Award for courage. (The award was named for the 1941 musical Western with Gene Autry.)

Both are driving in nature, show little concern for hazards," said the *New York Times*. "Their string of records all over North America confirms this courage."

Then on to California, and Rhona sitting out to nurse her ankle and give Rhoda a shot at first place, which she of course immediately takes advantage of, beating the nearest racer by a full four seconds. The American press doesn't only have difficulty figuring out who is who between the twins, they also have trouble figuring out their spirit—"Quiet, remote Rhoda Wurtele," the papers say, "this gal with her phenomenal build is proving herself to be one of the greatest of all women racers."

Maybe by the next year they figured it out, at Pico Peak. "This was the type of race made to order for Rhona and her sister. Both are driving in nature, show little concern for hazards. Their string of records accumulated over the past few years in North American ski circles confirm this courage." Rhona took the long hard course "at breakneck speed, her weight shifting neatly...down the last long grade where leg power counted and weariness began to take its toll, Rhona went flying and finished in a snow-throwing christie that had the crowds yelling with glee." She may not have "flashed the smoothness and effortless style" of Paula Kann, but the *New York Times* conceded it made little difference when you won by a huge margin of five seconds. The *New York Herald Tribune* found the same thing. "Both the twins are robust and powerfully built, but Rhona's extra dash and daring in every run she made was always marked."

But it would never be just one twin. The *New York Times*, on the 1947 Mont Gabriel International Meet, one week later:

> It will be some time before another eye-opening run like Rhoda Wurtele's first one will be seen. Skiing in

It was lucky the twins had made such a wise decision to follow a career in the delicate sport of downhill racing.

> typical manly fashion and showing absolutely no fear of trails or their condition, the Canadian came roaring out of the mountain at close to a mile-a-minute pace into the sight of the spectators....A hush came over the crowd.... could Rhoda hold her speed. Not to do so would mean a nasty fall, perhaps serious injury. Up the outside of the 'hollow' she came. She was off balance heading into the finish, actually skiing on only one leg, the other almost shoulder high. The onlookers held their breath and turned away. It appeared as though the 24-year-old Canadian ace would be down soon. Somehow or other she got out of the predicament, dashed over the finish, probably the most 'controlled' skier ever seen.

"Those Canadian girls ski like men!" Paula Kann said, "and what skiers!"

Rhoda greeted all the adulation with the aw-shucks nature of a test pilot. "Never had such a moment in my life," she said. "For once I did not know what to do with my feet, so I decided to let nature take its course and old gravity do the rest."

Rhoda had edged out her sister in that spectacular downhill; the next day in the slippery slalom, with most women falling, Rhona beat Rhoda by five seconds, and the US National Champion Paula Kann by ten seconds, "a terrific margin for slalom" that "will long be remembered."

Louis Cochand had set the flag run, and the Austrian ski whiz directing the ski school at Tremblant, Hans Falkner, wondered if it was maybe too tough "Sure, it's tough, very tough," Cochand replied, "but they might as well learn how to negotiate the hard ones here and not wait until they get to the Olympics."

"So they made it tough and the weatherman made it tougher with his icy top and slithering flats," Myrtle Cook wrote.

All in all, it was lucky the twins had made such a wise decision to follow a career in the delicate sport of downhill racing.

THE NEW WAVE

"Now that peace is here and the minds of men are once again turning to sport, there has been considerable talk of reviving the Olympic games." So said Louis Cochand in 1946. One of the first presidents of the CSIA, and manager of the pioneering Chalet Cochand at Ste. Marguerite, Cochand knew that Canadian skiers would not only have to negotiate tough courses on Olympic slopes. Battles would have to be fought just to get there, too.

Not lady-like and too dangerous: Rhona can't wait for the snow so attempts leaf-skiing, 1940s.

Cochand had a special attachment to the Olympics, claiming to have represented Canada in the 1938 Olympic Winter Games in Poland. There was an entire lack of planning last time, he said, and many of the Canadian ski team didn't even show up. This is understandable, since there never was a 1938 Olympics, nor has Poland ever hosted one.

Perhaps Cochand had mixed up the Olympics with a Fédération Internationale de Ski (FIS) competition—also understandable, since the Winter Games were still young and looking for their identity, especially after a twelve-year hiatus. The last Winter Games had been held in 1936 in Germany; the next would finally come to St. Moritz in Switzerland in 1948.

But what Cochand did get right was the state of Canada's planning for overseas competitions. There was no regular training, no team managers, no money. Cochand tells of the French coming to events with between twenty and thirty team members, plus trainers and managers; they even brought along their own chef. Skiing had certainly progressed in the last decade, Cochand said, but had sports organizations kept pace?

Changes came fast and hard to skiing after the war. Many of the former heroes of the slopes, especially Europeans, had died in fighting; many of the rest were ready to retire from racing and take up less punishing pursuits. Others had missed the best competitions at their peak because so many international events were cancelled. Some, like Quebec's unfortunate Olympic hopeful Germaine Prefontaine, saw their careers cut short by untimely accidents. Skiing down Mount Royal early in the 1945–46 season, she had swerved to avoid other skiers and instead smashed into a woodpile. Seeing the multiple leg fractures, doctors decided to amputate her leg above the knee. Prefontaine recalled one of her greatest experiences as she lay recovering in the hospital—that trip out skiing the Rockies the spring before with Rhona and Rhoda.

But there were bright spots, too. With the economy back on track after the war, time and money were freed up for families to spend on skiing. Stores were quick to capitalize on it. The father of downhill, Hannes Schneider, was appointed Technical Manager of Henry Morgan and Co.'s sporting department ski division. When Schneider made an appearance at the Montreal store he drew crowds of people eager and curious about the sport, and fielded questions about the hopes of Canadian skiers at the Olympics. Other ski stars were there, including Rhona and Rhoda. Schneider said the Wurtele twins "stood out in the best of ski company." When questioned about who would win the Olympics, he said it was "anybody's guess—the difference between the top skiers was in split seconds"—though the Wurtele twins had a good chance.

Montreal spectators could be forgiven for thinking that winners of ski races could be foregone conclusions. In post-war Canada, Rhona and Rhoda won everything they entered, and rarely had split seconds to decide it.

There were other bright spots on the sports horizon. Besides the continuing successes of Rhona and Rhoda, a tiny young Ottawa girl named Barbara Ann Scott was starting to come out on top in international figure skating competitions. Then, too, surprising things were developing among even younger girls skiing in the Laurentians. These girls had turned their idolizing eyes on Rhona and Rhoda, watching them sweep races wherever they went. In 1947, eleven-year-old Lucile Wheeler was graduated to Class B in skiing. "She still takes her teddy bear to bed at night," Myrtle

The "father of downhill skiing" Hannes Schneider meets Rhona and Rhoda at Morgan's department store, Montreal, 1946.

Cook noted, but she was besting many of the times of male skiers. Later, where both Rhona and Rhoda would take first and second, she would come in eleventh in the Lake Placid downhill, and sixth in the Dominion Championships. There was an even younger girl catching the eyes of the *New York Times*, too. "The performances of eight-year-old Anne Heggtveit and 11-year-old Lucile Wheeler... were eye-openers. Both bear watching in the future."

Canadians in general were now more aware of the importance of physical activity and amateur sport for health reasons.

The pros were right that time. Lucile Wheeler eventually won Canada's first Olympic medal in skiing, a bronze in downhill in 1956. On her team was Anne Heggtveit; four years later Heggtveit won Canada's first gold medal at the Squaw Valley Olympics, beating her closest rival by a record 3.3 seconds.

Canadians in general were now more aware of the importance of physical activity and amateur sport for health reasons. Wartime fitness training of soldiers had undoubtedly played a major part. "Perhaps," Louis Cochand hoped, "the newly formed National Council on Physical Fitness will have some answer" to the poorly run national sports teams.

That turned out to be wishful thinking. The Council fizzled out by 1954, more obsessed with politics than sport. So once again the onus fell on individuals to push for what they wanted. As Rhona and Rhoda had never doubted what they wanted, and had never been at a loss to get to that goal, women's skiing was in no immediate danger.

In the two years prior to the 1948 Olympics, the twins left almost all their competitors struggling to keep up. "Judging by the way Rhona and Rhoda were skiing today, it's going to be an occasion when both will taste defeat," the *New York Times* opined after an international race at Mont Gabriel. The only thing that could stop them, it turned out, would be the Europeans—better trained, coached, and managed than Canadians could ever hope for.

But who wanted the bitter flavour of defeat? For two years, Rhona and Rhoda tasted the sweet savours of success.

They began 1946 in classic style, Rhona taking first and Rhoda second at the McGill Red Bird's downhill. Still lingering in Class B, they nevertheless beat the times of 75 male skiers in a field of 79. Later at St. Jovite in the Snow Eagle slalom race, the girls must have smiled to see the weather: arctic temperatures, brittle winds, and patchy snow: just their kind of weather. Rhoda lost a ski at one point, and finished fourth with only one; her sister so confidently took first place that when the final tallies were made it was discovered she was second overall with the men too, and just 4/5th of a second behind the winner. They ended the month with Rhona taking the downhill, slalom, and combined at the Ontario Ladies Meet in Collingwood, Ontario, and Rhoda right on her tail taking seconds in all three.

The twins took the bobsled run designed for the 1932 Olympics at Lake Placid; two sleds had already gone over the edge that day.

After a quick dash down the Taschereau (Rhoda first, Rhona third after Margaret Burden), the twins headed off to Lake Placid to compete for the annual Kate Smith Trophy. Rhona won the slalom and downhill, and Rhoda took third in both, helping their Canadian team to a sixth win in ten years. But winning the trophy was not the biggest thrill in Lake Placid, apparently. "I went down the Olympic bobsled run," Rhona said. "It was wonderful!" It must have brought back memories of brother George's homemade bobsled cobbled together with scraps, and of racing down the steep hills of Westmount into traffic. It was no less dangerous either. In their scrapbooks is pasted a waiver the twins had to sign before going down the run; a hand-tinted postcard shows bobsledders "Riding high on Whiteface Curve," looking ready to ride right over the edge. It happened regularly. While they were there, two different sleds had overshot Zigzag turn, and five men shared amongst themselves fractured hips, knees and legs, broken ribs, shoulders, thighs, arms and collarbones, plus lacerations to the face and head. Underneath the twins' waiver is scribbled "Fun Times."

There were other thrills going on. As the women were racing at Lake Placid, over in Hanover, New Hampshire, the men were racing the Dartmouth University race; McGill represented Canada. The Redmen beat ten US universities to win the meet, but to the twins the real news was the appearance of the Denver men's and women's teams, straight from the Rockies after a "four-day transcontinental trip by automobile." Barbara Kidder had come out with them and raced at Lake Placid. After winning one slalom race but losing combined times to the twins, it quickly became apparent that the cherubic Kidder would give the twins more competition in the future. She had won the intercollegiate meet at Alta earlier that year; Jerry Hiatt won the men's division. The twins cut out their pictures and pasted them in their scrapbooks, but in particular there are full articles on Hiatt. He cuts a dashing figure in the photos, triumphing in the slalom, wearing a Norwegian sweater, his face tanned and proud, after he had captained his Denver team to victory.

There is also a telegram from Jerry to Rhoda: "Enroute to Hanover putting Barb on train in Albany wire your plans to me immediately love Jerry."

It seems Hiatt had fallen for one of what the *Times* called "the stylish skiing twins." It was certainly unusual for a team that far out west to make such a long drive across the country. Was it possible that Jerry convinced his whole team to come all that way just to get close to Rhoda? At the US Nationals at Franconia the next month, Jerry would get his chance. When Rhoda crashed into the trees after her hood slipped over her eyes, it was Jerry Hiatt who stayed up "till long after midnight," working on fixing Rhoda's ski with her. Rhoda would come in fourth the next day. Rhona, who had got less attention and more sleep, not only won the Nationals, but also in the slalom beat Barbara Kidder and Paula Kann by nine seconds. It was the first time a Canadian would take the title, and by doing so that year Rhona would hold both the Canadian and US championships at the same time. The *Herald Tribune* also noted, "Had she been competing in the men's field of approximately eighty contenders, she would have finished in eleventh place. When it is remembered that a majority of the speediest men skiers in the United States were competing, an indication of the Canadian girl's performance is obvious."

As usual, the twins pleaded little interest in the classification—all they wanted to do was race.

Before Lake Placid Rhoda had already taken first and Rhona second at the Laurentian Zone Championship downhill (the Burden sisters right behind them), and the same finishes at the Zone Championship slalom the next week. The Combined Zone Champion was announced at the end of the winter, and it was no surprise to see Rhoda crowned champ, and sister Rhona second. What was surprising was that the twins were still Class B, even though they were increasingly being touted as Olympic material. "Designating them as Class B skiers when they have certainly reached the acme of success at home and across the border is nothing short of denying them their rights," Myrtle Cook huffed.

As usual, the twins pleaded little interest in the classification—all they wanted to do was race. But they wanted to be challenged too, and the hankering for the big time and big mountains they had seen by brushing up against Denverites Jerry Hiatt and Barbara Kidder was becoming more imperative.

But first there were two more races to win before spring skiing began. At Mount Orford, Rhona took firsts in downhill and slalom, Rhoda seconds. And even though Rhona was the fastest skier overall, beating the senior and junior men's times, this time there was no outcry over faulty timing. Skiers in the Townships

It turns out the girls were cooling their heels in the deserted peaks of the Canadian Rockies.

counted themselves lucky just to have seen the fabulous Wurteles race. Later at the University of Montreal's St. Sauveur race, they pulled the identical one-two trick.

Then they were ready to conquer the West, 1946 style. Newspapers scrambled to get photos of the adventurous twins loading their skis on the train. This time Gaby Pleau accompanied them. And this time they wanted friendly revenge at Alta. Last year, Barbara Kidder had taken the combined from Rhoda by 33/100ths of a second.

Luckily, at Alta this time the conditions were ideal—a blizzard, threats of avalanches, poor visibility, a little rain thrown into the mix. Exactly what the twins thrived in. Alta had added the grand slalom that year, and in that first race, Rhona came first, Rhoda second—and Gaby twelfth, still "putting about 30 men to shame," said the papers. Rhona took the top spot again the next day in the downhill, with Rhoda fourth. They squeaked by in the slalom in third and fourth place, but it was enough to give Rhona the top combined prize. Behind her was Barbara Kidder, and third was Rhoda. Johnny Fripp had come out for the races too, and with his first place win in the combined, Quebec had swept the Rockies. The two shared champagne and a public kiss at the awards as Rhona blushed. Now, Myrtle Cook said, the twins were "the acknowledged Queens of North American skiing."

As befitted queens, then, they had to make the Royal Tour; and with invitations coming from all over, first they went to the "first post-war Great Divide Championship Cup Races" in Banff (Rhoda first in the slalom, third in downhill, but losing out to Gaby who won the combined). Rhona was conspicuously absent from the races. Where was she, and with whom? It turns out the girls were cooling their heels in the deserted peaks of the Canadian Rockies, really—and had quickly got in some 125 miles of ski touring to relax.

Next the twins headed off to Reno, Nevada, where as mentioned earlier Rhona sprained her ankle and took the Sierra

"The stylish skiing twins," in a photo by Helen Fischer included in her book on North American skiers, 1946.

Sue award, for courage. It was only much later she learned it was cracked too.

Courageous or not, by the time they headed over to Sugar Bowl in California for the Silver Belt races, Rhona couldn't race on that ankle. Twin watchers might have been wary of Rhoda going down—would she sprain something now too? She didn't, coming in first place by a wide margin of four seconds. But this time it was Gaby Pleau who took a mighty fall, right at the finish line. She broke her leg so badly doctors had to put a pin through the bone, and she faced a long stay in the hospital. It essentially put an end to her ski career.

When a light dusting of snow fell on Mount Royal, at 7:00 a.m. Rhona and Rhoda were out skiing.

The skiing season ending, there was nothing for the twins to do but wait—in the lush playground of California, accompanied by a sporty ex-marine turned business magnate with celebrity connections. "So we left her and went to go party," Rhona says. More on that later.

Two of the trio ended the season limping, but at least they had the summer to recuperate for the next winter of 1946–47. And in what looked like a good sign, that winter started with a bang—and would end with another, even bigger one. On October 1, a freak weather system hit Montreal, and the temperature plunged from 81 degrees Fahrenheit to 33.2 in two days. When a light dusting of snow fell on Mount Royal, at 7:00 a.m. Rhona and Rhoda were out skiing in Murray Park with Shadow, their cocker spaniel. After a season like the last one, they were anxious to get racing. And after taking the Ski Alliance instructors' course again that December (now under Luggi Foeger), they were kept turning down offers of instructor's jobs at resorts like Sun Valley and Aspen.

In Canada, it would be a season of firsts and seconds again for the twins, and some long overdue recognition. In January of 1947, after years of Myrtle Cook's and others' battles, with a new president in the Canadian Amateur Ski Association, Rhona and Rhoda were finally granted an A rating. It came just one year before the Olympics.

They immediately put it to good use, heading to Pico Peak

in New York for the US Eastern Ski Championships mentioned earlier. The Americans were in awe of the twins, holding little hope that they could win against the double threat. They were right. Rhona took first, a full five seconds ahead of Paula Kann. Then Rhona took the slalom too, and the combined. Rhoda was third in the downhill, second in the slalom, second in the combined.

"Looking the entire field over after the final run was completed," said the *Herald Tribune*, "the figure of Rhona Wurtele stood out as the premier skier of the meet... she scarcely ever slackened her swift pace, even when racing through the hazardous hair-pin turn and on the few straightaways she boomed along at a magnificent clip, drawing thunders of applause from every onlooker as she swept to victory."

For the twins, it was almost embarrassing. "You know, we didn't like going down there and coming home with so many prizes. But we couldn't help it." They lugged home a total of nine prizes among them, including cups, medals, and their names on the US Eastern Combined Trophy—which had to stay stateside.

Were the twins trying to be good neighbours, or were they really that modest? Is it possible to combine an athlete's supreme desire to win with that kind of down-home goodness? The next week might have answered that question. At the Mont Gabriel International (that tough course Louis Cochand had laid out, the one where Rhoda crossed the finish line with one leg above her shoulder), Rhoda had taken first in the downhill, Rhona second. Rhona then took first and Rhoda second in slalom, and the same pattern continued in the combined. But Rhona herself had written an article about the race for *Ski News*, and in it she is generous with her assessment of all competition—they are either "skiing very well," or "improving tremendously," or "making others nervous." By her account, it seems she swept the competition almost by accident. The editor had to take the extraordinary measure of adding a note at the end of her article: "The above account does not quite give the whole story on the meet between the Canadians and Americans since author Rhona Wurtele has told with extreme modesty about her exploits and her sister's."

It was left to others as well to talk up their near miss at getting the Canadian Sportswoman of the Year nomination that month. As in their races, they came in one after another in votes, losing only to their tiny nemesis, figure skater Barbara Ann Scott.

For the twins, it was almost embarrassing. "You know, we didn't like going down there and coming home with so many prizes. But we couldn't help it."

It certainly didn't affect their continued run on the slopes. Rhona won the Laurentian Zone Slalom Championships with Rhoda right behind, then they immediately repeated the finish at the Zone Downhill. They only missed finishing one-two at 1947's Taschereau Downhill because Rhoda had injured a knee; it was left to Rhona to take first all alone. By the time the Lake Placid meet took place in February, the twins once again led their team to victory over the Americans. Accompanying that event—which everyone had to admit was not turning out to be unusual—was a sign of post-war technology. The *Sunday News* covered winter sports in Lake Placid in a special colour supplement—the first time colour newspaper clippings appear in the twins' scrapbooks.

Another reminder of war's end came that month: the Dominion Ski Championships, on hold since 1940, were finally going to be held again, this time at Mont Ste. Anne in Quebec. It would be the twins' first kick at that can, and they wanted to make it a good one. A few challengers from outside Canada had shown up, including three Norwegians, two Chileans, and a handful of Americans. Even French women's champion Georgette Thiolières, the greatest woman skier in Europe and a student of Emile Allais, was rumoured to be on her way (but didn't finally, stuck training in Sun Valley with Friedl Pfieffer). More surprisingly, six skiers came from Canada's West—a hint of things to come, if anyone had the foresight to see it. Yet Quebec, and Montreal in particular, still dominated skiing in every way, from winning races to developing hills and using new technology. It fell to the Frenchman Emile Allais to set up the course, however—a sixty-gate course so exacting that the man who the *Montreal Standard* called "the greatest skier

The Dominion Championships, 1947. Rhoda on the left took second, Rhona took first at Mont Ste. Anne. "We had to climb to race," she wrote on the photo.

in the world" lost control and slammed into the bushes at one of his own toughest spots.

For the men, Montrealer Hector Sutherland won the championship, with Quebecers Pierre Jalbert and Harvey Clifford behind him. All three would go on to represent Canada in the Olympics the next year. In the women's, "of course," the papers said, Rhona took the championship, with Rhoda right behind. Rhona had won the downhill, though lost the slalom to her sister by 3/10ths of a second. Although she contented herself with second at the Dominions, Rhoda was starting something of a breakthrough. Close followers of the twins had seen them go back and forth between choosing first or second place. Recently Rhona had swept most races. But after Rhoda had two mishaps in that downhill (and still took second) things were going to go decidedly in her favour.

For now, however, it was Rhona who took top spot like no other skier before her. Not only had she won the Canadian championship, but because of her win at the US Nationals the season before, she was also the first Canadian skier to hold both an American and a Canadian speed title at the same time. It was a grand slam of skiing, that earned Rhona and Rhoda the sobriquet the greatest women skiers on the continent.

There was only one thing left to do. Tasting sweet success over and over in the east, and being proclaimed queens of the mountain was delightful, but it didn't make for a balanced ski diet. Like other great athletes, the twins wanted to be pushed to their absolute limits, the only way they could improve. It was time to meet the Europeans racing over in the American West in the coming spring. With the Olympics around the corner, the Swiss and French teams had come to the Rockies to test their competition. The Americans were getting their Olympic team into shape too, and would use the US Nationals at Alta, Utah, and races at Sun Valley as the testing ground. And that's where the twins headed, into the heart of the lion's den.

Despite all the Europeans descending on the Rockies, the American press was breathlessly awaiting the arrival of the twins.

The Dominion Championships, 1947: Left to right: Hector Sutherland, winner Class A Men's; Rhoda, 2nd Women's A; Emile Allais; Rhona, winner Class A Women's; Pierre Jalbert, 2nd A Men's; Lucile Wheeler, winner Women's B; Jack "Porky" Griffin, winner Men's B. Canadian Pacific photo.

They were probably a little breathless themselves—by the time the results for the Dominions were published, Rhona and Rhoda had already been seen on to the Trans-Canada Air Lines plane by the district manager, taking their first major flight (a picture shows them bringing their skis and poles into the plane, apparently as carry-on baggage).

In Utah, things looked ready for the international pack of skiers. The racecourses were well-packed thanks to the forest rangers of the area; famous American skier Dick Durrance had set the courses. The twins had two things to get adjusted to: the lack of trees beside the course—they claimed to use the trees to measure how fast they were going—and the high altitude. They had experienced these conditions before, of course. What was more of interest was the competition, judged to be even stiffer than last year. "Georgette Thiolières is marvellous, and then there are the Swiss skiers, and the American girls have been practising and are much improved this year," Rhona said. The Swiss trio of women, led by ninety-eight-pound Olivia Ausoni, was regarded as the best. Soon, though, Thiolières was out of competition after an early fall left her bruised and scraped. That took care of "the world's greatest feminine skier, and one of the prettiest."

And yet, at the bottom of the downhill course in Utah, the results looked suspiciously like Lake Placid: Rhona first, Rhoda second, and New Englander Paula Kann third (a full ten seconds behind Rhoda). The closest the Swiss came was Olivia Ausoni in fifth. Were the twins set to devastate the Europeans as they had all North Americans already? At least the Swiss had won the men's, with the shoemaker Karl Molitor handily sweeping first place (he in fact made high-quality leather ski boots for his parents' sporting goods store). Back in tenth place was an American name the Wurteles would become very familiar with: Gene Gillis, racing for the Sun Valley team.

Now the Americans were getting serious. Canadians and Swiss beat them on their own turf, and they had to get a crack team together for the Olympics.

The slalom would be another story. Excessive snow and a snow slide moved the course to nearby Snow Basin, and this time the Swiss showed their true colours. Rhona had earlier taken a bad fall and broken her skis, forcing her to ski on strange ones, and the closest Rhoda could come was fourth place—behind the Swiss trio and Paula Kann. Nevertheless, Rhoda's two finishes were enough to put her over Olivia Ausoni at the top for the Combined honours, a place she shared with Karl Molitor on the men's side.

Now the Americans were getting serious. Canadians and Swiss beat them on their own turf, and they had to get a crack team together for the Olympics. The tryouts were to be held the next week at Sun Valley, Idaho; Rhona and Rhoda followed the hopefuls, since there would be another race for non-Americans.

Before that, however, they got the news they knew was coming: they were named to the Canadian Olympic team, the only two women. They found out the day after Rhoda swept the US Nationals. For some it was a foregone conclusion, and among skiers there was no surprise. "It wasn't a surprise for us," Rhona says, "because we knew we had beaten them all. And we didn't know much about going on an Olympic team, but we were really excited about representing Canada, and going to see what it was like Over There. We hadn't raced there yet. So that was a thrill."

Whether it was the thrill (and heavy expectations) that came with being named to the Canadian Olympic team, or bad luck, or just the fact that the Europeans were hitting their stride, after that the twins found it impossible to hold on to first place—until the Swiss returned to their Alps. At the American tryouts race in Sun Valley for all skiers, Rhoda came in fifth and Rhona tied for sixth; the next weekend Sun Valley hosted the Harriman Cup and the Europeans hit with full force. With French champ Georgette Thiolières back on her feet, everybody else was forced to watch her sweep the slalom, downhill, and combined. With Swiss and American competition now primed, the best the twins could do was Rhona's fifth place in the slalom; neither made it to the top eight in the downhill. And although Rhona's slalom run helped her place fourth in the combined, for the twins the race was a washout—and a wake-up call.

Frustrated at losing, they may have pushed themselves harder than ever before and risked injuries.

Although much had been made of Rhona's using strange skis to replace her broken ones—her father shipped her another pair from Montreal by air express but they got lost in transit—there was more than that going wrong. Rhoda was disqualified for missing a gate, and wasn't allowed to race in another. Rhona, who rarely complained, called it "a pretty weak business." Frustrated at losing, they may have pushed themselves harder than ever before and risked injuries. Then there was the frustration of seeing that, while the Americans and the Europeans were busily preparing for the coming Olympics, the Canadians were still trying to raise enough money to get the team overseas.

For the American team, said Rhona, "Everything is free and they have two coaches in constant attendance. Paula Kann has her own coach with her, Toni Matt. Swiss and French skiers also have their own coaches along. If our Canadians hope to beat the

The twins on the cover of *The Standard*, Montreal 1948. It would be a difficult Olympics for every nation, but the Canadians had no coach, training or money.

Europeans we must have a lot of polishing and training. [Emile] Allais would be just the man!"

The Wurteles had had no coach since the loss of Hermann Gadner. The prospect of returning to Canada was hardly tempting. "Plans for training and coaching have not yet been completely formulated," Harry Pangman, the head of the team selection committee, said. That was an Olympian understatement. There was almost no money for the Canadian skiers, and the method of raising some—selling Olympic Ski Buttons—met a poor response. Pangman still clung to his plan, however: spring training in the Rockies, summer conditioning, then on to Switzerland in December. In the Alps, he promised, a coach would be hired. That would give the team just one month of coached preparation.

It would be a difficult Olympics for every nation, coming as it did on the heels of a world war. But for Canada, Pangman's plan fell apart before it could begin. Spring training was cancelled due to bad button sales.

While the Americans and Europeans were busily preparing for the coming Olympics, the Canadians were still trying to raise enough money to get overseas.

Wisely—and thanks to their family—Rhona and Rhoda chose to stay in the Western states as long as possible. Despite the losses and minor injuries, at least they had the opportunity to race against the pros and even get some informal help from foreign coaches. Still, out west that spring, the Swiss continued to dominate. At the Silver Dollar Derby in Reno, Nevada, that March, Rhoda managed to carve out a third in the combined. She had taken a fall, stumbling one hundred feet from the finish line and coming second in the downhill. Then Rhona took a bad fall in the downhill—the only one of thirty-seven entries to do so—and knocked herself unconscious after hitting a tree.

From there the twins went to the Far West Kandahar in Oregon. By now the Swiss names were sharing top billing with the Wurteles, deservedly. The trio of Swiss men led by Molitor swept the top three spots in the slalom, and Olivia Ausoni took the women's slalom, followed by Rhoda and Rhona. But that was all the West and North America would taste of the Swiss for now. The second day of the Kandahar, a terrible blizzard blew in, reducing visibility to zero, putting three inches of freezing snow on gates, and blowing so hard it almost stopped skiers in their tracks. The downhill was cancelled and the Swiss, on a tight schedule, left for their own hills.

Rhona and Rhoda were sorry to see them go. A great friendship had sprung up among the women in particular, and the Swiss had "showered the Canucks with lovely little gifts" and invitations to come visit next season. The Canadians were embarrassed, holing up together in a summer cabin without heating, newspapers on the bed for warmth and one person a designated fire keeper through the night; they had no coach, they had to lift sandwiches from the hotel, and they certainly didn't have presents for the Swiss. Still, even though they had to duck the laundry hanging in the Canadians' rooms, the Swiss might have felt more at home with them than with the Americans. In America, Ausoni said, the cities were crowded and the countryside empty, making her think Americans spent as little time in nature as possible. What really surprised her, "and which is totally natural there, is to find the hotel barmaids on the slopes. After work, she has everything she needs to train. Other skiers we met have all the best material needs, they all have cars and never come to the hills without their wives. You've no idea the clashing colours and clothes these ski-lovers wear!"

Now that the Swiss had gone home, Rhona and Rhoda knew they had to keep training.

Now that the Swiss had gone home, Rhona and Rhoda knew they had to keep training, and stretched out their Western tour as long as they could. At the Teton Derby in Jackson Hole, Wyoming, Rhona literally earned her spurs, receiving a silver pair after she won the giant slalom; Paula Kann took second, and Rhoda, fifth. Then they promptly left for Banff. While other Olympic ski team members were invited to train at Tremblant, the twins stayed out west in the big mountains and snow, and took Paula Kann with them to Banff: they were going to make a film with Luggi Foeger in the Canadian Rockies.

THE GOLDEN BOOK

The twins appeared in a number of films in their heyday; the ski film genre began as soon as skiing did. But it was still an event. At the end of the 1946 season, after Rhona had won the US Nationals at Franconia, something called the Electrical Club of Montreal invited the twins to a banquet as honoured guests, where they "saw themselves in movies in sound and colour." They had always loved movies since the silent films of the 1920s and the later Westerns, and seeing themselves on the screen was a kick; but they were a far cry from publicity hounds. Other celebrities of their day might well have capitalized on their fame by taking up offers to appear in dodgy Hollywood films. The twins had a brief flirtation with Los Angeles celebrity circles, meeting stars of film and art, but they were too shy to push themselves further. They much preferred that attention be directed to their achievements on the slopes.

In 1946, the *Montreal Herald* declared that the twins were "good enough to defeat most of the male competitors this winter, and although they don't seek it, they get full credit and publicity for their performances."

That was only partially true. They had had to wait years to get their A rating, and despite their unstoppable successes, had lost the Sportswoman of the Year award in 1946 to Barbara Ann Scott. In fact, the rise of the figure skater Rhoda calls "the little chickie" would continue to overshadow the twins outside the skiing world. Scott won the North American Figure Skating championships from 1945 to 1948, and at age nineteen was the first North American to win the European and World Figure Skating Championships. She was also petite and ultra-feminine, which may have mitigated her acceptance into the sports world. Apparently, one cute figure skater trumped identical twin skiers.

It was Scott who got talked up in Parliament, who was given a convertible by her hometown of Ottawa (but had to turn it down to stay amateur for the Olympics), and who came to Montreal to sign the "Golden Book" with Mayor Camillien Houde, using the same gold pen the Queen used.

The Montreal-born Wurtele twins were the undisputed queens of North American skiing championships, and through their incredible feats had promoted skiing in Canada, but they were barely honoured by Montreal. "Like Barbara Ann," Myrtle Cook wrote at the time, "they have brought great honour to the Dominion by their skiing accomplishments and good sportsmanship." Later that winter, it looked like Toronto would even beat out Montreal in honouring the twins; they were in the running for the coveted Lou Marsh trophy for athlete of the year (Barbara Ann had won the year before, and would win again in 1947 and 1948). "The twins are due for some civic honours here," Cook wrote. The Rose Bowl, awarded to the twins two years previously, was the "only official acknowledgement of their prowess so far."

The Montreal-born Wurtele twins were the undisputed queens of North American skiing championships, and through their incredible feats had promoted skiing in Canada, but they were barely honoured by Montreal.

The twins didn't get the Lou Marsh trophy—it went to Joe "King" Krol that year, a Toronto Argonauts quarterback who won six Grey Cups. Unfortunately, that kind of near miss on official honours has dogged the twins most of their career. After accidents kept them out of the running, neither of them was named to the Canadian Olympic Hall of Fame for the 1948 Olympics, but Rhoda did get named in 1953 for her participation in the 1952 Oslo Games. Neither have they been named to Canada's Sports Hall of Fame (where Anne Heggtveit and Lucile Wheeler are honoured), and attempts to get them nominated for the Order of Canada have been unsuccessful. Perhaps the gravest slight, to their minds, was not being called immediately to participate in the 1988 Calgary Olympic Games.

YOUNG AND FREE

In the heady times of post-war North America, the girls were giving little thought to any of this. They were still relatively innocent twenty-somethings, and their state of mind perfectly reflected what was going on in America just before the 1950s. It was a time to reclaim what innocence had been lost in World War II, a time to indulge in all things that had been rationed for too long, with no need to justify spending money or taking long trips. Women still clung to some of the relative equality they had enjoyed during the war; the backlash that was the 1950s hadn't yet become entrenched. And when Rhona and Rhoda headed west to ski the big mountains, they had every intention of enjoying themselves in a big way too.

The return to fun and frolic began with the reappearance of the St. Andrew's Ball, in the autumn of 1945. While Rhona and Rhoda had complained of how dismal the showing of eligible bachelors was during the war, now all the young men were returning heroes. Montreal girls had been patient; there were 185 debutantes "docketed for presentation to Canada's Governor General, the Earl of Athlone, and his Countess, the Princess Alice," *Time* magazine wrote. The photo the magazine chose to run, of course, was of identical twin girls being greeted by the Earl—Rhona and Rhoda curtseying. Rhoda, secretary of the ball committee this time, helped ensure that more than two thousand guests would wolf down three tons of haggis. Then, through the misty memories of an ancient Scotland most guests had never seen, with the bagpipes echoing through the hotel, the guests enjoyed a victory dance till breakfast.

For Rhona and Rhoda, these years held the joy of being young, unattached, modern post-war girls. In a way, they were ahead of their time—it was unusual for girls their age (twenty-three when the war ended) to still be unmarried, never mind without a beau. Their brother Wally had his first child that year, and their dear friend Libby had graduated from McGill and immediately got engaged to a sailor, Dr. Graham Taylor. But, says Rhona, "We were late bloomers. At least that's the way it was for me."

Up till now, with the best men fighting overseas, skiing, swimming, and sports had been their only concern. Had they even noticed the boys? "Oh yes, we did," says Rhona. "I went through a stage of about seven of them. But nobody compared to Gene."

Gene was Gene Gillis, the tall, blond, and bronzed American skier the twins had already met skiing at Sun Valley at the Harriman Cup. Rhona hardly had time to even smile at him the first year; he had immediately left for other ski meets. But it was inevitable their paths would cross again, and in the Rockies. Skiing in those mighty mountains with athletic young men must have been a heady mixture for the twins; since their girlhood days watching Nelson Eddy and Jeannette MacDonald chase each other over and over through the Rockies in the film *Rose-Marie*, the Wild West and its mountains had been infused with the promise of adventure and romance. They had already tasted the adventure. Now they were ready for more adult pursuits.

Rhoda had already been pursued by Jerry Hiatt, the Denver skier who brought his whole ski team east just to get close to her. She seemed less immediately susceptible to the ephemeral charms of men than Rhona; "She was kind of dating him," says Rhona. On the other hand, "Mother said I fell in love with all the boys," Rhona confesses. And now on one of those spring ski trips, Rhona would meet a fun-loving and unpredictable man who would introduce them to a bigger world, and be her "other great romance": Dick Steigler.

"Dick led us astray," Rhona laughs.

Rhona met Dick while they were on their second tour of the West in 1946—either in Sun Valley, Idaho, or Utah. After arriving with Gaby Pleau in Utah, the twins had met Johnny Fripp and Yves Latreille from Mont Tremblant, and the Americans were suitably impressed with "Montreal's stylish skiing twins." The twins were equally impressed with the US, and Dick Steigler was a perfect representation of all the promise America held after the war. And when the twins got in his great big Buick convertible with his famous German shepherd Minor, they soon discovered what it was like to live American style. A New York native, Dick was a big man physically, an ex-Marine who had been stationed in San Diego during the war. And he lived large too. An entrepreneur and businessman, he owned a string of stores of the dominant grocer on the continent, the Great Atlantic and Pacific Tea Company—more commonly known as A&P. In every town they went through with Dick, he stopped at the local A&P, swaggered into it wearing a Hawaiian shirt and shorts, and checked up on its staff. Then he came back out with a bunch of bananas, which he duly hung from the rear view mirror of the convertible.

Utah to Banff in Dick's great big Buick, 1946. "I had to sit in the back with the dog," remembers Rhoda.

"We had a great time," says Rhona. She found herself falling for his irrepressible energy—he was one of the few people who could keep up with the twins. When he challenged Rhona to a game of tennis, "I thought he'd kill me," she says. "After six sets I could hardly shuffle my legs—I was never so stiff in my life." That's saying a lot coming from a champion skier. On top of it, Dick was fifteen years her senior.

That age difference may have been one of the main reasons the family wasn't crazy about Rhona's announcement that she was going to marry Dick Steigler. When he visited Montreal, he brought Rhona to Birks to buy an engagement ring—but somehow she ended up getting a movie camera instead. "I thought it best because of the reaction of the family to him," Rhona explains enigmatically.

Dick had driven with Rhona and Rhoda throughout the West

and up to Banff, eventually bringing them down to the California he knew and enjoyed so much. Earlier, hearing about some of their escapades and the photographers and filmmakers chasing them down, Myrtle Cook had predicted that "you'll find them winding up in Hollywood some day." They did get there, but not because of any celluloid ambition. With Gaby Pleau finally out of the hospital after her disastrous spill in Sugar Bowl, California, Dick and the girls loaded up the car and took a proper California tour, going to Santa Barbara, swimming at Pebble Beach, and marvelling at wacky California trends such as restaurants serving a portion of spaghetti with every meal. Then Dick took them to his old navy post at San Diego, and to a big party in chic La Jolla at a beautiful home overlooking the sea. Among the guests were surrealist painter Salvador Dali, who had recently moved to the US, and actress Greer Garson, who had been nominated for an Academy Award every year during the war. "What do you say to these people?" Rhona asked herself. "We were just known in the ski world."

They didn't show up in Los Angeles. Could it be that the twins had been abducted and taken to Mexico? Rhona and Dick Steigler in 1946, not looking too distressed.

With all Dick's connections to California celebrities, the twins found it tough to make time to visit their Uncle Reverend Arthur in Los Angeles—he with the church on Hollywood and Vine. Even he and his wife had a touch of Hollywood eccentricity—his wife in particular was "a real weirdo," Rhoda says affectionately, both a painter and a poet who treated the twins to recitals. But this time they didn't show up at Uncle Arthur's when they said they would, and when he phoned their parents to check on them, the family panicked. It was only ten years ago or so that the highly publicized kidnapping of Charles Lindbergh's son had taken place. Their father immediately hired private detectives to track them down. Could it be that the twins had been abducted and taken to Mexico?

That was exactly what had happened, although it was Dick Steigler who had abducted them, and it could well have been their own idea. By the time they got to Uncle Arthur's in Hollywood with armfuls of Mexican souvenirs, they discovered the family was in a state. Not only had the family been frightened about their disappearance, but they also envisioned them missing their roles as bridesmaids for their friend Barbara Wickes' wedding back home. Their sister Jean was already sitting in for them for the rehearsal. Finally they got back, thanks to some last-minute scrambling. "It all went off very well," Rhoda says, "but we looked a bit funny with very dark faces and sunburned arms up to the biceps."

Rhona and Gaby working on their tans—and Dick Steigler and Major the dog working on their skiing—in Banff, 1946.

And Dick? "We were going to sail around the world," Rhona recalls. "But I never saw the boat. That never happened when we got back to reality." In the course of the next year Rhona ended the engagement.

The next spring in 1947 the twenty-five-year-old twins were right back at it, however, jumping at any opportunity that lay in their way. "The girls are off on a ski jaunt for up to seven weeks," their father told the newspapers after they'd left. "When they go off on a trip like their current one they get invited here, there and everywhere." He must have been thinking of their escapade in Mexico, too. "Last year they went away without much of a program just as they did this year, and they were away until May. It may be the beginning of May before they're back this year."

It was a likely-sounding prediction, but it didn't turn out to be accurate. This time, with pre-Olympic preparation going on all over the continent, they wouldn't be back until mid-June. And this time Rhona would come back with a real engagement ring.

With Rhona and Rhoda named as the only women on the Olympic Ski Team after winning at Alta in the spring of 1947, their stars rose even higher in the sports world; now the Americans were going to study their style and technique with even more scrutiny. Rhona, in turn, was keeping a very close eye on one particular American Olympic Ski Team member.

Toni Matt, left, and Luggi Foeger at Lake Tahoe. Both had been instructors at Hannes Schneider's School in Austria, and skiing soldiers of the 10th Mountain Division in the US. Foeger was well-equipped to make a great film.

But after winning everything they could in the American Rockies, the twins were ready to go back to the Great White North. With an invitation from Luggi Foeger to come to Banff, the twins loaded up their skis on the train, taking Paula Kann with them. "Everything under control meaning money," the twins said in a telegram back home. It looked like even more than money was under control: they were joining seven of North America's top skiers for Foeger's film *Rhythm on Snow*. Foeger had done silents and talkies with the groundbreaking German filmmakers and actors Leni Riefenstahl and Arnold Fanck. He had run ski resorts from the southern tip of South America to the American Rockies to Gray Rocks in Quebec, and was well equipped to make a great film. It was an intelligent decision, no matter the reputation of Foeger's films; the rest of the Canadian Olympic Ski Team was training in Quebec, where little if any snow remained, and staying on longer in the Rockies would give the twins extra snow time.

At the Brewster Camp in Banff they met the cast and crew, led by Austrian downhill champ Toni Matt, who would ostensibly be giving them courses at the Sunshine ski resort, Lake Louise, and at the Colombia Ice Fields. His wife, Helen, and their toddler, Chris, who was already on skis, joined him. With them would be Roger Trottier from Quebec and American racers Gerry Everett, Paula Kann, Colin Stewart, Herbie Schneider (son of the great Hannes) and Gene Gillis.

Seen today, *Rhythm on Snow* may not be great, but it certainly is fun. "We had a marvellous time making that movie," Rhona says. "We climbed so much we felt we could jump off mountains." The film is still available at the US Ski Museum in Franconia, NH.

To the eyes of a younger generation, the film is a wild foray into 1940s "sexism lite." It has a jaunty tone, like cartoons shown before the main feature (it was intended to be shown in specialized places where there were ski fans). There is no dialogue between the skiers that we can hear; it was less complicated and less expensive to lay over the narrator's voice in the studio. It was up to him to hold together the flimsy vaudeville story, really just an excuse to show the artful skiers in the beautiful Rockies.

It goes like this: three pretty girls arrive at the Brewster Ranch in a latest model Ford Woody, the precursor to the minivan and a perfect ski bum vehicle, a nine-seater with genuine wood panels on the outside. Immediately two cowboys spot the girls and begin moving in "for the round-up." The cowboys can't figure it: there's no snow around and the girls got them strange ski things on top of the Woody. Turns out, "It's those feminine annihilators of skiing competition, Rhona and Rhoda and Paula Kann." They're going skiing at Sunshine, but first they go horseback riding with Johnny following them, looking for all the world like a real Hollywood cowboy. Then he tries to go skiing with them, and "the snow maidens" make him look a fool next to their prowess. To our eyes today, that prowess may look rough, and indeed so does the film—there certainly aren't any overhead helicopter shots here à la Warren Miller. Something that keeps the times in perspective, too, is that the "fireball twins" ski up to Sunshine Lodge. Ain't no helicopters—nor cars, nor people. Just the handful of skiers and the grandiose silence of the mountains, a completely different picture compared to today's high-traffic ski resorts. After the twins show "an old idea coming back," that of the suicide leather strap that angled the heel straight down instead of diagonally, the skiers execute some choreographed rhythm down the runs. Although they're heading down Sunshine runs, they may as well be skiing virgin territory. But it's not deep-powder skiing—there's a promotional film Rhona and Rhoda made for Canadian Mountain Holidays when they were seventy-two years old that shows the twins heli-skiing through that years later. But that was spring skiing in the Rockies in the 1940s. The film has charming views of landscapes, especially after the group climbs to the top of 11,000-foot Mount Athabasca and surveys the peaks below, then skis down the narrow glaciers of the Colombia Ice Fields. And if you watch closely, you can see Rhona eyeing other views: "the tall

Ain't no helicopters nor cars, nor people. Just the handful of skiers and the grandiose silence of the mountains.

During the filming of ***Rhythm on Snow*** **in May 1947, in Banff, Rhona is all smiles and flirtation at the beginning of her "Great Romance" with Gene Gillis. Left to right: Harvey Clifford, Rhoda, Gene Gillis, Rhona, Gerry Everett, Paula Kann, Herbie Schneider.**

pine from Oregon," as the narrator calls him, or the "Greek god," as Rhona's mother preferred.

Rhona fell hard for Gene Gillis during the making of the film—"the Great Romance," she calls it. In 1947, she says, "I had complete faith in Gene. I depended on Gene the almighty." Before long, he proposed to her out on the balcony at Sunshine. She wanted to marry him, but she wondered what her family would think about this second attempt. She wasn't worried about being separated from Rhoda, she says; she thought it was time. And her sister Rhoda "really cared for Gene." She thought about it for a minute, then she answered Gene, "I guess so." He laughed, and never let her forget it.

THE 1948 ST. MORITZ OLYMPICS

The promises made to the Canadian Ski Team were not extravagant by any standards, but even so Harry Pangman and his Olympic ski committee had trouble delivering. Pangman had formed McGill's ski teams in the 1930s, representing Canada in the Olympics of 1932 and 1936. Full of excitement that Canada would get behind its ski team, he hoped to raise $25,000 by selling "attractive contributor's buttons at a dollar each." The team would then work out in the Rockies in the spring of 1947, train at Mont Ste. Anne in Quebec in early winter, then spend a month before the Games in Davos, Switzerland, training under a Swiss coach. Eight men and four women would represent Canada.

Raising that kind of money from selling one-dollar buttons (a dollar got you a haircut or lunch in those days) was a pipe dream. As the Games approached, Pangman suggested that "difficult financial problems have to be solved before the team is ready; a small fraction of the $25,000 needed was raised." In the end Canada was only able to support a team of eight men (plus one cross-country skier) and two women, Rhona and Rhoda. Margaret Burden was named as an alternate, but preferred to get married instead.

As for training before Europe, there had been no funds for spring training, and those who could went to the Rockies on their own (the twins stayed as long as they could in the American West). And instead of training on Mont Ste. Anne at the end of the year, the team went to Valcartier near Quebec City. It was a small hill, a 400-foot descent compared to the 3,500-foot descent they'd face in St. Moritz, and that year there was little snow. It was hardly preparation for the Alps, but the twins made the best of it, climbing the hill for conditioning. "But the best part," Rhoda said, "was Emile Allais as coach, a wonderful Worlds champion, soft-spoken and a great inspiration." The appointment of Allais, originally suggested by the twins, would give them their first coach since the loss of

The 1948 Olympic **Ski Team**

ALPINE SKIERS

Rhona Wurtele
Montreal Qc

Rhoda Wurtele
Montreal Qc

Harvey Clifford
Ottawa On

Bert Irwin
Princeton BC

Bill Irwin
Princeton BC

Pierre Jalbert
Quebec City QC

Hector Sutherland
Montreal Qc

JUMPERS

Laurent Bernier
Quebec City Qc

Lucien Laferte
Trois-Rivières Qc

Tom Mobraaten
Vancouver BC

NORDIC SKIER

Thomas Denis
Lac Beauport Qc

TEAM MANAGER

Louis Cochand
St. Marguerite Qc

COACH

Emile Allais
France

The twins **at Carnegie Hall**

Rhythm on Snow was introduced at Carnegie Hall by celebrity radio- and later TV-broadcaster Lowell Thomas, who had gained fame by publicizing the battles of Lawrence of Arabia. A "fanatical" skier, he had also helped develop Mont Tremblant. While on a honeymoon with his second wife in 1977, he broke a leg skiing. He was 85 years old at the time.

Lowell Thomas, left, skiing on Mount Washington in New Hampshire in 1936...

...and posing with Lawrence of Arabia, left, in a dryer climate in 1917.

Hermann Gadner. As the team prepared to leave, Allais was the picture of the European dandy, wearing a blue homburg, a coon coat, a yellow scarf, and "a suntan inches deep." He was "hopeful" for the team, but also quite aware that the Europeans had been training in the Alps for months now. The twins had only been seriously training for three weeks. As usual, they worked during the week and crammed all the skiing they could get into weekends.

The lack of support and training suggested Canada still wasn't quite ready for a national skiing team; since most skiing was still concentrated in Quebec, the team was something of a novelty, like the sport itself. There was loads of talent, but until Emile Allais signed on one month before, no coaching. And yet without all that, Canadian skiers did amazing things internationally. They had an indomitable spirit, led by the Wurtele twins. In the *Montreal Gazette*, the twins were featured at the end of 1947 among the sports personalities of the year, alongside such titans as Joe DiMaggio, Jackie Robinson, and of course Maurice Richard. Barbara Ann Scott was among the illustrious list as well; in fact, Canada's indisputable best hopes for medals or top-ten finishes were all women: Rhona, Rhoda, and Barbara Ann. The country had come a long way since the debate about whether women should even be allowed to participate in the Olympics.

In contrast, across the ocean, even though the Europeans had gone through a debilitating war, their ski teams were highly organized, and were funded either privately or by government. And stateside, the Americans had proper training and coaches, and, if they didn't have financial support, were able to raise individual funding. During the pre-Olympic races at Sun Valley where Gene Gillis was a team member, for instance, $2,500 was raised in two days. Among the fundraising events was the premiere of Foeger's *Rhythm on Snow* at Carnegie Hall in New York in January of 1948; all the profits were put towards the US Olympic Fund.

What the twins—and the rest of the Canadian team—received was publicity. "The team's selection, training and itinerary received

The 1948 Canadian Olympic Ski Team: Left to right: Manager Louis Cochand, Tom Mobraaten, Hector Sutherland, Harvey Clifford, Pierre Jalbert, coach Emile Allais, Rhoda, Morna Cochand (wife of Louis Cochand), Rhona, Bert Irwin, Luc Laferte, Tom Denis, Laurent Bernier, Bill Irwin, chef de mission Thorney Pickering.

Ski training **1947 style**

Summer Training Hints to the Olympic Ski Team, from the Canadian Amateur Ski Association, 1947:

a) Work outside at manual labour if possible.

b) If you have an indoor job get regular exercise during the evenings and weekends, but watch that you do not overdo it.

c) Get eight hours of sleep nightly.

d) Eat well but do not over-eat.

e) Cut your consumption of alcohol and especially smoking to a minimum or eliminate entirely.

f) As the fall months approach, try to get regular workouts in a gym, concentrating on the general conditioning of the body and particularly the legs. Mountain climbing is excellent leg exercise.

coast to coast publicity on a scale never before achieved with a Canadian Olympic Ski team," the *Montreal Herald* reported. Of course, the last time the press could report on an Olympic team had been twelve years earlier, and back then the team's selection was arbitrary, their training non-existent, and itineraries were left up to the individual. Still, the twins were everywhere—in American *Vogue* in a feature on skiing in St. Sauveur; in *Chatelaine*; the *Saturday Evening Post*; the *Montreal Standard* magazine; every Quebec newspaper, French and English; and most Canadian newspapers. *Rhythm on Snow* premiered in Canada, too, albeit at a much more modest venue than Carnegie Hall, and was hosted by the newly formed Westmount Ski Club. The result was that each team member was handed cash for their expenses at the Olympics: fifty dollars.

Finally, the day after Christmas the twins and the rest of the Olympic Ski Team gathered up their luggage—limited to "as much as they could carry"—and boarded the train for New York. The twins' parents, plus Edgar, George, and Jean came to say goodbye, but otherwise it was a small crowd that saw them off during the holidays. At least they were there to help with the luggage, with Edgar making a last-minute dash to retrieve a forgotten binding. Although money had been scarce for the team, sponsors did finally come through for the team in clothing and equipment. In the luggage were trench coats and toques, ski boots and shoes from the respected skiwear company Tyrol, blazers and flannel shirts from the Tooke Company, and "best of all, skis from Attenhoffer"—the brand was the choice of the day, with eight other European teams racing on the laminated, steel-edged skis too. Then the team got to race in those "wonderful" Irving ski suits, "which by the way," Rhona says, "were among the most handsome ski suits (besides the German Bogner ones) of all the Olympic women's teams."

The train took the twins straight to New York City, where they and the team (and Gaby Pleau, who came along as a supporter) were set to board the RMS *Queen Mary* and sail to London, England.

Only, irony of ironies, the day of their arrival the skies decided to dump the heaviest snowstorm ever seen in the city, and the metropolis ground to a halt. Two feet of snow stopped almost all traffic, kept the *Queen Mary* from going anywhere, and led the fire department to declare a state of emergency. Unfortunately, the ski team didn't have their skis with them—they had already left for Europe. Said jumping coach Thorney Pickering, "We probably would have got more training skiing through the streets to the *Queen Mary* than we have had in the past few weeks at Valcartier, Quebec." The team finally made it to the ship by alternating taxis, subways, and then hitching and finally trudging through "some of the finest snow conditions we've had this year," said Pierre Jalbert.

Sports Personalities of 1947 in the *Montreal Gazette*, December 31, 1947: on a par with the Rocket and Jackie Robinson. When the twins went to see Robinson step on the field as the first black man in professional baseball, "the crowd booed him" even in supposedly cosmopolitan Montreal, Rhoda recalls.

Meeting a snowstorm like that upon arrival in New York could almost be construed as a bad omen—although for a ski team going to the winter Olympics, it might equally be seen as a good sign. But then five fur-lined mackintoshes the ski team was bringing over for Barbara Ann Scott and other Olympians went missing, probably stolen. Worse still, even before the team left Bill Irwin had taken a bad fall at Valcartier during training; he was still nursing a concussion. It would not be the last the team would see of injuries. But the twins weren't looking for any signs at this point, other than the ones pointing towards the *Queen Mary*.

Right now, though, the world's grandest ocean liner was stuck in a snowstorm, covered with two feet of snow that the crew had to shovel for eight hours; and once they finally got moving the storm continued at sea. Tables were chained to the floor, tablecloths were wetted to keep dishes from sliding off. Up on a draughty and chilly deck, Rhoda was the first to get seasick, then Rhona followed the next day. The twins were eager to try the swimming pool, but the water kept sloshing from end to end, "so diving wasn't too great," and the pool had to be emptied. There was a gym, but the guy in charge was grumpy, and anyway, they'd just had shots so were feeling queasy—or was it the lurching seas? Mostly the girls tucked away in their cabins with the bestselling novel of those years, *Forever Amber*. Still, it *was* the *Queen Mary*, the true queen of the seas in those days, and on board there were stars and celebrities like Burgess Meredith and Ida Lupino and even Mickey Rooney, celebrating New Year's Eve and putting on an act and strutting around the deck, waving his hat.

The New York papers showed how the blizzard of December 1947 had ground the city to a halt.

On New Year's Day they docked in London, then made their way to Paris, Emile Allais showing them around—"Emile is a tin god here in Europe," Rhona wrote. The Canadian team's headquarters before the Games began was in Davos, Switzerland, so they headed there. The twins were thrilled to finally be in the Alps (and off the ship), and to finally be taking on the world's best skiers. In turn, the Europeans were thrilled to finally see the famous twins, whom they crowded around and followed to the ski runs. Switzerland was trying as best it could to throw a party after years of deprivation; parades of horse-drawn sleighs went between the train station and the Hotel Seehof, and for the first time the twins looked in awe at the magnificent scenery around them, and caught the excitement of the Olympians around them too. One of the runs went right by their window, and they watched the lift going up the mountain from their room. This ski area would become a model for American developments, with railways to mountaintops, twenty-five miles of downhill trails, and a $16 lift ticket good for eight days. The best part, Rhona said, was their big fluffy eiderdown beds. Coach Emile Allais immediately put them on a schedule of breakfast, wax, ski, and rest.

Now everybody wanted to know what the twins thought their chances would be of getting medals at this Olympics. "Let's just wait and see," Rhona said. "We're going to try awfully hard. We'll do our best and we'll hope it's good enough to get us near the

Rhoda and Rhona proudly posing in their blazers; Davos and the Swiss Alps in the background. January, 1948. Behind and to the left is the Hotel Belvedere, the first hotel the Twinski Club later stayed at in Europe.

Warming up: Rhoda, Emile Allais, and Rhona take a pause from training for the 1948 Olympics in St. Moritz, Switzerland. They're wearing "those wonderful Irving of Montreal ski suits."

top—or maybe head the list."

Yet there were already problems. The Americans were in town, and Rhona's fiancé Gene Gillis came right over to see the twins. Even though he had suffered a concussion four days earlier, he was "impossible to keep down."

The Americans in general were already suffering "stupid accidents" during training; the US captain Dodie Post had broken her leg. And now days after the twins' arrival in Switzerland, the twins' skis that had been shipped separately had still not shown up. And Rhoda had forgotten her favourite wax in a drawer of her dresser back home; a panicked telegram to Montreal got the Olympic uniform designer, Irving Margolese (head of Irving of Montreal), to bring it when he came over. Luckily the twins were already chummy with the American team; Paula Kann and Andrea Mead lent them their extra skis.

THE DISFAVOUR OF FATE

It was a colossal task, putting on a worldwide sporting contest so soon after the end of a worldwide war. As can be imagined, the organizers and the athletes encountered all manner of new situations: the good, the bad, and the ugly. For the most part, athletes didn't have to deal directly with the geopolitical manoeuvring, but they would have to negotiate the politics being played by Olympic committees.

Commemorative stamps and envelope from the 1948 Olympics in St. Moritz.

Those politics almost got the Games cancelled only hours after they opened. Hockey, the most lucrative and popular of the winter sports, was the culprit. It was specifically squabbles over which of the two hockey teams that the US sent would represent America, and which had true amateur classification, that frustrated officials. Then the IOC cancelled the hockey tournament—most Canadians had only slim hopes for the RCAF Flyers anyway, a team pasted together at the last minute with university students and pilots—and finally it looked like hockey would never again be included in future Olympics.

War and Peace **in Switzerland**

The *New York Times*: "In this peaceful Alpine resort, a thousand athletes, some of them former enemies in the war that twice postponed the games from 1940 and 1944, will decide the champions of the hickory ski, the silver skate and the racing bobsled..."

Gretchen Fraser, the US skier who won the special slalom at the St. Moritz Olympics.

Many of the problems in the 1948 Olympics were directly related to the war. Nations and individuals brought their still fresh wounds to the Games, and organizers had to slalom through hazardous territory. Equipment was at a premium; audiences were hard to come by with travel restrictions still in effect in some countries and hard currency scarce. Germany and Japan weren't allowed to participate, and Soviet Russia chose not to show up. Then there were accusations that some of the Austrian athletes had been Nazis; one skier in particular, it was said, had driven a car for the Gestapo in Norway, and this delayed publication of official results of the men's slalom race by more than six hours. There were few Norwegian athletes on the once-strong Nordic ski team—war had taken care of that—so the neutral Swedes swept the competition. There were accusations that the Americans' bobsled had been tampered with. *Gazette* reporter William Weintraub, who was now in St. Moritz covering the Games, quoted an observer there: "The trouble with the Olympics is that they can become too Olympian, with everybody just standing around and hurling thunderbolts."

If nothing else, it is comforting to know that previous Olympiads were just as bogged down in controversy as our current Olympics. Only the details have changed.

Back on the ground level, however, the athletes were experiencing problems of their own. Right from the moment training began in Switzerland, these Olympics would be plagued by injuries. *Ski News* magazine would report on "The disfavor of Fate that has seemed to haunt this Olympics." As mentioned, the Americans had already suffered too many accidents. Soon, the strongest hope for the Canadian men, Pierre Jalbert, would take a trial run down the St. Moritz course, fly over a huge bump, and break his leg.

After a first glance at that course, the Olympic committee had come to the conclusion that the men's course wasn't difficult enough. To make it more challenging, several huge mounds were piled up on the run, making for some astounding jumps. Many racers weren't happy about it, including Jalbert. But now he was off to the hospital with the others. Fortunately for him, it turned out to be pretty exciting, as movie stars and celebrities visiting the Olympics came by to express sympathy.

The movie stars must have been kept busy. Particularly in skiing, before the Olympics had even begun there was what seemed like a rush for the emergency rooms of Swiss hospitals. After American Dodie Post broke her leg, two US jumpers were hospitalized, two men's downhillers had ankle injuries, and Gene Gillis nursed his concussion. The Swiss men boasted a broken leg, a fractured leg, an unspecified injury to a jumper, and a spine injury that left one skier temporarily paralysed. In this area at least, the Canadians kept up. To join Jalbert and his broken leg, Lucien Laferte had chipped his anklebone and Harvey Clifford sprained a ligament. Those were added to Bill Irwin's injury lingering from training in Quebec. Even someone travelling with the team in an unofficial capacity tore a ligament. That meant six Americans, four Swiss, and four Canadians (out of ten) were down. Then there were broken legs among the smaller ski teams of Australia, Austria, Norway, Romania, and Czechoslovakia.

Hearing of the skiers falling like soldiers, a panicked Sydney Dawes, president of the Canadian Olympic Association and still in Canada, cabled his ski team manager Louis Cochand. He was instructed to "supervise training as to eliminate further accidents." There had been hardly any money to send this troupe of skiers overseas; there was absolutely nothing left to send replacements (though over on the ice rink, the skating and hockey teams had managed to get all their expenses paid). "In the past years, the Canadian Olympic Association (COA) has contributed nothing to Canada's Winter Olympic teams," Dawes had told reporters before the teams went overseas. "This time, the COA is endeavoring to collect $600 for each approved competitor...for both the 1948 Winter and Summer Olympics. We estimate that this amount will be sufficient for the summer teams if proper economy is exercised." When Dawes finally did make it to Switzerland that

The Queen Mary's **long voyage**

By 1948, the *Queen Mary* had been retired from a stint as a troop transporter during World War II, having ferried 800,000 soldiers. She was one of the fastest liners around, and because of that often travelled without convoy or escort during the war. Hitler offered $250,000 and the Iron Cross for the sinking of "the Grey Ghost," so named for her camouflage and elusiveness. The ship was never hit. At war's end, she made seven voyages to bring war brides over the Atlantic. Today, the *Queen Mary* serves as a hotel, museum, and restaurant in Long Beach, California.

year, he claimed that he had $100 for each winter team member. Rhona and Rhoda say that he handed them $50 each. That would cover their expenses for the time they were in Europe. So like any good black-market dealer in post-war Europe, the team went to work raising funds on their own. The radios they bought in New York for $33 each they sold for $50 each in Switzerland; Gaby Pleau was offered 2000 francs for her fur coat.

And still they plugged on. By January 14 it was reported that the Canadian Olympic skiers were gamely continuing with their training despite one hobbling man and two confined to bed. And then the next day things would get even worse.

With sixteen days until the Olympics were scheduled to begin, Rhona and Rhoda were training at Davos, taking the practice runs with calculated risks. There were small crowds gathered to watch the unique spectacle of identical superstars on skis. Coach Emile Allais was justly proud of his girls; they were training with Emile and the men, and easily holding their own. But that was exactly what would lead to problems. Emile led a group down a practice run, with Rhoda and the remaining men's team behind him. All of a sudden, one of the men (Rhoda remembers it as Pierre Jalbert) took a sharp turn in front of Rhoda; she tried to avoid him, and he skied over the back of her skis. It ended with a wild tumble for Rhoda, and wearing only the standard leather boots with flimsy bindings, it also meant her ankle hurt when she got up. It meant another visitor to the hospital, this time for Canada's best hope. The doctor pronounced a crack in her right anklebone. After the swelling went down in nine days, they would put a cast on, six days before the Games.

Rhoda was predictably optimistic. The *Montreal Star*: "Rhoda is 'browned off' with the inactivity. It is the first accident the brilliant Montreal skier has had. 'It's a nuisance,' she said from her bedside where she was knitting a sweater and practicing on Cochand's accordion." For his part, Louis Cochand was confident that the "silly accident" would not put her out of the Olympics;

Emile Allais didn't comment.

But if Cochand wasn't worried, at least not publicly, there was someone else who was getting nervous. Back in Montreal, the Wurtele family was very closely following the news out of Switzerland. Hunter Wurtele was worried about Rhoda's injury, but he knew his daughters' iron will, their ability to finish anything they started. But his wife was nervous. One of the twins had been hurt. "It will affect Rhona too," she told Myrtle Cook. "It always does when one or the other is hurt." But how exactly would it affect Rhona?

Mrs. Wurtele didn't have to wait long to find out. Exactly two days later, Rhona was skiing the Parsenn run in Davos through deep soft snow and caught a ski on a hidden rock; her ski flew up and hit her on the back of the head. "In other words, she knocked herself out," wrote Cook. "As has been the case all their lives, one twin rarely does anything without the other following suit. Accidents are apparently no exception."

In fact, Rhona hadn't quite knocked herself out, but the ski made a nasty gash on the back of her head. Still, being a Wurtele, she picked herself up and continued to follow the rest of the team down the run. Perhaps she was still a little dizzy; she skied over a ridge too fast and flew through the air. Emile Allais was watching from below; she was heading towards a fence post, so he skied in front of it so she would crash into him instead, saving her from two accidents on one run. Rhona finished the run, then stopped at the hotel. Rhoda told her to go see the same doctor she had, Dr. Frei. So Gaby bundled Rhona off to see the doctor—only they found the wrong Dr. Frei, in a dingy little clinic ("Who would have thought there were two Dr. Frei's in that little town!" laughs Rhona). When they did find the right doctor, he must have been equally surprised to see an identical twin with another injury.

While he cleaned it up, Gaby took a look at the wound and saw what she thought was a piece of black plastic from the edge of Rhona's ski. The doctor sewed up the gash with three stitches and

A homeless **Olympics**

During the war years, the Olympic Games had been bumped around like an unwelcome relative during the holidays. The 1940 Summer Olympics had been scheduled for Tokyo, but Japan withdrew in 1938 when they were at war with China. The International Olympic Committee (IOC) transferred the games to Helsinki, only to see Finland invaded by the Soviets in 1939. With global conflict raging, the Games were cancelled in 1940 and 1944.

In 1948, the IOC woke from a long sleep, and offered the Summer Games to London. Much of the city had been laid to waste in the Blitz, but the English gamely accepted. With a no-frills approach, and with no invitations to Germany and Japan (and the Soviet Union choosing not to show up), the show went on.

Part of the "Cripples Club" on the Sporthotel Seehof at Davos, 1948: From left, Hec Sutherland, Rhona with bandaged head, Rhoda with cast, Harvey Clifford.

wrapped a white bandage around her head. "It looked a little startling," Rhona says, "so he changed it for a black one."

That was it for Sydney Dawes. He now told Cochand that there would definitely be no more pre-Games races for the Canadian team, as the skiers had hoped. His ski team was currently operating at 40 percent, and Canada's biggest hopes for medals, besides Barbara Ann Scott, were both walking wounded. Of course, as soon as she could Rhona was up and skiing. In two days she was out daily with the other members of the team; her own skis had still not arrived. Rhoda was also putting up a brave front, and "walking like nothing happened." Of course Rhoda would have walked like nothing happened even if she was missing a foot. "You should see our parade into the dining room of cripples," Rhona joked.

Luckily, there were plenty of things to distract "the Cripples Club" before the Games began. The twins celebrated turning twenty-six on their birthday, January 21; Rhoda got a nice big white sock for her cast. Their cake had so many candles Rhona's hair caught on fire when she was blowing them out, but Luc Laferte leapt into action and put it out. The injured girls and Gaby spent their time in Davos reading *Forever Amber* on the balcony outside their room, watching the sleighs and skiers go by. Their first time in Europe, despite the injuries, was "so much fun and exciting and beautiful."

Then the Canadian Hockey team arrived at Davos, causing a lot of excitement among the Swiss; the Swiss were pretty confident they had the best team in Europe and could finally win gold in hockey.

When the snow was finally shovelled off the ice, they could practice; and when they were finished, a tiny nineteen-year-old girl came on the chipped and slashed ice after them, carving circles and figure eights and leaping in the air, her every move followed by an adoring crowd. It was Barbara Ann Scott, who had just recently won the European and World Championships in figure skating. "Everywhere we went we heard 'B.A., B.A.,'" Rhoda says.

The twins with Barbara Ann Scott at the ice skating rink in Davos, Switzerland, 1948. Luckily, the injured twins had someone to hold them up.

"She was a very sweet little thing," remembers Rhoda. "She looked like a little chickie. She went around in bonnets and was very dainty. She was about that high, and she had this sweet little smiling expression all the time, and would skate by the officials like that."

Of course, the twins were attracting almost as much attention as Barbara Ann Scott, and in the spirit of camaraderie the Canadian team was building up in Switzerland, she invited Rhona and Rhoda over for tea. First, however, she told them she'd run through her Olympic program on the ice for them. Rhona was still feeling woozy, so caught some of the program and headed back to the hotel; Rhoda and Gaby stayed on and did tea with Barbara Ann and her mother. There they found out the skater had had infantile paralysis (polio) when she was young; Rhona had also been diagnosed with polio when younger but was never severely affected. Barbara Ann had overcome the disease by exercising on the ice, she told them. "And apparently her mother was a great pusher, and knew how to handle the officials, and she was in there fighting all the time," says Rhoda.

There were certainly similarities among the three young women: dedicated athletes at the top of their form, overcoming

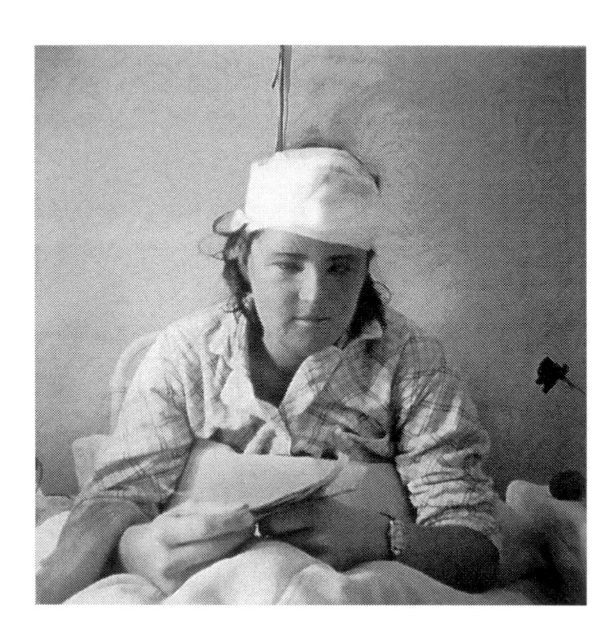

"One of Rhon's better days" after her head wound became infected, wearing a "wee bonnet" of her own. After eight days in the hospital, she would race on one of Europe's toughest courses.

odds to reach the Olympics. But there were also differences. Fancy skating never caught the twins' imagination, although they had tried it when young on the Murray Hill rink normally reserved for hockey, and later were members of the Montreal Figure Skating Club, with whom they skated in a recital at the Forum. But with their skiing and swimming, there wasn't much time to concentrate on other sports. Perhaps as well figure skating was too tame, and there was less chance of breaking one's leg, or they didn't like having to wear skirts. Now, where Barbara Ann Scott was delicate and tender, the twins were said to "ski like men," and headed into the riskiest ski runs without a second thought. Scott won the hearts of the audience with her charm and grace; Rhona and Rhoda won their races by skiing the fastest. When the three first met in Switzerland, after all, sweet Barbara Ann was wearing a wee bonnet atop her curls; Rhona's head was swathed in a heavy black bandage and Rhoda's foot was in a cast. One can only imagine that Miss Scott was made slightly nervous around these unpredictable double threats.

The next day, however, Rhona could have scared away most brave men. She woke with her face and neck ballooned to a terrific size, swollen so that even her eyes were squeezed shut. A doctor was rushed to her room, and after sorting out the confusion—the doctor had treated Rhoda's ankle, and wasn't sure which skier he was dealing with here—Rhona was taken to the *Krankenhaus*, the hospital at the other end of town. The wound had become infected, and now had to be drained. Fortunately for her, penicillin had just been developed and used during the war years (one of its first major uses had been during the D-Day invasion in 1944), and so Rhona was given massive doses every three hours day and night. "Moaned and groaned all night," Rhona wrote in her diary, "can't lie on head." If it hadn't been for the penicillin, Rhona believes she might have died.

The team stayed on in Davos slightly longer than they had expected because of Rhona's and other team members' injuries; two days later Rhona's eyes were still swollen shut. Finally the team gathered up its wounded and headed to the Games, only to find themselves placed far from the town of St. Moritz by Sydney Dawes, who felt his team too delicate to deal with the distractions of European festivities. Emile Allais was horrified—the team had to be in St. Moritz. With his connections he quickly got them into a ramshackle hotel closer to the centre of excitement, where the poverty-stricken Austrian team was staying too.

Gene Gillis and Rhona strolling the streets of Davos during the Olympic Games in Switzerland: "A nice social event."

But while they were closer to the Games, Rhona and Rhoda were no closer to being in shape to race. Louis Cochand was still publicly confident that Rhoda would be able to race, and proudly spoke of Rhona training with the team, but the reality was quite different. Rhoda's foot had been in a cast for only five days. As for Rhona, the day before the opening ceremonies she wrote in her diary, "Left hospital after lunch—eyes blurry and hard to see—terribly weak." They nevertheless took the sleigh to another hospital to see Rhona's fiancé Gene, still bed-ridden and recovering from his concussion. He would soon develop a diabetic condition from his injuries and have to take insulin.

By the time the opening ceremonies and Olympic parade were held on January 30, the procession of athletes must have looked like a veteran's parade. Hobbled, on crutches, with heads bandaged, the athletes were nevertheless thrilled with the ceremo-

St. Moritz: **Countesses and Kings**

"The Olympics are a nice social event," wrote William Weintraub for the *Gazette*, "and for those who like sport there are also competitions." The reporter was being only slightly sarcastic. Having been spared most of the horrors of the war because of its neutrality, Switzerland swung in the post-war years. "Countesses were gazing at the reflections of their jewels in martini glasses," Weintraub noted. *Ski News* saw the same scene: "St. Moritz is the last redoubt of a vanished epoch. All the rich and the proud who remain unruined by war and revolution still come here to admire each other—deposed kings, Indian princes, haughty dukes, fabulous merchants... and of course, black marketers from all over Europe, with attendant butterflies." The twins had a ball parading through the Alpine town.

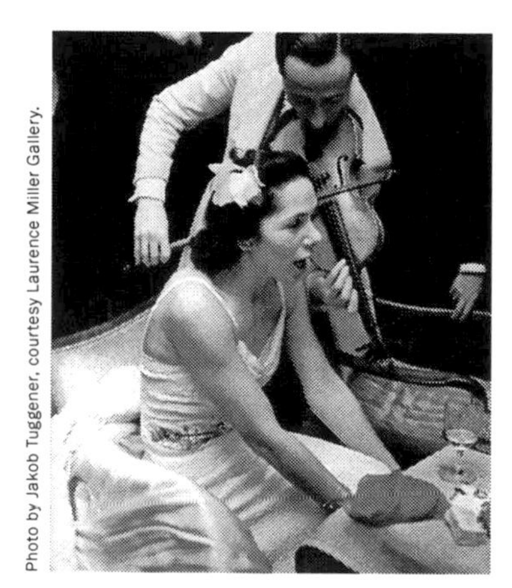

Photo by Jakob Tuggener, courtesy Laurence Miller Gallery.

"Palace Hotel, St. Moritz, New Year's Eve, 1945/46."

nies—"Impressive," says Rhoda, "but nothing like the extravaganzas that take place now." About fifty Canadian athletes marched down onto the ice of the lake below the Palace Hotel, led by the hockey team, the ski team, the speed skaters and figure skaters. When Barbara Ann Scott's feet touched the ice she drew a tremendous round of applause, and a phalanx of photographers gathered as close as they could. The twins, meanwhile, came limping into view. Rhoda had somehow managed to stuff her cast into the pliable leather ski boot of Canadian jumper Luc Laferte, and pretended all was as it should be; Rhona was grateful that the ski team got to carry their skis in the parade, as it gave her something to lean on. From the news photos of the time, you wouldn't guess anything was amiss. But soon it was public that Rhoda's ankle injury would keep her out of competition in these Olympics.

And Rhona? "Exhausted," she wrote in her diary. "Have never felt so weak in my life before." Two days later, she would race down the toughest women's course in Europe.

First, however, the twins decided they had to check out that downhill course—it was the first time downhill and slalom ski events were held in the Olympics, and they hadn't even seen the hill yet. Still fitting into Luc's ski boot and having adjusted the bindings, Rhoda figured she was fit enough to ski "after a fashion." As they headed off, Louis Cochand saw them leaving. "Where do you two think you're going?" he asked. Maybe he didn't believe them when they told him, but he let them go anyway. Yet at the top of the hill, the trail was closed, so the twins skied down beside it. "Nothing to it," they thought, compared to what they'd been doing. So Rhona was game for the Games, and Rhoda would film with their new 8-millimetre camera from below.

RHONA RACES

There seems an incredible casualness to the Olympic races of the time; to hear descriptions from the twins and others, some of it sounds no more official than schoolgirl races at St. Sauveur. Sometimes it's hard to tell whether the times were so different or whether it was the twins' casual treatment of what to others would be life-altering moments.

The day of the women's downhill, Rhona wrote in her diary, "Rested—all went to see Men's Downhill. I drank eggnogs and rested and waxed. Sandwiches to Ladies' Downhill."

Bringing her own sandwiches to the hill? But that wasn't all. Before embarking on the race of her life, Rhona was sitting in the snow waiting, as if this was an afternoon excursion with friends. Worse, a man came by holding his skis over his shoulder and swung around, precisely walloping her on the back of her head as if to remind her of her injury. "Which I really didn't need," Rhona understates.

So Rhona was ready: Her first Olympic downhill, on borrowed skis; having had an accident two weeks previous that left her with a bit of Attenhoffer ski stitched into her skull; which a week later got infected and swelled her head so that her eyes were shut; and having been on a weakening diet of penicillin in the hospital for the last week; and having just been freshly whacked on the back of her head by a pair of weighty hickory skis; and most importantly of all, entering a race without her shadow, her double, her constant companion in almost every race in her lifetime, who was sidelined with an injury at the bottom of the hill; yes, Rhona was ready. She was ready to try and break that magical spell that binds twins in good and bad; to tempt fate and see if one of them could finally run a race without her twin and win.

"You could hardly call it a race," says Rhona.

Rhona gathered all her strength and began the downhill

course with a fiery burst of speed, and all seemed to be going to plan. At the end of the course was a long steep hill, followed by a sudden sharp upgrade and quick turn to the right; she couldn't see what was coming around the corner. Normally Rhona would have had the strength to plow to slow a bit, or jump slightly to lessen the impact, but by the end of the course she had used up whatever reserves she had managed to find so far. And with that she found herself flying out of control through the air. There was a loud crack—her skis hitting each other?—and just as suddenly she came down over the ridge and landed in the merciful powder of a ravine. There was no immediate help—she probably would have refused anyway—and Rhona waited while her acquaintance from the US team, Andrea Mead, made a similar detour on her way down. Then she climbed out of the ravine and finished the race. "We were taught to finish what we started," Rhona says, repeating the Wurtele mantra. They always finished, no matter what. Their German-Scottish father and mother had driven that lesson into them. And that is all Rhona says about the race, her first and last time racing in Europe.

Tellingly, she doesn't mention what the *Montreal Standard* reported on underneath a photo of Rhona on February 7. "Rhona Wurtele, wrapped in blankets and teammate's coat, is revived after fainting at the finish of the women's downhill races at St. Moritz. She was found to have finished on a chipped anklebone."

It took every bit of adrenalin to get down to that finish, and finally she collapsed. That loud crack she heard had been one of her skis imitating what had happened to her twin sister Rhoda two weeks earlier. It had taken longer than usual, but eventually the "twin effect" had caught up to her. She—and Canada—finished in last place, and no one was left to race the women's slalom. They took her away on a stretcher to the hospital, put on a cast "that weighed about ten pounds, and that was the end of that," says Rhona. She must have had the doctors wondering if the Canadians were identical triplets.

Barbara Ann **the Living Doll**

Barbara Ann Scott's miracle on ice—she had already become the first North American to win the European and World figure skating championships in 1947 before taking Olympic Gold—turned the diminutive Ottawa native into Canada's Sweetheart. She immediately became a cultural commodity. Besides being honoured by parades in Canada's major cities when she returned, Scott took centre ice in a show celebrating the returning Olympians at the Montreal Forum. Rhona and Rhoda were invited to take part too. Scott became a professional skater for years, touring with ice revues like "Rose Marie on Ice," and capitalizing on her popularity with as much fervour as today's sports stars. The most lasting product was the Reliable Toy Company's Barbara Ann doll, made from 1948 to 1954. Sold for $5.95, the doll met with overwhelming demand.

Barbara Ann Scott shows the twins her form during practice at St. Moritz before the Olympics.

When the races were over, the Combined results put two of those equipment-poor Austrians and one unexpected US skier, Gretchen Fraser, on the podium (the pigtail-sporting Fraser took the Silver, the US's first-ever skiing medal at the Olympics). The Canadian men, even without Pierre Jalbert, fared better in the Combined. Behind an avalanche of Europeans and one American, Harvey Clifford came twenty-first and Hector Sutherland came twenty-third.

Fate would have it that at this Olympics other sports would take medals for Canada. The men's hockey team, the Air Force Flyers, would wrest the gold from the Swiss, as would (to no one's surprise) the doll of St. Moritz, figure skater Barbara Ann Scott. Indeed, for North America it was the women who kicked European butt in 1948—specifically, Fraser for the US and Scott for Canada.

Special Collections Department, J. Willard Marriott Library, University of Utah

Four members of the 1948 US Women's Ski Team: From left, Silver medal–winner Gretchen Fraser, Andrea Mead, Paula Kann, Brynhild Grasmoen.

When Barbara Ann skated her final program, an air force jet had screamed overhead, the ice was rutted and scraped after two hockey games, and the above-zero temperatures made the ice soft and slushy. She hardly noticed. "When you have to skate outside in the elements, you tend not to worry about the small stuff," she said. Scott took the gold, the first Canadian to ever win Olympic gold at the senior women's figure skating level—and still the only Canadian skater to do so to this day. It was those kinds of triumphs—and the courage of athletes like Rhona and Rhoda—that made people forget world and Olympic politics for a little while. In fact, Canada got so swept up in Scott's victory, the nation almost forgot the rest of the team (besides the upstart Air Force Flyers hockey team—the other medal, a bronze, was given to Suzanne Morrow and Wallace Diestelmeyer for pairs figure skating, another Canadian first). Prime Minister Mackenzie King sent Scott a telegram telling her how she gave "Canadians courage to get through the darkness of the post-war gloom," according to the CBC.

THE OLYMPIC LEGACY

The injuries and spills that caused Rhona and Rhoda to miss out on capturing Olympic medals were drastically disappointing for the twins, especially after smashing all other records and taking trophies throughout North America. But no matter the scale of tragedy, they had never been the kind of women to sit and moan about what might have been. Instead, there are sighs and shrugs—"Going into the Olympics was the thrill of a lifetime," Rhona says, "but winning was not in the books."

There were questions, naturally: "We had a lot of minor accidents," Rhoda says, "but why did the big ones happen then?"

"We were always lucky," answers Rhona. "But not at the Olympics."

Image courtesy of Vintageskiworld.com

1948 Winter Olympics poster, St. Moritz, Switzerland.

The twins prefer to think of the positive aspects. "Fifty-seven countries took part in these 1948 Olympic Games, which is amazing when you realize it was so soon after World War II."

The twins are not the type to search out culprits and lay blame, either. "Of course it was disappointing," Rhona says. "The whole team was facing injuries. They were smashed up. They hadn't had any experience over there. A bunch of characters from all over. Emile Allais was coaching, but what could he do in two weeks?"

What then was the reason for so many injuries? The whole Olympic field of skiers were affected at St. Moritz, not just the Canadians—could it have been that skiers were pushing themselves harder than ever after an eight-year hiatus? The answer is probably more prosaic. When the training of future Canadian skiers in the Olympics is studied, the difference is glaringly obvious. After 1948 much more time and money was spent on the athletes; today they are in better shape, are used to higher altitudes, know about international competition, have safer and more reliable equipment. And while Rhona and Rhoda trained as much as they could, and, unlike most other Canadian skiers, were familiar with high mountains and European and American skiers, the fact remains that when they schussed down the Alps, they had on flimsy leather boots with even flimsier bindings, no shin pads, no goggles, no helmets, and rather arbitrarily laid-out race courses. It's a wonder any of the racers at all got down in one piece. "We did have a few suggestions on our return to put forth to our ski association about training for future Olympians," Rhoda says.

On top of it, Rhona had to battle with the separation of twins. "I was alone," she told Myrtle Cook. "I remember racing before without Rhoda and feeling lost, but that was years ago. This time she was there in spirit. I tried not to let it make any difference." And yet, this important Olympic crucible would hardly be their biggest trial. Soon, the twins would first be separated on different continents—when Rhona finally left Europe to go home for medical treatment, Rhoda would stay to race, and do quite well on her own—then they would move to different ends of the continent to raise families and begin the long and sometimes difficult process of becoming two unique individuals.

Rhona and Rhoda's lasting legacy from the Olympics, however, has nothing to do with winning or losing. It has everything to do with the example they set for the women who followed them. In a CBC-TV segment during the 2002 Salt Lake City Olympics about the "Heroes and Heartbreak of Canadian Alpine Skiers," most of the women skiers interviewed cited examples of the skiers who came before them as inspiration and the reason they felt they could actually win a medal. Rhona and Rhoda had no such heroes. They had hardly heard of the 1936 Olympics when they were children, even though they later raced with the monocled Diana Gordon-Lennox; their heroes went a little further back, to the ancient Greeks (and those were men, to boot). Today, it is thanks to the Wurtele twins that women's alpine skiing in Canada has always been more fascinating than men's skiing.

Women **in the Winter Olympics**

1924 Chamonix, France
13 women of 258 total - 5%

1928 St. Moritz, Switzerland
26 women of 464 total - 5.6%

1932 Lake Placid, NY, USA
21 women of 252 total - 8.3%

1936 Garmisch-Partenkirchen
80 women of 668 total - 11.9%

1948 St. Moritz, Switzerland
77 women of 669 total - 11.5%

1952 Oslo, Norway
109 women of 694 total - 15.7%

1956 Cortina d'Ampezzo, Italy
132 women of 820 total - 16%

1960 Squaw Valley, CA, USA
143 women of 665 total - 21.5%

1964 Innsbruck, Austria
200 women of 1091 total - 18.3%

1968 Grenoble, France
211 women of 1158 total - 18.2%

1972 Sapporo, Japan
206 women of 1006 total - 20.4%

1976 Innsbruck, Austria
231 women of 1123 total - 20.5%

1980 Lake Placid, NY, USA
233 women of 1072 total - 21.7%

1984 Sarajevo, Yugoslavia
274 women of 1274 total - 21.5%

1988 Calgary, AB, Canada
313 women of 1423 total - 21.9%

1992 Albertville, France
488 women of 1801 total - 27%

1994 Lillehammer, Norway
522 women of 1739 total - 30%

1998 Nagano, Japan
814 women of 2302 total - 35.3%

2002 Salt Lake City, Utah, USA
886 women of 2399 total - 36.9%

2006 Turin, Italy
1021 women of 2663 total - 38.3%

1948 OLYMPIC **HOCKEY GAMES**

The 1948 Olympics also had problems outside the political, and some of them seem awfully quaint from today's perspective. Whereas conditions were good for the Olympic skiers, the Canadian skating team couldn't get in a lot of practice before the Games, but it wasn't because of injuries or politics: there was just too much snow falling on the outdoor rink for shovellers to keep up with it. One news photo from the time shows Toronto figure skater Marilyn Ruth Take helping to shovel the knee-deep snow off the ice. Though the outdoor rink was nestled in one of the most beautiful locations underneath the Alpine peaks, there were other drawbacks for skaters. Figure skating competitions followed on the heels of hockey, meaning pirouettes had to be perfect on the chewed-up surface, with no Zamboni between sports. Hockey games were still being played—on day three the US beat Italy 31 to 1—but the confused Americans not only had to contend with playing as an unrecognized team in an unrecognized event, they also had to deal with a flash snowstorm.

Despite controversy, the wondrous seeped through. The games unravelled in the literal shadow of the mountains. Wildly uneven scores in hockey were fairly normal as the sport was still being learned in Europe (in 1924 the Canadian Olympic team beat the Swiss 33–0 and the Czechs 22–0; in 1948 the Czechs beat the Italians 22–3. Shades of Olympic women's hockey today...). But although in these Games the Americans crushed the Italians, a rare camaraderie arose between the teams. "Eleven members of the winning team are former soldiers," wrote the *Gazette*, "and five of the Italian side fought as their enemies in the Second World War. But only one penalty was called in a surprisingly cordial match. Every time two opposing players brushed or collided heavily, they stopped and shook hands. And when Arnaldo Fabris banged Fred Pearson of the American team with an inadvertent stick, Italian players apologized and helped pick the American up."

An outdoor venue gave spectators the delight of watching the games while perched on mountain ledges, with the added bonus of being able to throw snowballs at players and referees. This became essential for the biggest game of the

The hockey arena in Davos, Switzerland at the St. Moritz Olympics, 1948: The newly arrived Canadian players dealt with snow-storms, former war enemies—and snow-balls from the audience.

Olympics: Canada's RCAF Flyers against the Swiss. Hockey was finally back on again, the Americans having made up their minds (and lost their games), and all of St. Moritz shut down and headed to the stands, confident in the best ever Swiss team. The twins went to the big game, of course, with the whole Canadian Olympic Team. "The Air Force boys were still blue in the face from just coming over," Rhoda remembers of the fatigued team.

"When decisions went against the Swiss in the vital game with Canada," wrote the *Herald Tribune*, "a chorus of shrill whistles echoed through the Alps and a barrage of snowballs came down from the hillside." And yet when the flying snow cleared, to everyone's surprise the Canadians managed to win the game 3–0—and take the gold medal.

"So what happened," Rhoda says, "is that nobody would talk to us Canadians. There was complete sadness as the town dispersed from around the rink." It was the opposite when the team finally got home—a hero's welcome awaited them, with a parade and thumping marching bands in Ottawa.

THE TWINS' OLYMPIC LEGACY **THROUGH THE YEARS**

Kerrin Lee-Gartner, winner of Canada's first downhill ski gold in Albertville, France, 1992.

It was in the 1950s, and due to the pioneering of the Wurteles—"These remarkable twins," the CBC said, "who are credited with starting it all"—that Canada finally started winning Olympic ski races. Rhona and Rhoda did more than set an example; Canadian women's medal-wining achievements in Olympic skiing over the last half century can all be directly linked to the Wurteles.

The first link is Lucile Wheeler. As a youngster, she had been coached by Hermann Gadner and watched the Wurtele twins take all the prizes at her parents' Gray Rocks ski resort. At fourteen she represented Canada at the World Championships. On the Olympic team at the 1952 Oslo Olympics, she roomed with Rhoda; at the next Games in Italy, in 1956, she won Canada's first ski medal, a bronze for downhill. In 1958 she won the FIS world championship in Austria in downhill and giant slalom. Her wins finally helped to get increased funding for skiers at an international level and boosted skiing's popularity in Canada.

On the 1956 Olympic team with Wheeler was Anne Heggtveit. In 1959 Heggtveit toured Europe with the National team, with Rhoda as manager. The next year in the slalom she won Canada's first gold skiing medal at the Olympics in Squaw Valley, California—with a margin of 3.3 seconds, a record that still stands. She was also the first non-European to win an FIS slalom and world championship, and the first North American to win the Arlberg-Kandahar.

On that 1960 Olympic team watching Heggtveit win was Canada's "Female Athlete of the 20th Century," Nancy Greene. In 1967, she won the World Cup; at the 1968 Olympics in Grenoble, she won the gold in the giant slalom and silver in the slalom, making her the first Canadian to win two medals and the most decorated ski racer in history.

Canada's next medal came from Kathy Kreiner at the 1976 Games in Innsbruck, Austria, when she pulled an upset to take the giant slalom gold; she had already won the giant slalom at the world cup in 1974.

Finally, Kerrin Lee-Gartner won gold in the downhill at the 1992 Olympics in Albertville, France—the first gold for Canada, male or female, in the downhill. Lee-Gartner cited Nancy Greene as a major influence in her career; Greene was her next-door neighbour when she was a little girl.

COMING HOME

After the Olympics most of the Canadian ski team, including Rhona and Rhoda, weren't about to leave the best skiing in the world—and they didn't have enough money to get home anyway. It would take awhile for money to be sent. So they immediately headed for St. Anton am Arlberg in Austria, the birthplace of Hannes Schneider and modern skiing, and the site of the Hannes Schneider Cup. The trip was organized by George Eisenschiml, an Austrian living in Banff who was also in the process of installing the first chair lift in the Canadian Rockies. The American team went with them too, including Rhona's fiancé Gene, who by this time had found Rhona a proper ring for their engagement, although it didn't fit.

Despite the difficulties in post-war Europe, the twins were able to travel in style. As guests of US Generals Collins and Bergan, they were invited to use the US military train and stay in the biggest (empty) hotels. Still recovering from injuries, the girls had to be content to watch the races. But they saw they had little to complain about. At Bad Gastein, they watched, fascinated, as soldiers with amputated legs skied with outrigger poles, a brand new innovation after the war. The men climbed up the hill and came down again. Rhoda took home movies of the event. "I didn't limp much after seeing that," Rhoda says.

Rhoda was in fact champing at the bit to race again. Rhona was still healing, so near the end of February, Rhoda and Gaby Pleau said goodbye to her sister and Gene and headed off for a race near Nice, France. With her weighty cast finally cut off, Rhoda entered the slalom—and came fourth. The separation from her sister didn't seem to have the usual traumatic effect this time. It was as if the girls were practising at pulling away from each other, bit by bit, preparing for adult life. And at the next race, Rhoda would do even better.

A magical moment: **Margie Gillis on her mom, Rhona**

"I remember the magical experience of seeing *Chariots of Fire* [the 1981 film about the 1924 Olympics] at the cinema with my mom—she sat there and whispered the whole time about her experiences in the Olympics. Some people would have hated it, but I loved it. The twins don't talk about it normally; they talk about the basics, the fundamentals. But they had the feeling, and taught us this, that the most important thing was being there for your country, and with respect—and that winning was not the most important thing. So they had learned and applied this lesson already. When they went to the Olympics they were expected to win, they were at the top of their form; but there was never a moment of bitterness. They were there, and they did their best."

Brochure from Austrian Spa and Winter Sports centre Bad Hofgastein, 1948.

At Chamonix, France, Rhoda entered the famed Arlberg-Kandahar. This was the site of the first-ever ski championship in downhill and slalom, which British ski enthusiast Sir Arnold Lunn had organized with Hannes Schneider in 1931. There, Rhoda finally got revenge for missing the Olympics. "Her legs were still wobbly as a result of breaking an ankle two months ago," the *Montreal Standard* reported, "and she had been advised not to enter the race." But that was unthinkable. "I was really out of practice," Rhoda said, "and did not really get the feel of the course until about half-way down—and then I let go." It took her to third place in the downhill—the first time in history a North American had cracked the top three in the race. "Sir Arnold was there," Rhoda recalls, "and was rather surprised a Canadian had done that well." Rhoda also took fifth in the slalom and the combined. She had in fact floored a lot of Europeans, who had missed seeing the twins at their peak because of their accidents at St. Moritz. The French papers called her run "a magnificent demonstration of pure style."

Rhona, meanwhile, had quite another kind of experience in her European journey. While unable to do any skiing at Zermatt, she could not be kept down, and found a Rodel sled to ride down the icy spring tracks. Riding somewhat hampered by her ankle cast (complete with an iron bar inside it) and her head still bandaged, Rhona's sled sailed over a ridge; she landed seat first on some rocks, bruising her bottom. She felt ridiculous wallowing in snow up to her hips in the ravine, trying to retrieve the Rodel. When she got to a slight slope she tried to get the sled to get her down the hill. As she flung herself stomach first on the sled it immediately sank in the wet snow; once again she went flying off it, this time bruising herself down the front of her body. She shuffled back to the hotel, even more broken and bruised than before.

Later in Austria she was just able to attend a dinner thrown by the American generals in a nearby castle without wincing too much when they passed the salt. But when an American military

The famed Arlberg-Kandahar. Rhoda has traced the line of the "Gal's course" on the Brevant. It was down this wild run that Rhoda came in third, surprising everyone. It was her first race since the Olympics with her cast off.

Post-war **Austria**

After the relative glitz of Switzerland, Austria was sobering, still reeling from the effects of war. An occupied zone, the St. Anton district was filled with French soldiers quite aware of being on hallowed skiing ground. They greeted the arrival of Canadian coach Emile Allais "as a sort of minor deity," William Weintraub wrote. You almost had to be a god to get into the district; tourists still had a hard time getting in, and the twins were among the first civilians into the area since the end of hostilities. Greeting them was the St. Anton band, dressed in Tyrolean costumes, reading from sheet music held up by young boys. The sight moved the girls: "They had waited a long time for visitors," Rhona says. Among the destruction, stores had mostly bare shelves and were only open two hours a day, and most things were to be had at a bargain. Austrians got by on only a pound of meat per month. The twins tried to help out by buying wool for sweaters and giving it to a woman to knit—who the next day presented them with the completed sweaters. She had delegated knitting parts of the sweaters to all of her friends who also needed money.

doctor examined Rhona, he recommended she go back home to Montreal for treatment as soon as possible. With that, the couple found some plane tickets (a princely $350 from Geneva to New York), and that was the end of Rhona's racing career in Europe. But it certainly wouldn't be the last time she'd ski there.

Rhoda and Gaby followed some time later. First they took a brief tour through Paris, dropped in on Gaby's relatives in Belgium, and visited the English family of the children the Wurteles had taken care of during the war. Rhoda also took Gaby to Westminster Abbey and found the plaque honouring her relation Jonathon Hunter, the founder of modern surgery. Then the pair took the *Queen Elizabeth*, the *Queen Mary*'s sister ship, back to New York and Montreal.

$350 from Geneva to New York.

Back in Montreal, Rhona was kept busy getting new casts for her ankle, getting her engagement ring resized, and recovering from her numerous aches and pains. From the combination of accidents in Europe, Rhona developed "a bad hematoma" on her hip which resulted in an infection and two operations that put her in the Royal Victoria Hospital for three weeks each time. "A great summer," she remembers sardonically.

The worst ache of all was watching Gene leave; he had gone out west "to make a pot of money, a little nest while I recovered in the hospital. I could have died to see him go," Rhona wrote in her diary. They had intended to marry in the spring, but now delayed the wedding until Rhona was well enough.

Yet even that postponement couldn't keep her down. At the end of April the twins were invited to another post-Olympic celebration, this time at the Montreal Forum where they skied down the ramp on the ice. Rhona had only got her ankle cast removed that day. A short while later, they did the same trick in Ottawa—accompanied by "little Anne Heggtveit," an up and coming nine-year-old skiing prodigy.

Rhoda, having fully recovered from her ankle injury by the summer, took the opportunity to amuse herself with a little track and field during the Zone Olympic Trials—and subsequently won the javelin, high jump, and baseball throw, then set records in the shot put and discus.

It was quite a show, and, shockingly, for some it was too much. In a column in the *Montreal Standard* that summer, Andy O'Brien talked about what a shame it was that the Wurtele twins were injured in the Olympics. But then he seems to hit a time warp and regress forty years or so. "Extreme exertion sport can find little justification in milady's realm," O'Brien wrote. "A doctor friend of mine who rates as one of Montreal's leading obstetricians is quite definite on the point. 'In the main,' he says, 'an inhibitory effect of sports on development of young girls is to be noted. The reason is that, in general, girls must exert much more effort than boys to accomplish the same physical work. It has been wisely pointed out by foremost men of obstetrics and gynecology that women would be wise to turn away from strenuous sports and direct their strength and accomplishments into channels which are not measured by a stop watch.'"

That must have been laughable to the twins; they probably could have advised the journalist to direct his strength towards writing not measured by chauvinism. Yet however reactionary O'Brien's comments seemed, there was still a large segment of the population who believed a woman's place was in the home—preferably in the kitchen, feeding her man and her brood. And that backlash against women's increasing freedom during the war years would only build through the upcoming decade. Still, through the 1950s and into the new millennium, the Wurtele twins stood as irrefutable proof that exertion in sports did not inhibit the development of girls. It only turned them into women.

What is the quality you like most in a man?

Rhona:

A good physique—handsome! Kind, gentle, thoughtful, intelligent, has gumption—strong, sharing, caring, loving, blah blah, blah. And a sense of humour.

Rhoda:

Honesty and a sense of humour. And respect!

SEPARATION BY LOVE

That summer after the Olympics, Rhoda had entertained ideas of going to Chile to ski with Dodie Post of the US ski team. She had to get a little money together first, of course, so logic prevailed and she applied for a job as a stenographer at RCA Victor. That would change everything. Because on her walk from Westmount to the office downtown—which she did every morning and every lunch too—she kept seeing one of the young men from accounting drive by.

Image courtesy Ford Motor Company

Ad for 1950 Mercury—*rebel without a cause?*

Now Rhoda is not one given to florid statements. Much of her recounting of her racing years—and her recent years of heli-skiing, bungee jumping, and windsurfing—are told with the matter-of-fact tone of test pilots and bucking bronco riders. It follows then that she brings the same approach to romance.

"Well," she says, "that's where I met Arnold and then we got married." And what made Arnold Eaves, the car-driving accountant, stand out for her?

"He gave me rides," she says.

She accepted Arnold's proposal because he gave her rides? Of course he had just bought a 1949 Mercury (with a hot new design) for two thousand dollars—the kind of car James Dean would drive a few years later in *Rebel Without A Cause*. But Arnold was no rebel.

"He was very pleasant," Rhoda concedes. "He was attractive and had a good sense of humour and lots of fun. He skied a lot and we had mutual friends."

"It was timing," Rhona interjects.

The twins had done well to wait until after the war to be married, it seemed. While they had bemoaned the lack of worthy suitors at the St. Andrew's Ball in earlier years, now they had snagged a couple of prizes. Besides being on the US Olympic Ski Team, Gene, the six-foot-three Greek god, had been a sports hero back at the University of Oregon, an outstanding football player; he had also served with the Marines during the war. Arnold had spent three years in Europe during the war as a Lieutenant with the Royal Montreal Regiment, and later in Sherman tanks with the 28th Armored Division of British Columbia, and was involved in many sports. After graduating from McGill University in Commerce, he settled into the dependable and steady job of being an accountant with RCA Victor for the rest of his career.

Arnold Eaves in training at Trois-Rivières, Quebec, 1942.

It was already clear that summer that after Rhona and Gene would get married, they'd be moving out to the Northwest US, Gene's stomping grounds. Gene had also got a car, but on an athlete's salary settled for a 1941 Cadillac. He used that car a lot that year, driving back and forth out west and going to Alaska to work. Rhona was in and out of the hospital, getting operations on her inner hip, in no shape to have a wedding. So with Rhona putting her wedding off till later, and now Rhoda newly engaged, eventually it seemed logical to have their weddings together.

So on November 13, 1948, the inseparable twenty-six-year-old twins took another large step together, and had a double ceremony at St. Stephen's Anglican Church in Westmount; appropriately, the priest was Reverend Love. Just a little wedding among friends, with three hundred people invited, including skiers Paula Kann, Johnny Fripp, Harvey Clifford and Lucile Wheeler; Gaby Pleau and Nancy McKean were bridesmaids. However offhand the twins may be in describing it, the wedding turned out to be one of Montreal's biggest social events of the day. Besides the news photographers and reporters pushing through the church doors, an additional seven hundred people tried to get inside. According to the *Montreal Standard* magazine, which covered the event in a four-page spread, "They jammed the aisles and vestibule and many waited outside in the rain during the entire service." Excited spectators ending up standing on the pews to see the nuptials; it was difficult to hear any "I do"s above the din of revellers. Then: "Ushers and Westmount police had to clear the aisles to let the

Hits and **Mrs.**

Although most media now began calling the twins Mrs. Arnold Eaves and Mrs. Gene Gillis, as was the custom, Myrtle Cook insisted on calling them Rhoda Wurtele Eaves and Rhona Wurtele Gillis. Myrtle was a "Lucy Stoner"—the name for someone who followed nineteenth-century feminist pioneer Lucy Stone, who continued to use her maiden name after marriage.

Lucy Stone, circa 1850.

wedding party out." Reporters were unable to report how many broken hearts looked with jealousy upon Gene and Arnold.

Already before the ceremony, the twins had so many presents that "Mother made us put one twin's away." One of them was a certificate from the Montreal Amateur Athletic Association that read "I hereby promise to coach your children to swim (2 only) for the next sixty years. Your old Scotch coach, Jimmy Rose." (Unfortunately, Rose would die the following September at age sixty-five). Then the girls, bedecked in green coats trimmed with beaver fur and green hats festooned with ostrich feathers, held tight to the arms of their husbands and emerged into their new lives as Rhona Gillis and Rhoda Eaves, and more than their names split them in two.

"Wasn't it remarkable we ended up with a double wedding," Rhoda says. "It hadn't been planned that way but fate seemed to work for us. It would have been pretty drastic to be separated suddenly from someone you had spent every waking day with all your life." Rhona thought it would have been "dreadful for one of us to be married and the other not."

While both twins were deeply in love with their husbands ("We went along with anything because everything was happiness and darling," Rhoda says with a smirk) it was still a drastic separation for the girls. Teachers, noting their almost identical grades, had tried to split them apart as far back as Trafalgar School and it hadn't worked. The longest separation they had had was after the Olympics—just a few months before—when Rhona flew home early. Now the twins were adults, and they had begun to shape their lives as individuals.

"I guess we'll manage to ski anyway," they told the *Daily Star*. "We'll each have our husbands instead."

Years later, Rhoda went to a conference about twins while Rhona was recuperating from another operation for fused vertebrae. At a discussion about whether twins should be kept together throughout their childhood or schooled independently, Rhoda had decided it

At the double wedding, November 1948. From left, Rhoda and Arnold; Rhona and Gene: "Everything was darling and lovely."

was a great thing for twins to stick together through everything. "I wouldn't change it," she says, "We had too much fun."

Rhona offered a different opinion from her hospital bed. "I said no, twins should be treated as individuals because then they can stand on their own two feet later on. And that's very important." When Rhona would be left alone with her children at the beginning of the 1960s, she would discover the importance of self-sufficiency to its full extent—a lesson she would rather have learned an easier way.

And yet, "We had a wonderful time" growing up inseparable, Rhona says. "We did have a way of communicating, when we would start a sentence and talk about something entirely different, and each understood. Of course when we got married it was a little difficult for the husbands to understand. The kids I think still don't

SKIING **CHANGES TOO**

The big change in the twins' lives coincided with a big change in skiing in Canada. As the 1940s drew to a close, it was the end of an era for the "glamour pros" in Laurentian ski resorts, *Canadian Sport Monthly* said in another article in the

"The Glamour Pros" of the 1940s: Schneider in front, Luggi Foeger on the right, unidentified men behind. Back to newly peaceful Europe, and giving the Canadian pros a chance.

issue announcing the twins' marriages. After the war, the Austrians and other European instructors began to leave—some to return to a newly peaceful Europe, some to jobs in the massive new resorts springing up in the Rockies. Hannes Schneider had been a regular visitor to the Laurentians, and even before the war's end there had been a world-famous coterie of instructors with charming accents, including pioneers Benno Rybizka, Luggi Foeger, Emile Allais, Heinz von Allmen, and Hermann Gadner. Now, although respectful of the primary and immense contribution the European pros made to setting up skiing in Canada, Canadian skiers were anxious to take charge of their own affairs. It was hardly coincidence, since Canada had come into its own after proving its mettle in the recent war. So now, "When Banff wanted a pro, [Montrealer] Harvey Clifford went." Then too, there was no new "name pro" coming this year with "a breathless new message on technique." In years before there had been the "Gadner Stemm Emphasis; the Pseudo-Parallelism of Fritz Loosli; the Rotation of Foeger and finally the mixture of Skating/Parallel of Allais." This year, under Quebec natives Louis Cochand, Réal Charette, Roger Trottier and Clint Melville, the magazine promised there would be "More Skiing, Less Talk." All that, and *Sport Monthly* was also sure that skiing was becoming a "new and remarkably stable industry. The magic of ski has transformed what was once regarded as the tedium of snow bound winter into new freedom, a new prosperity."

understand us, and sometimes don't know what's going on."

Rhona's daughter Margie Gillis has her own take on the twins' connectedness. "They have a big-little sister relationship," she says, "even though one's older by only five minutes. So Rhona, the older one, is saying we're twins and trying to be independent. And Rhoda, the younger one, feels left out sometimes, and loves to be recognized as a twin. Rhona doesn't acknowledge this big sister thing; she is a twin struggling for her independence. Rhoda is independent; but she's struggling for twindom."

Today Rhoda admits that's the way it was when they were kids. "She was the boss," she says of Rhona.

So Rhoda looks back on the double wedding as "very good it happened that way, because it was a major break. Suddenly everything was divided in half. That was an adjustment to make. But it was okay, because we were in love."

Rhona meanwhile says she wasn't worried about the separation, and thought it was time. She had complete and utter faith in Gene.

Whatever they felt, after the wedding Rhona acknowledges, "Everything changed."

After the wedding, it changed: suddenly, everything was divided in half. From left, Gene, Rhona, Rhoda, Arnold.

THE END OF AN ERA

If the twins' marriages were the end of one era and the beginning of a new one for them, for the public and skiing in general it was also a watershed year. On hearing of their upcoming wedding, *Canadian Sport Monthly* proclaimed "The 'Team' Breaks Up!" and offered "a final salute, before the break-up by marriage, to the finest competitive combination in our skiing history."

The magazine bemoaned the "prime disappointment of the Olympics" and the missed chance for the twins to "show their real form on the Corviglia Run in St. Moritz. When they were hot in competition, both 'got going' and it was then they seemed virtually unbeatable." In what seems like a backhanded compliment, the magazine also said, "There were probably never two top athletes who got more publicity with less color or temperament injected into their performances."

But now that they were getting married, the magazine assumed that would be the end of their careers too. "It is more than likely that they will have other interests than blasting some tremendous slope. Rhona will move to far off Oregon as a 'G.I. Bride' since Gillis is a member of the U.S. Marines."

It wasn't quite that simple, of course—it never was with the Wurtele twins. For now, Rhona and Gene were off to Whitefish, Montana, to run a ski school with Toni Matt; Rhoda and Arnold moved into a duplex on Clanranald Avenue just down the street from their Westmount home. The twins didn't compete *together* as much in the next few years, that was true, but both kept entering—and winning—big races until 1953. As they began to have children, they had less time for racing, but then they simply turned their attention to getting everyone else on the slopes, including their kids, other children, and finally the mothers of those children.

Rhona and Gene Gillis during the filming of *Rhythm on Snow*, 1947: an idyllic life.

ROCKY MOUNTAIN CABINS AND WESTMOUNT DUPLEXES

Rhona was living what seemed an idyllic life. She was alone with her husband, Gene, in a bright and cozy little cabin perched on the edge of a beautiful lake that reflected towering Big Mountain. It was a mile's drive to town, and five miles up to the skiing lodge and chairlift of the resort. Her husband ran the ski school at Whitefish with former Austrian racer Toni Matt, while Rhona and Toni's wife, Stella, ran the ski shop. Rhona even got to teach once in awhile. "Recently she had 24 kiddies under her wing," Myrtle Cook reported.

It looked like she could do no better: living on a ski hill with a ski pro in the Rockies. When the local paper, the *Whitefish Pilot*,

I tried to be a darling housewife. Once a week I'd get the car. I could leave and do anything and he wouldn't complain.

interviewed the new star in their midst in February of 1949, they revealed that "living the quiet life of a housewife is one of the most prominent athletic lights of North America." Rhona thought the area beautiful, and said they planned to build and settle there. And her plans?

"I haven't much to say about that anymore," she answered. "I go where Gene's business carries him."

Gene's business would end up carrying him all over the American West, including Montana, Idaho, Washington, Colorado, and, the last stop, Oregon, where the couple finally settled and Gene led a coaching camp for American ski racers. It was a wonderful life, Rhona says, always mixed up with sports, coaching, and teaching. In winter they skied; in summer they taught a variety of sports, including trampoline, swimming, tennis, golf, and diving.

Back in Montreal Rhoda was settling in too, in a duplex a stone's throw from her parents' house. Arnold had joined the Red Birds Ski Club. Geographically close to her parents, Rhoda also ended up fashioning a home life very similar to theirs. Arnold, she discovered, "was kind of like Dad. He had his office job that was very important to him, and Mother did all the work at home. I certainly didn't get any help from Arnold. He would say, 'I don't care, choose the furniture, I don't care what we have.' And I tried to be a darling housewife. Once a week I'd get the car. See, Arnold is very good but very much his own person; yet I could leave and do anything and he wouldn't complain."

Surely iron-willed Rhoda was her own person too?

"I suppose," she says. "But I certainly looked after him."

Like any marriage, the first year for both newlyweds must have involved plenty of adjustments. That is, until the snow started to fly. Then the twins began to fly down the slopes again.

In January of 1949, a new name appeared at the top of the Laurentian Zone's first major race results: a certain Mrs. Arnold Eaves had won at St. Donat (and fourteen-year-old Lucile Wheeler

Rhoda and Arnold on their honeymoon, Hotel Annapolis, Washington, D.C., 1948: "I certainly looked after him."

was not far behind at third). Those reading the sports pages would have to get used to this new reality—not only the new name, but the appearance of one Wurtele twin all alone at the top. Yet now Rhoda didn't seem to have a tough time racing without her twin. After taking that first race, she not only won the Zone championships at Mount Baldy, taking the downhill, slalom, and combined, but she beat her nearest female competitor by ten seconds, and allowed only one male competitor to have a faster time than her.

Then Rhoda set out for Lake Placid and the Kate Smith Trophy—this time not only as a racer on the team, but also as captain, team manager, and chaperone. The many roles didn't seem to affect her concentration either: she took first in the downhill, the slalom, and the combined.

FRENCH **SAVOIR-FAIRE**

Emile Allais in France. The French had reworked everything, and were in superb physical condition.

Crowds at the Dominion and Quebec Kandahar championships were astounded by everything the French did on the slopes in 1949. First of all, they poled all the way down the hill, even throwing in the occasional skate step to keep their speed up. When they looked closer—as many surprised competitors later did—it was found the French had reworked everything in order to gain speed. While skiers in North America still raced with relatively baggy clothes (sometimes, like Rhona and Rhoda, with hoods that could flip back over their eyes mid-race), their ski clothes were radically designed with no extra material that might catch wind; they had tight-fitting jerseys, silk caps, and stretch trousers. French ski equipment had somehow taken a great leap too, making North American and even Norwegian and Swiss models look like antiques. The advances French design had made over others, said a ski column in the *Daily Star*, "are as obvious as the difference between pre-war and post-war aircraft." Their skis had Lucite plastic on the bottom that glided easily over any kind of snow, and also eliminated the need for constant heavy-duty waxing. Emile Allais had designed the skis with edges of hardened steel, hollow-ground like skates. They had apparently changed their methods of skiing as well, no longer strictly keeping to Allais's teaching. The Star reported with wonder the team's ability to simply keep vertical over their skis, and their economy of movement as they followed the fall line down the hill. Everything had been reduced to its basics—except for two important areas. All the athletes were in "superb physical condition, a luxury which few amateur competitors around these parts enjoy." And there was no way Canadians could now catch up to this international competition, the *Star* opined, until they had the same kind of financial backing the French did.

Emile Allais in action.

Everything looked rosy for Rhoda as she approached the Dominion Championships in February—until it was learned the French were coming. In Europe, that team had been on a steady rise after the war, beginning an ascendancy over the historic favourites of Switzerland and Austria. "Five men and a girl" (Lucienne Schmidt-Couttet, who would go on to win World Championship medals) descended on Mont Tremblant for the championships, and before anyone knew what was happening, took almost all the honours away from the hometown heroes. The only one to come out relatively unscathed was Rhoda, who came first in the downhill, and missed capturing the slalom due to a wipeout.

Other exciting news came when the McGill Red Birds Ski Club finally announced that the Quebec Kandahar race would, for the first time, be open to Class A and B women (they had previously raced only as forerunners or special guests). But by the time the race would be held, Rhoda would be out west, joining her sister in even bigger races.

Lucienne Schmidt-Couttet, 1950.

REUNITED

The first stop, of course, was Whitefish, Montana. Not only was Rhona there, but the US National Downhill Championships were being held there that year too. And one of the first things Rhoda saw when meeting her sister in the Big Mountain Ski Shop was Rhona surrounded by "all these American kids applying their wax using Rhona's travelling irons." So they had found a use for those wedding gifts after all. And one "American kid" in particular turned that wax trick to her advantage at the Nationals. Andrea Mead, who at sixteen was already experienced in international competitions (and had competed against the twins at the Olympics), took first place in the downhill, keeping Rhoda in second place and Rhona one-fifth of a second behind in third.

Gene also raced at the Nationals; he was intent on winning the downhill and slalom, and had a good shot at it. But when he didn't win, the twins were astonished at his reaction: "He brooded for four days," remembers Rhoda. "With us [when we didn't win] it was just something that happened, there'll be another race, you know. He didn't do that."

"He just grew quiet," Rhona says.

But eventually Gene got over his disappointment, and life got back to normal. Normal, as in the twins would start taking first place in the races they entered again. The Canadian girls Rhoda had brought with her had the special advantage of training with Gene and Toni Matt, too. That winter and spring, Rhoda won the Roch Cup in Aspen, and Rhona came third. At the North American Championships, Rhoda was first in the downhill, but had to settle for second in the combined—the unstoppable French had taken that again. Rhona wasn't quite back in shape yet. After a few broken body parts and half a year of operations, she came fifth in the downhill.

This time, the twins didn't extend their western trips as they had before—they had husbands to get back to. Or at least that was the excuse. When Rhoda returned to Montreal that summer, she competed for the Mercury Track Club again, travelling to Rhode Island to win a javelin throw, then going on to defend her record in Toronto.

By the time the winter of 1949–1950 loomed, Rhona had a major decision to make. Both the Canadian and the American National Teams claimed her as their own. Her sister Rhoda was assured a place on the Canadian team for the upcoming World Ski Championships. Would twin end up racing against twin? The question was tantalizing, even threatening to be "a serious breach between the national ski association of this country and Canada," wrote the *New York Times* in December of 1949. Rhona waffled back and forth, divided between loyalty and nostalgia for her Canadian team, and loyalty to her new husband and chosen country. Gene wasn't going to race for the US team that season; a bad accident in the spring still had him using a cane and limited to teaching. Finally, Rhona sent her answer to the chairman of the US team committee. "As a matter of choice," she wrote, "I have thought it over carefully. I have decided I would like to ski on the American team."

The sisters reunite in Montana, 1949. Rhona greets newly arrived Rhoda for the US Nationals. "We were so happy, we laughed till our faces ached for two days after," Rhona says.

What had finally given her the push towards the US FIS team, joining her old rivals and friends Andrea Mead, Paula Kann, and Dodie Post?

The answer may have been revealed by the scribe who had for so long chronicled the fortunes of the Wurtele twins, Myrtle Cook. "No matter which team she skis for—Canadian or U.S.—the former Rhona Wurtele of Montreal won't be skiing against sister Rhoda. It's this way: by the time the championship date at Aspen rolls around in February [1950], Rhona may be a full-fledged citizen and on the U.S. Women's team. But Rhoda won't be there. 'You see, there's going to be a little skier at our house sometime next March,' said Rhoda."

Arnold, David, and Rhoda in 1951, after water-skiing in New Hampshire. At the lakeside reunion for the US ski team, Howard Head had just unveiled his "tin-can snow skis"—the first aluminum skis.

In the months leading up to the 1950 FIS World Championships, the event was the talk of the ski world. Like the Olympics, the Championships had been put off since the war, an eleven-year hiatus. The location of Aspen, Colorado, was an unusual choice for the event. It was the first time the championships were held outside of Europe, perhaps due to a still-recovering continent. Still, it didn't seem to affect their skiers. Both Canada and the US were kept way off the medal list: in the women's races Austria easily dominated, with France contributing a few familiar names like Georgette Thiolières-Miller (like Rhona and Rhoda, recently married) and Lucienne Schmidt-Couttet; a more mixed European bag swept the men's races.

But with the twins kept out of the medals, in the Wurtele family, the real big news that spring was the arrival of Rhoda and Arnold's new baby, David. Waiting for him had kept her out of the February Championships in Aspen, and his arrival in March kept her fully occupied. Within a few months, by that summer, and thanks to her Quebec record-breaking entries in the javelin, discus, and shot put the summer before, she was named to the Canadian track and field team heading to the British Empire Games (now the Commonwealth Games) in New Zealand. Her new son kept her from attending that as well.

On their return to the States, Rhona and Gene moved to Idaho near Sun Valley—and Rhona quickly left her mark on that state too. With Gene's coaching and instruction, she learned seven new dives in two weeks, then immediately won the Idaho State Diving Championship that summer, *and* the 100-yards freestyle race. Then it was Gene's turn to shine. When in 1951 Rhona had her first child, Christopher, she convinced her husband to go back to Montreal for a winter, where Gene could study at McGill and coach the Laurentian Zone team at the same time. "So there we were in a tiny Crosley car with six-foot-three Gene and Vic Allen [Gene's best man] and me in the back with a new baby trying to feed it, and we drove it across the whole damn continent." In Montreal, Gene began attending McGill University and developing the Canadian National Ski Team. Forming a national team was a new idea he had taken from the Europeans and developed for the US.

Visiting granny in Westmount. From left, Rhoda with David, Rhona with Christopher: their first children, 1952.

Having already missed out on a voyage to New Zealand for the British Empire Games, it didn't take long for Rhoda to get back on the hills and start competing again. In 1951, the year after David's birth, Rhoda won the Kate Smith trophy again, taking the slalom and combined; she then took home the trophy for the second running of the Women's Quebec Kandahar, won the Dominion Championships in downhill and combined, and for good measure took the downhill and combined at the Harriman Cup at Idaho's Sun Valley. Gene Gillis was coaching her Ladies team to victory after victory. That Rhoda had "retired" long enough to have a child, then come back as a housewife and mother was still unusual enough for the press to comment on it every chance they could. "Canadian Matron wins," read one less than flattering headline.

By 1952, Rhona and Gene had moved again—this time to Bend, Oregon. This was Gene's stomping ground, and he and Christian Pravda set up a coaching camp for America ski racers. Like her sister, Rhona didn't take long to get back on the slopes after her son's birth, taking first the combined at the Golden Rose Cup in Oregon's Mount Hood, then snatching the Harriman Cup back from Rhoda in the downhill (she was in Norway at the 1952

Rhona in 1951 with the Fédération Internationale de Ski US National Team, with whom she won the first American Giant Slalom race.

Olympics). Rhona also won the Silver Dollar race in Reno, the Eastern Nationals in Vermont, and an international meet back at Mont Gabriel in Quebec. Finally, in Alta, Utah, Rhona entered the first running of the US Nationals Giant Slalom, and handily won it too.

Like Rhoda, Rhona seemed to be getting the hang of racing without her sister just ahead or behind her. She also seemed to enjoy being part of the American team. "But I didn't join the club," she says, and never officially applied for citizenship. "I thought if anything ever happened I would go back to Canada. I don't know what made me think that."

Perhaps Gene's moods already made her suspect what might happen in the future. But at the time, she had so many things on her plate it would have been an almost superhuman feat to second-guess her husband. "He was a wonderful husband," she insists. "So good to me, encouraging and helping me at all kinds of things. He was wonderful with the kiddies, reading to them and playing with them. Though I must say, after I did the garden I did have to say, 'At least come and see what the garden is like now.'" She had an infant, a husband often on the road, a ski shop to run, children to teach on the slopes, and the odd race to win—and things would just get busier. "They asked me if I would coach their teams for the US Nationals," Rhona remembers, "but I was kind of bogged down then." The next year was the 1952 Olympics in Oslo, Norway. She'd have to miss that, too. She was pregnant again.

THE 1952 OSLO OLYMPICS

In previous Winter Olympics, it had always been the Scandinavian countries that walked away with the heaviest load of medals in their baggage; now that the the Games were finally coming to Norway, their athletes could leave the medals at home. Its people were thrilled.

There was someone else quite excited about the coming Games. Rhoda had been named to the Canadian Alpine Ski Team, with Lucile Wheeler, Rosemarie Schutz, and Joanne Hewson. Thirty years old and with a child, Rhoda was the hen mother of them all; Wheeler was only seventeen. Yet Rhoda wasn't quite as preoccupied at home as Rhona; her David was already a year old. He could stay with her parents, and Arnold could take care of himself—although Rhoda promptly began a half-year program of convincing her new husband to come with her. He refused, so Rhoda would go neither with her twin, nor with the person she now looked to for support. Had Arnold been stubborn about not returning to Europe because the battles fought in World War II were still too fresh?

1952 Oslo, Norway, Winter Olympics poster.

For Rhoda, the coming Olympics would be a rare second chance to make up for the "stupid" accidents of St. Moritz in 1948. It bothered her more that she hadn't been able to prove herself than whether she had won or lost. She had learned a lot from those first Olympics, and was determined not to repeat her mistakes.

"Sometimes I lie awake, shuddering over St. Moritz," she told Toronto's *Star Weekly* before the games. "We tried too hard and suffered accordingly. This time a smooth even pace will tell the story."

Once again, though, the team didn't have the training they should have had. They began at Mont Tremblant in December of 1951 with Harvey Clifford as their coach, and "Porky" Griffin and Bob Richardson helping out. Harry Wheeler, the proprietor

Sunday best? The 1952 Canadian Olympic Ski Team, left to right: Joanne Hewson, Rosemarie Schutz, "host" Harry Wheeler, Rhoda, Lucile Wheeler. The size of the team had doubled since last time, but the uniforms were worse: "Flap pants and a nylon shell," wrote Rhoda. "Wow."

of Gray Rocks (and Lucile's father) helped the Women's Team in whatever way he could. Rhoda was less impressed with their uniforms this time around—cheap thin slacks and a nylon pullover—but that wasn't the important thing. The important thing was to get over to Europe and start training there.

This time the team flew over the Atlantic, ending up in Oslo where they met their coach Franz Gabl, the first Austrian to win an Olympic medal in skiing. And in the birthplace of many winter sports, in the native land of Jackrabbit Johannsen, of Arctic and Antarctic explorers, the Canadian team found that there was hardly a lick of snow to be found. Scandinavia was experiencing one of its worst winters ever: it was warm, dry, and cozy. Even though the Canadian team had been invited to train in continental Europe, there was little they could do—once again, either money or disorganization prevented them from going where the snow was. There were no other Olympic teams in Norway—even the Norwegians were training in the Alps.

Without sister or husband to support her, Rhoda found it tough adjusting to Norway. The Norwegians themselves were "wonderful" and entertained them well. But not only was there no snow, there only seemed to be about two hours of daylight before darkness fell again. Neither was Rhoda used to the dampness that pervades a northern European winter. And those Vikings ate the strangest things—a smorgasbord till ten in the evening, which seemed to still be there the next morning for breakfast, and a big bowl of gruel with "fish stuff floating in a sort of soup. Smelly goat cheese. Then we were given a piece of wax paper, a piece of black bread, some jellied fish stuff on top, another piece of wax paper and another piece of black bread on top. I mean, I can eat almost anything, but we just ended up throwing a lot of it away." It wasn't long before her discomfort started manifesting itself in the body. "I wasn't feeling that great," Rhoda says. Soon, she started getting gall bladder attacks, the kind brought on by eating fatty foods; more esoteric beliefs say the gall bladder stores our fear of making mistakes, or the fear of failure.

But Rhoda had overcome adversity before. Now she prepared for the pre-Olympic races in Norway. At her first slalom race, she drew the "honoured" #1 bib; skiers don't like to be the first down the hill, since they have to work extra hard to find the ideal path. Surprising even herself, Rhoda ran a great slalom, with the best time overall. But officials at the final gate saw that she ran around something that wasn't a gate at all—a ski pole someone had planted near the finish line. She was disqualified. Her coach yanked the pole out of the ground and threw it away in disgust. "Yuk, what a start," says Rhoda.

Then came the races in famed Holmenkollen, which were also the final trials for the Norwegian team. Along with the usual downhill and slalom, this would be the first time the women would encounter the new giant slalom.

With an eye on the patchy hill, a discomfited Rhoda took the downhill course at a good clip. But she ran into problems near the end again. "My tips caught when I made too sharp a transition, and the next thing I knew I was up in the air, but upside-down—I did a complete flip, hit my head on the way around—but landed on my feet and, wow, I'm still going. I had lost the grip on my pole but managed to grab it and finished the race, sixth place. There was a cartoon about it in the Norwegian papers. But I won the slalom and the giant slalom, so I won the combined."

The snow still refused to fall on the Olympic hills in Norway, and the Canadian women's team was getting anxious. But finally the ski teams from other countries began arriving in Oslo, and with them the Olympic spirit began to grip the country. Or perhaps it was the arrival of the Norwegian army, which was called on to pull snow out of the surrounding woods and line the race hills; then

Don't even try **to outdo the twins**

Rhona's daughter Nancy Gillis Andersen was a top acrobatic and freestyle skier in the 1970s—but she quickly learned how tough it was to impress her mother and aunt. "It was a little intimidating with the twins, because they had already done all these crazy things. The first time I did a flip on skis I was so proud, and I went over to tell Rhoda. She said, 'Oh yeah, I *accidentally* did my first flip on a downhill race in Norway once. Came in sixth.' So you're kind of deflated. They've already been there, done that."

CCCCAABC MONDAY, MARCH 19, 1951 **PAGE 3 H**
SAN FRANCISCO CHRONICLE SPORTING GREEN

(P) Wirephoto

MOMMA DOES BEST—Mrs. Rhoda Wurtele Eaves, Montreal mother, was a surprise victor in the women's downhill event Saturday at the Harriman Cup races at Sun Valley, Idaho. The housewife captured the women's combined yesterday when she annexed a fourth in the slalom. Mrs. Eaves, named to the Canadian Olympic squad, is shown here bowling through Roundhouse Slope on the downhill run in which she flashed a time of 1:54.4.

"Montreal mother" Rhoda was a surprise victor.

they iced the mountain down with water hoses.

Rhoda drew #1 again, this time for the Olympic races. Normally, she says, racers aren't allowed on the trail beforehand, "but with the lack of snow they wanted us to have a look." So she and her teammates got on the course and sideslipped down. By the time they got to the bottom Rhoda realized it was almost time to run her race. She was next, but there was a huge line-up to get up the hill; at the last minute she saw a man alone, so pushed her way to the front and flung herself onto the T-bar beside him. And as she turned to apologize to the man, she saw it was Emile Allais, her old coach from the last Olympics.

At the top she rushed to the starting gates and almost immediately flew out of them too. The gates were scattered all over the hill—wherever there was a bit of snow left. Then down near the end, her skis hit a stump only partially hidden by snow, spinning her around. It cost her a lot, putting her in a distant fourteenth—or ninth, depending on what day you ask her. "The whole thing was stupid," she says. "The slalom wasn't difficult but excitement and everything piled up and my run wasn't the greatest."

So Rhoda again watched others mount the podium—in particular her sister's new, American teammate, Andrea Mead Lawrence, now nineteen years old (she had been fifteen in the St. Moritz Olympics), newly married, and in her prime. No one expected the "American housewife" to take the gold in both the slalom and giant slalom, least of all the twins, who regularly beat her in other races. But that was the Olympics. Rhoda could take cold comfort in the fact that Canada did miserably all over in those Olympics, taking just the expected gold in hockey, and a bronze in the men's 500-metre speed skating. Canada had more snow and ice than any other country—why couldn't they win at winter sports? The Norwegians, despite their funny diet and stranger weather, again had the most medals.

As consolation, Rhoda gathered the younger girls around her after the Olympics and got them off to continental Europe.

Their first stop was at Davos, Switzerland, the site of the twins' training for the last Olympics, and the place they both were injured. It was as if at these races Rhoda wanted to prove something, even though the disadvantages were once again building up against her. Her husband and first child were waiting for her back in Montreal, her gall bladder was continuing to bother her, and she hadn't eaten or slept well since arriving in Norway. And yet, the results of Rhoda's races were astounding: second place in the Parsenn downhill, and second place in the Dorftalli giant slalom.

1952 Canadian Women's Olympic Team in Voss, Norway, before the Olympic Games. From left, Lucile Wheeler, Rosemarie Schutz, Rhoda, Joanne Hewson.

Perhaps buoyed by a better showing, Rhoda now took her ski chicks on a pilgrimage to the skiing Mecca of St. Anton, Austria. There was a running of the seminal ski event, the Hannes Schneider Pokal, and again the best skiers in Europe were congregated there, and this time the American Olympic team too. The last time Rhoda had been there Rhona had been there with her—both with their ankles in casts. It was another chance at redemption.

The day of the races, the snow came down hard on the Kandahar run. And as soon as the women started racing, they also started falling, spectacularly. "And these were Olympic racers," Rhoda says. "The race was disastrous." One particular "crazy corner" was giving everybody trouble, and so far there were two broken legs because of it—one of them belonging to the twins' good friend Paula Kann. But once again Rhoda gathered up her strength and headed up the mountain, trying to ignore the pains in her stomach. "I was glad I had on my goggles," she says, "so other people couldn't see how miserable I felt going up the lift." All that, and she had a good downhill run—until she sprawled near the finish on a steep transition "and managed to crawl through the finish." She took second place.

But it wasn't over yet. After a number of racers had come down, Rhoda noticed Harry Wheeler (who had been following his daughter around Europe) was in a panic: Lucile still hadn't appeared. It was Rhoda, the hen mother, who once again dutifully trudged up the slope to find Lucile. She had taken a bad fall and was all right, but had to go to the hospital to be checked out. It was Rhoda who accompanied her and her father there, too. "Finally by about nine p.m. I removed my boots and fell into bed. Quel jour! Next morning I woke up and put my feet on the floor and my ankles were huge." It was only then she realized she had sprained both in the last race.

By then even Rhoda realized it was time to head home. She booked her flight, and a little while later got a telegram from her father: "Congratulations for your fine showing in Pokal...Arnold will meet you in Chamonix." *Now* he was coming. Rhoda headed for the French resort at the base of Mont Blanc, but another gall bladder attack put her in the local hospital. And that's where they had their romantic reunion. Rhoda did manage to limp over to southern Switzerland to Zermatt at the base of the Matterhorn; she wanted Arnold to actually enjoy some of his holiday, and they did get to Paris for a few days too. But doctors advised Rhoda to return home and get a gall bladder operation as soon as possible.

Rhoda wouldn't race in any more major races again until 1959, seven years later in Austria. And Arnold would need a lot more coaxing to go back to Europe with his wife; he would return in 1975 to ski in Austria and Switzerland. "He had already been there," Rhoda explains mordantly. Back in Montreal, Rhoda learned of more sad news. Rhona, whose second pregnancy stopped her from going to these Olympics, had watched as her twin lost the races, and now the child she carried had been lost as well.

It was a frustrating time for both twins. But as far as the Olympics went, somehow the 1948 St. Moritz Olympics was still the disappointment of their career. Yet despite the losses—or worse, the injuries that kept them from competing—for the twins, being involved in the Olympics was the highlight of their career.

"We have always been exceedingly strong and able to overcome adversity," says Rhoda today, "but on reflecting on our lifetime ambitions and Olympic hopes, I guess it wasn't in the books. After all, figure it: it's a one-day race, and you wait four years for your abilities and luck to peak. That's the way it was. Now with the World Cup tours, skiers race all through the season and build points and maybe come through one or two meets—the points are the big proof of their ability. And yet at the Olympics, with all the different sports and all the best athletes in the world, you still have to pay on your one great day. It's quite different from any other competition, with the excitement of all those athletes from so many countries and their training programs. I still say you cannot surpass the hype and thrill, especially if an athlete from your own country stands on the podium to receive an Olympic medal, and you listen to your own anthem being played for you. Performing or being at the Games as a real part of it cannot be surpassed in athletic circles.

We have always been exceedingly strong and able to overcome adversity, but on reflecting on our lifetime ambitions and Olympic hopes, I guess it wasn't in the books.

"Now of course there's the fantastic opening and closing ceremonies, huge publicity and TV coverage, and the payoff for the winners. There's the amazing difference between being first and losing, sometimes within fractions of seconds; winning still grants that athlete a fine future, with sponsors and everything. And I still say even though we had to pay our own way, and had no doctor or psychiatrist or physiotherapist or manager, we had desire, love, caring, sportsmanship above all and fairness, and friends and memories never to be forgotten. It was worth it all."

NEW LIVES IN A NEW SOCIETY: THE WOMAN OF THE 1950S

From the distance of the new millennium, and especially for those who did not live through the post-war era, the changes the 1950s wrought in women may seem strange. Why would previously independent women who acted as if the world was theirs suddenly abandon everything to their new husbands? The twins had worked in many office jobs until now; and in earlier years, Rhona and Rhoda had no qualms about immediately quitting jobs that interfered with their skiing and swimming. They knew they could beat men in races on the slopes, and they did. From their earliest youth, from their first soaring launch off the senior men's ski jump on Mount Royal, they had tasted absolute freedom. And the expectation that they could do what they wanted, when they wanted, looked like it would stay with Rhona and Rhoda forever.

Yet when they married they instead tried to be "darling housewives." Rhona admits that she left all the decision-making to Gene; and Arnold, outside of his accounting work, had Rhoda to look after him and the entire household. What happened?

While many countries were literally rebuilding after the cataclysmic world wars, society in North America was also going through a reconstruction. Men retired their uniforms and put suits or overalls back on, and more than two million women in North America threw down their welding torches and rushed to put on ruffled aprons and high heels. Well, maybe half of them rushed; the other half were quite taken with the freedom that came from earning their own paycheque. Yet the world they had worked to change was now out of their hands: those rare women who had been pilots, for example, like Rhona and Rhoda had once dreamed of becoming, were now offered jobs as stewardesses. Where Katharine Hepburn had pursued a career in *Woman of the Year* in the 1940s, now June Cleaver was content to sacrifice her life for her family on TV in *Leave it to Beaver*.

As the economy once again strengthened, the housewife of the 1950s was presented with myriad new inventions and opportunities to make that nesting life easier. Eventually it seemed the only difference between the modern housewife and her grandmother was that today's woman had *electric* appliances in the kitchen. Even clothing styles had swung back from the tailored looks of the 1940s to narrow waists and billowing skirts that resembled the constraints of the housewife's grandmother.

A woman's job now was to rebuild the nation. The best way to do that, according to propaganda in advertising and the fantastic new medium of television, was to get married and make babies. In the 1950s the marriage rate hit an all-time high, and couples married younger than ever before, often right after graduation from high school. Within seven months of the wedding, the majority of women were pregnant. Three- and four-child families were the norm.

Had Rhona and Rhoda lived up to the expectations of society—or what were purported to be the wishes of men? They had already bucked the trend of early marriage, single-mindedly pursuing their sports careers until they were twenty-six years old. That was almost an old maid in some circles. But when they did marry, they both began having children very soon. Between 1950 and 1955 Rhoda had three children; by 1957 Rhona had four.

And what did their men expect from them? The men the twins married were quite different from each other, but it appears neither locked up their wives in the kitchen. Gene was built for the ski slopes and athletic fields, and having met his wife on the mountain may have expected her to keep up with him there. Arnold was (and is) a private man whose work was very important to him. His niece Margie Gillis says, "He's a cocktail person, and I mean that in the best way possible. He knows how to talk and hold a cocktail and be charming. The twins were more active. They were born that way—born to be wild."

Should married women **work?**

In the late 1940s Toronto's *New World Magazine* featured the twins in a photo story about ski school.

A "Picture poll" in the same issue asked, "Should there be jobs for married women?" Answers ranged the full spectrum.

1. Mme. Pierre Casgrain, Montreal: "A good social and economic equilibrium can be achieved only when the whole population, regardless of sex, is free to work according to each one's needs, taste, capacity and circumstances. Married women, by working, can enrich the life of the community."
2. Hugh R. Haughton, Toronto: "Certainly not. Too many women right now are neglecting children, husbands and homes to grab every loose dollar. Let married women stay home."
3. L/Corporal Shirley Lawson, CWAC, Parry Sound: "Married women should leave the jobs for those who have to have them in order to live. Girls who marry should be sure—in advance—that their prospective mates could support them. No woman can work and run a home as well."

Man is a **Woman's Work**

Dorothy Carnegie, wife of Dale Carnegie (author of the best-selling *How to Win Friends and Influence People*, 1937): "The two big steps that women must take are to help their husbands decide where they are going and use their pretty heads to help them get there."

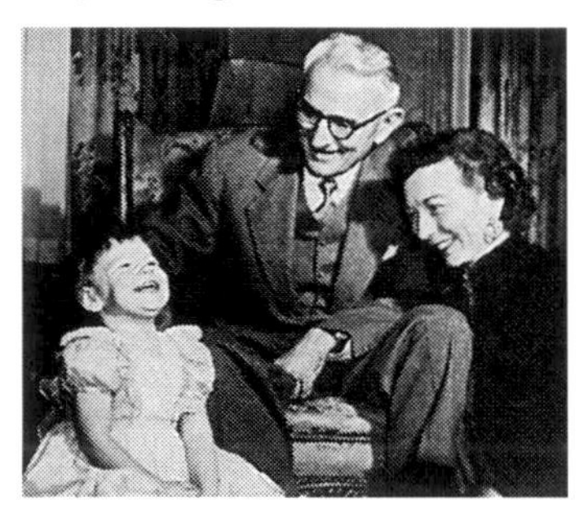

The Carnegie family.

Much of the twins' leap into marriage and attempts at being "darling housewives" probably came in large part from their own desire to fulfil that 1950s fantasy—and like everything else they did, they did it with gusto and verve. Of course they weren't alone. Even their old nemesis, figure skater Barbara Ann Scott, left professional skating at the end of the 1950s to try and be, in her words, "the perfect '50s housewife. I want my white picket fence." Popular culture said raising children and taking care of a household were a woman's "natural destiny"; whatever the truth of that, the task was (and is) extremely important, even though the same society often relegated the housewife to the lowest rung on the ladder. Yet the limitations of being ***only*** a housewife would become obvious in the next decade, not only for the twins but also for women throughout North America.

The prevailing belief that women should stay at home and not get distracted from their natural destiny, says Bruce Kidd, author of *The Struggle for Canadian Sport*, "had its reverberation in sports. Women fought against that, but it became harder and harder. At one point CCM stopped making hockey skates and baseball gloves for women." The progress of women in Canadian sport, he says, can't be thought of as a steady line. "Huge gains were made until the 1940s; they were followed by huge reverses." Women's sports associations like the Women's Amateur Athletic Foundation collapsed and were melded into men's organizations, with disastrous results for women's organized sports.

People who had followed the twins' careers through the years had no doubt that even those wild Wurteles would do the expected thing for women, and only have time left to ski for amusement. But the twins proved that after having one child, they could still compete in international races. Didn't it follow that after having numerous children, they could compete in numerous races? Although they never *actively* tried to change things, in the 1940s Rhona and Rhoda watched and inspired changes in the status of women at home and in sports; they had no reason to expect things would stop changing.

While Rhona and Rhoda had all of their children during the 1950s, and tried in their own words to be "the darling housewives," the reality was that they were as active outside the home as ever. In that way they followed the real trend of the decade: more women than ever before were entering the work force. Even while they were raising their own children, both twins were active in teaching skiing; soon they would formalize their instruction and begin the first ski school for children in North America.

Rhona, Gaby Pleau, and Rhoda at Sunshine, Banff, 1947. Like the twins, Gaby was blessed with seemingly unlimited energy. The neighbours called her "La Diablesse"—the little devil.

By 1953, both twins had another child—Rhoda's John Ironside and Rhona's Margie, born within three months of each other. Some health complications after the delivery meant that Rhona wasn't able to breastfeed, so Rhoda ended up doing double duty, nursing both John and Margie (just like having twins). "Rhoda came to the rescue because I was having a tough time," Rhona says. "Elsie the cow," Rhoda interjects.

"So," Rhona says, "that was the only daughter she ever had. Arnold didn't let her have any more children at one point because they wouldn't fit in the car! That's true! Then he thought it was a great idea to have a two-door to keep the kids from falling out."

GABY PLEAU: **IT WASN'T ALWAYS EASY**

Gaby approached life the way she approached ski racing—undaunted by obstacles. Here, George Jost of the Red Birds Ski Club starts her out of the gates, St. Sauveur, 1944.

The neighbours called her "la diablesse." Like the twins, as a child Gaby Pleau had unlimited energy. She also preferred the rough and tumble company of boys. It prepared her for the rough world of business and sports, too.

Her favorite sport was alpine skiing, which she did with the twins every winter, and which made her a star in Quebec—she was the first female francophone on the Canadian alpine ski team. But after a serious broken leg in California in 1946 while skiing with the twins, her career ended. Undaunted (and at a time when French Canadian women were meant to stay at home), Gaby set up her own ski club for girls and women, the club-école Saint-Castin du Lac-Beauport (the largest club for girl skiers in the world at the time, with 163 members), helped run the family fur business with her mother after her father died when she was five, and eventually turned it into Gaby Pleau Inc., a maker of sports clothing and accessories. Both the club and business are still going strong today; Gaby died in 2002. Her daughter runs the business and sponsors the Gaby Pleau Cup in Lac Beauport every year.

But as a pioneer for women's skiing in Quebec, it wasn't always easy for Gaby. "Everything she tried to do other people just pushed her backwards," says Rhoda. She attempted to import Rossignol skis after meeting Abel Rossignol with the twins at the 1948 Olympics. After giving her four pairs to bring back to Canada for a test, Gaby threw a party to promote the brand, but never was able to corner the market.

Perhaps the biggest shock to Gaby came when she got married. Earlier, Gaby had told the *Toronto Star Weekly*, "Skiing is my life. I'll ski until I marry and when I have children I'll bring them up in snowbanks." While she attracted many admirers because of her beauty and energy (among them world champion Emile Allais, who asked her to marry him), the man she ended up marrying was very traditional. As soon as they got home from their honeymoon, he informed her that she could no longer be a part of the ski association, let alone compete. Rhona says that he told her, "You're not going to do this or that, you're my wife now. She cried for the next two weeks." After they had two children, the couple divorced.

BUSIER THAN EVER

Perhaps with the appearance of Wurtele children, Canadians of the 1950s thought the twins would now retire from active life, and decided it was time to honour them. In 1953 the Amateur Athletic Union of Canada named both twins to their Hall of Fame, citing both their skiing and swimming feats. It would be the first of many accolades. But an even stronger recognition of their contribution to women's sport in Canada came the next year. Their skiing protegé fifteen-year-old Anne Heggtveit, who had skied with the twins at the Dominion Championships, and watched as they went to the 1948 and 1952 Olympics, now was setting out on her own. At the 1954 Holmenkollen Giant Slalom in Norway, "Little Anne Heggtveit" came in first, the youngest winner in the race's fifty-year history.

Although the twins' famous scrapbooks start thinning out around this time, it certainly wasn't because things were slowing down in the twins' lives. In fact it was just the opposite. The next year, the twins once again had children born in the same year—Rhona's Nancy Gillis and Rhoda's Bruce Eaves. Both mothers still found time to race and teach, too. Rhoda was now teaching kids in Murray Park, the slope in the middle of Westmount where she had learned to ski. "I was doing that on my own, because the kids needed teaching," she says, "and I had to get out once in awhile."

Over in Bend, Oregon, Rhona, Gene, and Christian Pravda were running a very successful training camp for potential Olympic skiers. "I was running ski schools and coaching, studying art at University, and raising the children while Gene was leading these camps."

It was that year that a pregnant Rhona went to the Olympic trials at Alta, Utah. Among the competitors was a girl considered a shoe-in for the 1956 Olympics, who had won the junior *and* senior women's slalom title that year. Her picture already gracing the cover of *Sports Illustrated*, the "sweet little girl" that Rhona knew

Men **in the 1950s**

Life in wide-open Montreal was starting to change too. Brilliant young senator John F. Kennedy and his glamorous wife, Jackie, had been the guests of honour at the 1953 St. Andrew's' Ball. And while premier Duplessis's goons were still using archaic methods of getting re-elected, like stuffing ballot boxes and burning down their competition's meeting rooms, young lawyer Jean Drapeau was starting to do some serious clean-up in Montreal, getting rid of bordellos, gambling rooms, and other dens of iniquity.

Boulevard St. Laurent above Duluth Street in Montreal during a 1950 election campaign. Election signs in Yiddish, English, French and Russian.

very well was skiing with Buddy Werner, the finest American skier at the time. "Someone asked me about it at the bottom of the lift, and wondered who did I think would do well for the team? And I said this kid could but she's skiing over her head. She'd either do well, or she might get hurt. Get hurt!? For three days they thought she would die. Poor little thing." The skier was Jill Kinmont, and on her next run down she had hit a tree and broken her back. Her tragic accident left her a quadriplegic.

Yet even highly publicized accidents like this one couldn't do anything to dampen the growing enthusiasm North Americans had for skiing. After all, not everybody wanted to be a racer like Rhona and Rhoda, schussing fifty miles an hour down an icy chute. Until now, however, even casual skiers had to overcome a host of obstacles to enjoy themselves. Wouldn't it be great if skiers could just spend a leisurely afternoon having fun without having to get all complicated? Now, thanks to innovations in equipment and clothing, things *were* getting easier. The 1950s saw the introduction of buckle boots that meant no more lacing to get the right fit. When the boot started stretching, too, the Lange Company began making the plastic boot we take for granted today. Bindings were now step-in, ski poles were aluminum, and skis were metal with plywood cores. When Jean Vuarnet won on Emile Allais's aluminum skis at the 1960 Olympics, hickory became history. Artificial snowmaking began in this decade too, making skiers somewhat less dependent on fickle Mother Nature. And when better ski clothes came along—like quilted parkas and Bogner's "stretchies" in 1953—people could finally enjoy a winter weekend of fresh air and exercise *and* look good doing it.

Across North America, ski resorts began opening up, introducing novel amenities such as gondolas that only increased skiing's popularity. Rhona's husband Gene Gillis would note the popularity of gondolas in the American West and make his move in that new direction. In Quebec, an improved economy meant more money to spend on leisure, and cottages and cabins began popping up around previously quiet hills in the Laurentians. With improved roads, more and more cars were making the journey; and when the old Highway 11 became too crowded and slow, Quebec would lay down the first Autoroute toll-road up north in the summer of 1959.

Rhoda would take notice of how much easier it was to get up into the Laurentians. And when she put skis on her two-year-old David and pushed him down the hill, she wondered if a children's ski club might actually become a very popular thing—despite her child's vocal protests all the way down.

Sports Illustrated

Jill Kinmont Boothe: this cover appeared while she was racing at the Olympic trials with Rhona in 1955. The story of her triumph over adversity after becoming a quadriplegic was told in the book (and later film) *The Other Side of the Mountain*, as well as in a sequel.

Escaping **bad accidents**

At the 1955 Olympic trials in Alta, Utah, Rhona had an accident of her own—but thankfully nothing compared to Kinmont-Boothe's. A man had skied in front of her while she was coming down, and she ran into him, breaking *his* leg ("Left a scar on Nancy's face," Rhona claims—she was five months into her pregnancy with Nancy at the time). In a lifetime of skiing the twins have seen their share of serious accidents, avalanches, and lost a number of acquaintances. Friend Germaine Prefontaine broke her leg so badly it had to be amputated; Gaby Pleau had a horrible broken leg when they were competing in California in the 1940s. Their friend and first coach Hermann Gadner was lost in an avalanche, as was Buddy Werner (in St. Moritz). Perhaps the worst was still to come: Rhoda not only witnessed the death of Quebec skier John Semmelink when she was in Europe with the National Team in 1959, but also had to break the news to his family back home. And yet, claims Rhoda, "We never thought it would happen to us; it never occurred to us. And besides which we seemed to be very strong, and not prone to accidents." Rhona, who suffered through a number of operations says, "though lucky, I seemed to get warnings which I ignored and plowed ahead anyway. Our friends did get hurt when with us and it bothered us."

Rhona and Gene's children, 1958: left to right, Nancy, Christopher, Jere, Margie.

THE SKI JAYS... AND FINALLY, AN OLYMPIC MEDAL FOR CANADA

As Rhoda was readjusting to life with more babies and fewer ski races, she continued to look for some way to keep close to skiing. Her sister in Oregon had a husband who would always be on the slopes, but in Montreal Rhoda's husband, Arnold, was kept busy with his office work. Now she had three young boys, David, John, and Bruce (born in 1955), and she felt she had to get out of the house once in a while, or go crazy. She started with getting her boys on skis, wobbling down through Murray Park. At the same time, the Penguins Ski Club had begun giving classes for girls thirteen years and older. Immediately Rhoda jumped in, eager to give

Rhoda and Arnold's children, 1957: left to right, David, Bruce, John.

young girls the chance for instruction that the twins themselves had never had. And so, in 1956, Rhoda took on the directing of the Ski Jays and their many Penguin volunteers.

As a racer, Rhoda saw the club as a place to form girls into racers too. When the twins had joined the Penguin Ski Club in the 1930s, clubs were seen as places to mold racers, so she took the same approach. Today, clubs are seen more as places to get people interested in skiing; potential racers are then chosen from among them. But whatever the intent Rhoda had in encouraging young girl skiers, the opening of the club was perfectly timed. The first children's ski club in North America coincided with the mass popularity of skiing, and the numbers exploded. The job "was colossal," Rhoda says. There was racing, coaching and teaching. Rhoda mainly directed and managed the club, finding and developing the many instructors. Tiny Murray Hill and Mount Royal could no longer contain the hordes, and Rhoda began making regular outings with the club to St. Sauveur in the Laurentians north of Montreal. Rhoda had volunteer help from other women skiers, including former Olympic teammates Rosemarie Schutz and Joanne Hewson, then moved the classes permanently to the St. Sauveur hill. What began as a class with five girls had become a massive caravan of nineteen buses heading up to the Laurentians, with more than one thousand kids in a season. In the meantime, Rhoda (and soon Rhona) were not only introducing the sport to thousands of children, but also encouraging numerous adults to become ski instructors and fall in love with the sport themselves. The irony, of course, was that Rhoda's own three children—being *boys*—couldn't join the club.

The irony, of course, was that Rhoda's own three children—being *boys*—couldn't join the ski club.

Where did they find the energy to pour so much time into teaching skiing? "We were into skiing because it was fun," Rhoda says, "but when we did our club we had to be serious. Skiing got us into all the different aspects of running a business, coaching, that kind of thing. We had so much given to us," says Rhoda, "it was time for us to give back to other people."

All those years of teaching—the Ski Jays and its offshoots lasted until 1981, twenty-five years—were pretty close to a gift the twins made to the next generation of skiers. "We never made a thing," Rhoda says. "And I drove up that stupid highway all the time. Eventually I got money to cover the tolls. At first we worked out the organization with recreation people, then later we did it on our own with Twinski. We had a great many volunteers. We got the kids and found people to teach to be instructors and wrote books about how to teach, so we were always learning too. But we enjoyed it."

But even today Rhoda wants to make sure everyone knows how much work was put into the club. "It was a major colossal overpowering thing," she sighs.

The Ski Jays kept expanding, and after 1960 led to a plethora of associated clubs: while the Jays were for girls 13 to 16 years old, there were also 200 Ski Chicks, girls eight to twelve years old, run by Rhona; the Baby Bears, for four- to eight-year-olds and run by Sue Casey and Liz Carrique; the Ski Jets, the boys' equivalent of the Ski Jays; and later the Ski Hawks, for younger boys (taken over by the Red Birds and Bob Griffin); the Nancy Greene Leagues (a racing class) with nine teams, each with their own coach; there was also a travelling school, Freestyle Groups, Instructors In Training, and annual five-day Christmas Camps. Among the volunteers were Bev Waldorf directing the many buses, Claire Robinson in charge of finances, and especially Rhoda's honorary secretary, "Mackie" (Betty Polis), who was invaluable to her all through the years of the Jays and later with the Twinski Club.

For now, in the 1950s, Rhoda was still able to manage; eventually Rhona would join her sister again in the 1960s, managing the Ski Chicks on the slopes with her. But while it would be an exciting time for both recreational and competitive skiing in Canada, the next decade wouldn't be the easiest of times for Rhona.

Almost 50 Ski Jay instructors pose for a group photo at Hill 69, St. Sauveur in the 1960s. Rhoda at right in front.

LUCILE WHEELER: **THE LADY IS A CHAMP**

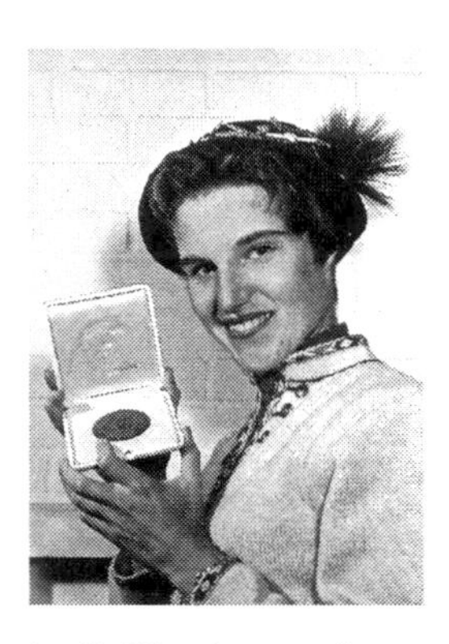

Lucile Wheeler proudly displays the first ever Olympic medal won by a Canadian Alpine skier. She took the bronze in downhill at Cortina d'Ampezzo, Italy, 1956.

The same year Rhoda began managing the Ski Jays, the fruit of many years of early training in the Laurentians was already paying off for another young girl—and for Canada. The 1956 Winter Olympics were held in Italy, in the beautiful Cortina d'Ampezzo region. Canada's triumph was an unlikely third-place bronze in the downhill, from the twins' long-time friend and protegé Lucile Wheeler. Wheeler "Beanie", as they called her, had looked up to the twins since she was two years old—since she had first put on skis. She had then used the same coach as the twins, Hermann Gadner, at what was considered one of the best ski schools in North America. But she had also come late enough after the twins to take advantage of the groundwork Rhona and Rhoda had laid down. Unlike the twins, Wheeler had been able to train in Europe during winters in the 1950s. It was still her family, however, that paid for the training.

The bronze medal at Cortina, the nineteen-year-old Wheeler said, was "an unexpected, beautiful surprise." But the World Championships were her real goal. Two years later in 1958 at Bad Gastein, Austria, Wheeler proved herself again: she won both the downhill and giant slalom and took second in the combined, ending European domination of the event. In her career she had been the first Olympic downhill medallist, the first Canadian Olympic skiing medallist, the first North American to win the Hahenkammen in Kitzbühel, Austria, and the first world ski champion in North America. She reaped the awards, too, from the 1958 Lou Marsh Trophy as outstanding athlete, to the Rose Bowl as outstanding female athlete, to the Canadian Press Award as woman athlete of the year. In 1976, Lucile Wheeler was awarded the Order of Canada. After retirement, Wheeler again followed in the twins' ski trails by starting a school ski program for children, hers in the Eastern Townships of Quebec.

It was a long way from the young racer that Myrtle Cook said "still brought her teddy bear to bed." The publicity from her wins would send even more people into the Laurentian hills to see what all the fuss was about.

"One of the finest people in sport that I have known is Lucile Wheeler," Rhoda says today, "and we've known a lot of people in sport."

THE END OF THE FABULOUS FIFTIES

"Dad wasn't around ever, even before he left," remembers Margie Gillis. "I have strong memories of my youth, but I remember my dad from his knees down. He used to put ointment on his calves."

In 1957 Rhona and Gene Gillis had Jere, their last child; Gene was working hard to make a living for the growing family. And while the kids might have wondered where their dad was all the time, Rhona was still "very happy" with her young husband.

Rhoda, Lucile Wheeler, and Rhona at Lake Placid, 1946: a racer who "still brought her teddy bear to bed."

One of their favourite things to do was a new sport Gene had introduced to Rhona: golf. Both twins remembered their parents playing golf back at Drummondville and Senneville, but going along with them seemed more a chore than fun. What was so great about having to keep quiet? When they took a few lessons as kids, it seemed a stupid idea, hitting a ball with a stick and going to look for it. But in Oregon Gene had worked on golf courses as a young man, and next to skiing it was his favourite sport.

It was in 1957 too that Ben Hogan published his bestselling guide, *Five Lessons: The Modern Fundamentals of Golf.* "Gene read that book forever," says Rhona, "probably memorized it, and treated it like a Bible. He could hit a ball and it would rise and take off like a comet." A scratch player (one who hits par or better), Gene encouraged Rhona to take up the sport too wherever they moved throughout the American Northwest. Natural athlete that she was, she excelled at it. She and Gene often played together in competitions, winning many of them.

In Bend, Oregon, Rhona found a tumbling, gymnastics, and dance class for her older kids, then eagerly took off to try her hand

Christopher and Margie Gillis all smiles in Bend, Oregon, aged 5 and 3; they were having a ball.

at the new sport. She would take along two-year-old Jere, handing him a sawed-off club to practise with. Jere got so good at hunting for golf balls that when the golf club had an Easter egg hunt, he found the most eggs. As the years went by, Jere would become exceptionally good at golf; he had a handicap of three (shot three over par) by age 15.

Meanwhile, Christopher, Margie, and Nancy were having a ball in their gymnastics class. Not surprisingly, all of them had a natural aptitude for it. Margie shone brightest the fastest, but while Nancy took a little longer to figure it out, "she was almost better at it," says Rhona, "sort of double-jointed. They danced very differently." Then Chris took quite an interest. He already had a predilection for flight and fancy. When he was younger Rhona had taken him to the circus, and the girls up on the high wire and trapeze had fascinated him; they wore butterfly costumes and magically turned somersaults in mid air. He was thrilled—until an animal escaped from its cage and he and Rhona had to make a run for cover.

The head of the gymnastics school, noting the kids' enthusiasm and natural talent, began to teach Margie and Chris an adagio dance while they were still quite young. "Chris would lift Margie in the air, throw her up and catch her," Rhona says, "and she'd giggle and laugh and tease him." The kids were doing so well Rhona was asked by the school to take them down to Los Angeles and get them on the TV show *Ted Mack and the Original Amateur Hour*, a forerunner of talent search shows like *American Idol*. The kids would never make it to that show—they would leave America before it could happen—but their talents would appear on much bigger stages in the future.

And yet, even as the children were growing and learning to

Rhoda and Rhona preparing to golf at Senneville Golf Club, Quebec, in 1936—and none too happy about it, either. What was so great about having to keep quiet?

Christopher and Margie dancing together in 1957 ...and on the cover of the 1991 *Dance Magazine*: a natural aptitude.

test their new talents, and as Rhona enjoyed her life as a mother, housewife, and ski instructor, it seemed the father and husband of the family was growing further and further away from them. Although Rhona says Gene "adored his children and was very sweet with them," he brought a Marine's sense of discipline to the family. "He was very strict," Margie remembers. "I just wanted to be *adored*."

Family dinners became an ordeal. "Can't we sit through a meal without someone crying?" Rhona wondered. What was happening to her family? She was confused: she and Gene never fought, "we just had a great time, always mixed up with recreation. We were coaching, lifeguarding, raising the kids. He taught me all sorts of things and got all the ski stuff ready and put it in the car and everything; and I collected the children and ran the ski school." But at the same time Gene suffered some kind of breakdown "and got quiet. He had many concussions and migraine headaches so bad that he couldn't speak clearly," Rhona recalls.

Today Rhona believes that these warning signs came about because Gene, three years younger than her, had far too much pressure on him. Skiing less and less, Gene was now looking to import ski lifts and erect them throughout the continent. He had found the business opportunity through working with an Oregon "lumber king" who wanted him to import heavy-lifting equipment from Switzerland—and Gene discovered they made ski lifts there. Rope tows and T-bars were all over the hills in North America, but chairlifts were still rare. But international importing was a very complicated business, perhaps more so than Gene (who had up till this point concentrated only on the business of ski schools) was prepared for. There were border complications, language barriers to cross; coaching and instructing continued on the ski hills. There was also a wife and four young children at home.

When Gene had to go over to Switzerland to check out some equipment, he wanted Rhona to come with him. "And I said, I didn't want to take those *four* kids over there. I didn't usually stand

The team was young—so Rhoda set the pace. The 1959 National Women's Ski Team in Kitzbühel, Austria, with Rhoda as manager and assistant coach. Left to right, Rhoda, Janet Holland, Claire Monaghan, Nancy Holland, Faye Pitt (with broken foot), Anne Heggtveit.

up to these things. He was the boss; he knew everything, and I was just the dumb mother. But I said, No, it's not a good idea. What if I get sick and I don't speak the language? So he said I'll go, and you stay."

Rhoda remembers those days clearly, too. "People have concussions, they change," she says to explain Gene's behaviour. "Over the racing years, Gene had seven very bad concussions from ski races."

Gene left to go to Switzerland, without Rhona. But he wasn't alone. A woman from Montreal they had known through the years was with him, ostensibly as an interpreter of German.

"She just took over with him. Of course I wouldn't believe anything," says Rhona, still with a tone of incredulity in her voice forty-five years later. "But when he came back from Switzerland,

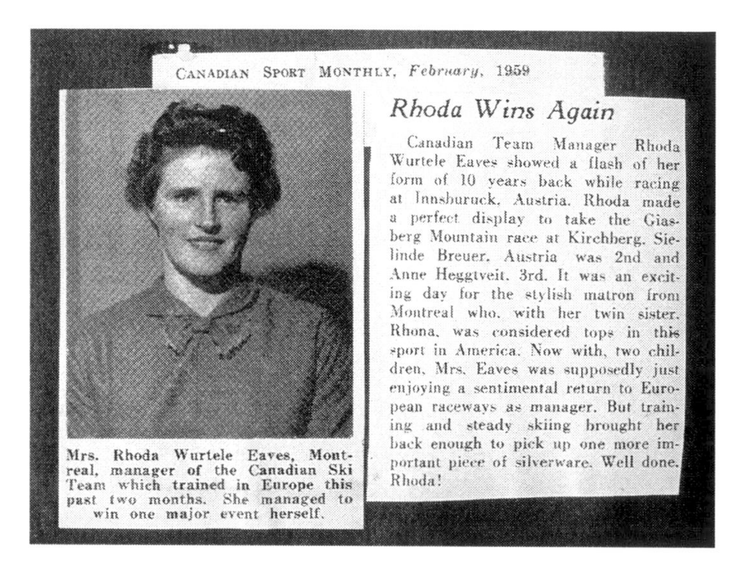
CANADIAN SPORT MONTHLY, *February*, 1959

Rhoda Wins Again

Canadian Team Manager Rhoda Wurtele Eaves showed a flash of her form of 10 years back while racing at Innsburuck, Austria. Rhoda made a perfect display to take the Giasberg Mountain race at Kirchberg. Sielinde Breuer, Austria was 2nd and Anne Heggtveit, 3rd. It was an exciting day for the stylish matron from Montreal who, with her twin sister, Rhona, was considered tops in this sport in America. Now with, two children, Mrs. Eaves was supposedly just enjoying a sentimental return to European raceways as manager. But training and steady skiing brought her back enough to pick up one more important piece of silverware. Well done, Rhoda!

Mrs. Rhoda Wurtele Eaves, Montreal, manager of the Canadian Ski Team which trained in Europe this past two months. She managed to win one major event herself.

One for the scrapbooks: At age 37 and mother of three, Rhoda finds she has to get down the hill—and racing down "was the fastest way." She beat the women's team she was coaching, and everyone else too. *Canadian Sport Monthly*, February, 1959.

we'd get these calls from her. 'Why don't you tell this woman to back down,' I'd say."

Rhona, still deeply in love with Gene, told herself that her husband wasn't having a love affair. They kept running their ski school, and Gene continued to make trips to run his ski lift business, often to New England and the Montreal area. When he would return from month-long trips, everyone would be delighted to see him again. But he drifted further and further from them, seeming not to care about anything, not wanting a wife and family. "It's ghastly," Rhona said at the time. He was keeping everything inside.

But finally one day Gene came back from a trip and said "I won't be back."

To say Rhona was devastated is an understatement. Yet to this day Rhona believes Gene did it "in a friendly way"; she would have taken him back any time, and never puts the blame on him. In her typical way, she confronted a huge event in her life, got through it, and retained her optimism about life.

Yet things would never be the same. When Rhona heard the news, she literally became ill, contracting typhoid fever. Margie says her mother went into a temporary state of amnesia. Rhona wouldn't believe it was happening to her; she believed Gene would get over it and come home. But it was happening, and there was nothing she could do about it. As if to prove it to her, the diamond in her wedding ring came loose and fell out soon after Gene's announcement.

THE FASTEST WAY DOWN

While Rhona was going through a tumultuous time in Oregon, Rhoda too was going through some learning experiences in Europe. The Canadian Amateur Ski Association had named her as team manager and assistant coach of the National Ski Team, and now both the men and women were heading off for winter races in Austria and Germany. Rhoda had to do some quick juggling to get her young family taken care of: David was nine, John was six, and Bruce was four. With the help of her parents, and her godparents, she finally managed to get away. But she was only giving up the responsibility of looking after one family to look after another.

Some of the men's team had already gone out to Europe on their own, including twenty-year-old John Semmelink (who came to train with the French team) and Dave Jacobs. The head coach was Pepi Salvenmoser, who in Kitzbühel, Austria, had coached Lucile Wheeler to her 1956 Olympic medal; two years later Wheeler won the world championship in downhill and giant slalom, then retired. Inspired by Wheeler's shattering of the European monopoly on the Worlds, Canada began sending a national ski team the next year, 1959, when Rhoda was manager. Taking Wheeler's place on the very young women's team were Anne Heggtveit, a senior at nineteen; Faye Pitt and Janet Holland, both seventeen, and Nancy Holland and Claire Monaghan, both sixteen.

Rhoda quickly set the pace. On the first day out in Kitzbühel, Pepi led the team to the top of the mountain, then skied down without stopping. At the bottom, he turned around and with some surprise found only Rhoda behind him. After that, the National Team took their training more seriously, and the slopes of "Kitz" improved their skiing immensely.

Although some of the team had been in Europe before (Heggtveit had already won a big race in Norway), for most it was an exotic introduction to the old world. The team filed down to the store to get milk in their own jug each morning, and watched, fascinated, as the locals patched their leaky jugs with pâté. Christmas in Austria was magical, with twinkling white lights on all the trees, chimney sweeps visiting their hotel, and the townsfolk, gathered on the church steps, holding candles and singing. To get inside the church you had to weave your way through huge boiled-wool curtains, hanging there to provide warming insulation since there was no heating. But while the team was introduced to the quaintness of Europe, they also saw the modernity. They made a side trip to Munich to visit the Bogner ski-clothing factory, which had been at the forefront of the business since Marilyn Monroe modelled the designer's stretch pants in 1948. There, Willy Bogner Sr. gave them "beautiful white Puff Bogner jackets and slim ski pants, which had only just become the vogue." Bogner's son, Willy Jr., was also competing at Kitz and won the men's title; years later, when Willy would go into filmmaking, Rhoda's son John would continue the family connection, working with him and starring in his films.

But the girls weren't there just to sightsee. The team raced in nearby Grindelwald in Switzerland, then went on to Kirchberg in Austria for a giant slalom race. Rhoda, preoccupied with getting "her kids" prepared for the race, found herself at the start gate close to the end of the race. Coach Pepi found he had an extra number for a racer. "Why don't you take a run?" he asked Rhoda. All her team was safely down the hill. "It was the fastest way down anyway, so why not?" Rhoda thought.

And seven years after her last major race, at age thirty-seven and now a mother of three, Rhoda Wurtele Eaves handily took first place. "I guess it was a hurry-up call to the gals," she says. Behind her in third place was Anne Heggtveit, who the next year would win gold in the slalom at the 1960 Olympics.

Despite her little star turn, Rhoda took her responsibility as manager quite seriously—and during this tour she would be tested to the limit. Pepi left to return to his retail business in Kitzbühel during the Christmas rush. Training continued at Kitzbühel, the

John Semmelink in Austria, 1959. Today the Canadian Ski Association gives out the John Semmelink Memorial award to a skier who, through sportsmanship, conduct and ability, best represents Canada in international competition.

home of the Hahenkammen downhill and known as the most difficult run in the World Cup circuit. Pepi had named a local boy as the temporary coach to the men while he was gone. "I can't remember his name now," Rhoda says, "but he was absolutely thrilled to be the coach of the Canadian National Team." Then on the first day out for the Kitzbühel native, Rhoda was taking the teams on runs down the hill, when she heard someone faintly calling for help. Shushing her chattering team, she sent two boys back up the trail; eventually the ski patrol arrived and discovered their new coach. He had taken a shortcut off-*piste*, fallen over a rocky cliff, and broken his back. They got him to the hospital in Kirchberg, but it was "very sad for him," Rhoda recalls.

Then, Pepi received a telegram from the Canadian Amateur Ski Association, telling Rhoda to represent the men's team at meetings for the races. Although it might have been a regular duty for Pepi, "I wonder if they ever knew how much it meant to me," Rhoda says. "I had only spent one day in my life alone." The only woman among all the competitors and officials, Rhoda gamely got the men's team set up for the Lauberhorn downhill in Wengen, Switzerland, the longest course in the world. There were fun responsibilities, too. Once she collected all the team's warm-up clothes at the top of the run, then tied them onto herself and skied down; when she took the men's team to Wengen, she watched as some of the French team skied behind the train. Finally, she returned to St. Moritz, the site of the twins' disappointing Olympics, and cheered as Anne Heggtveit won the slalom and came in fourth in the downhill. Things seemed to be looking up for the team as they headed off to Garmisch-Partenkirchen in Germany for the famed Arlberg Kandahar races.

It was a thrill for Rhoda to come to the site of the 1936 Olympics; she had been fourteen years old then, and it was here that a haphazard team of diplomats' wives had formed the first Canadian women's ski team. Rhoda took her young team to visit the Marker factory, Marker being one of the first companies to make modern safe bindings; Hannes Marker greeted them personally, and Rhoda felt he treated them well. Then they retired to have a hearty dinner on the night before the race. Pepi had once again suggested Rhoda should race, but this time she refused: her first responsibility was to the team, and anyway, the race committee had elected her to the jury. So the team, in good spirits from recent wins, enjoyed the hospitality of Germany. John Semmelink, in particular, was in fine fettle; he talked about having lived in this town when he was young, and how he loved the place; he thought he might even move back one day.

Race day began with Rhoda carefully watching the men coming down; the women's course would be later that day on another slope. Soon she noticed many racers weren't completing their runs, taking bad falls on what was turning out to be a troublesome course. When John Semmelink's number came up, the skier was nowhere to be seen. Rhoda made some quick inquiries about him, but her German wasn't good enough to get a clear answer. Finally she came to understand he must have had an accident: a fall on a steep and sharp turn. Spectators had moved out of the way as he came crashing down, and he slid over the edge of a trail and tumbled down a frozen waterfall. He was in a hospital, but which one? Rhoda ran to the only German speaker she knew in the town, Hannes Marker, and he found out John was at the American Military Hospital. She found a doctor, who handed her the goggles she had lent to the racer that morning. Through an open door she saw John lying on a table: he had serious head injuries, and the doctor gave him a fifty percent chance of recovery.

Rhoda collected herself; though it was a shock, she had to phone his parents in Montreal. John's father answered, and she told him the news. "You must come over right away," she said. There was a long pause, and then he hung up. Twenty minutes later, Rhoda had to call again. This time, it was to say that John had died.

The event hit Rhoda hard. She had three sons herself at home;

she could imagine how his parents felt. And John was special. He was a brilliant student who spoke six languages, and also a gifted athlete who was the big hope of the Canadian team. What Rhoda liked best about John was that when things seemed to be getting too much, John would walk in and everything would become easy.

That afternoon, Anne Heggtveit won both the downhill and combined. Again it fell to Rhoda to give her the sad news. The funeral was held in Garmisch, and Rhoda visited the chapel. They had put John's racing jacket on him, and he was lying "like a knight on a high-sloped slab in the middle of this cold, high-domed round room," she remembers.

"It was a growing-up time for me," says Rhoda. She had never experienced death first-hand, and she admits it took her a long time to accept why this had happened to this young and bright boy. This time, she couldn't wait to get back to Montreal, and to see her three little boys and Arnold. And, sooner than she thought, she would be seeing Rhona again too.

Family 1960–1980

THIRTY-EIGHT YEARS TO FIFTY-EIGHT YEARS

1960: LEARNING TO FALL

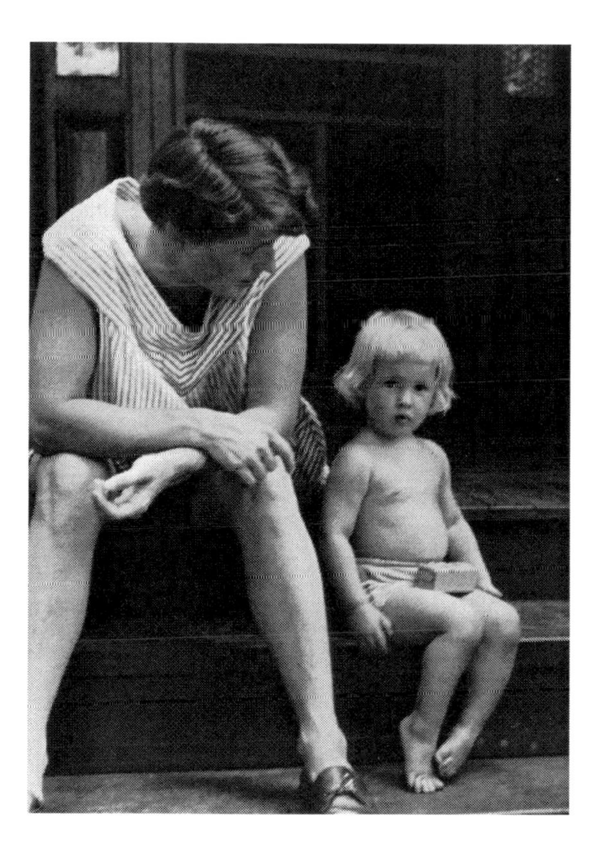

Rhona and Margie at Acton Vale, 1955.

"This is how it was at our house: if someone fell, at the dinner table we would all sit around and discuss the fall," says Margie Gillis, Rhona's daughter. "How did you fall? Did you have a choice? How do you think you could have fallen better? They would discuss it for an hour, break down this moment of a few seconds into forever."

"I watched my brothers walk up and down stairs on their hands," says Nancy Gillis Andersen, Rhona's second-youngest child. "We didn't think twice about jumping out of windows; and if we fell we didn't cry and call for Mummy, we just got up and dealt with it."

"And eventually if you fell really well," Margie says, "you would get a birthday cake, with candles and everything! It was an understanding of the body. They said, 'If you cannot fall down, you cannot stand up.' So if you are unafraid of falling, you can run, you can jump, you can fly.

"There is also a psychic, emotional side to it, an approach to life. In life you're going to fall, inevitably. So you have to know how to get up again. Of course, the twins do as they please. The rest of us mere mortals need wings to fly."

In 1960, Rhona and the Wurtele family as a whole would have

a spectacular fall, and it would have nothing to do with skiing. It was, as Queen Elizabeth II famously described a year in her own life, an *annus horribilis*—a dreadful year.

With Gene's sudden departure from his family in Bend, Oregon, Rhona had developed a number of illnesses, including typhoid fever; later she would suffer from anxiety, depression, and colitis. Her back seized up and had to be operated on; once when Gene called her she lost the feeling in her hands for a few hours afterward. Another time, on receiving a letter from Gene, she lost consciousness. When she came to, she found herself on the living room floor; her eight-year-old son Christopher had covered her with a blanket, dressed the kids in their pajamas, and was reading to the children.

That was the year, says Rhoda, when "all the men left us."

Back in Montreal, the twins' brother, flying ace Edgar, by then appointed to the Joint Intelligence Staff in Ottawa, had come home to visit the family. Still strong and with the physique of a man twenty years younger, Edgar had bent over to tie his shoelaces and suddenly collapsed. At the hospital they found he had a brain tumour. After a nine-hour operation they removed the tumour. "That was the end of Edgar," says Rhoda, and seeing his son so near death "just about killed Dad." In fact, their father was ailing.

Now Rhoda was confronted with her family all around her suffering, and in the meantime she was running the Ski Jays. She was organizing an upcoming Christmas ski camp, lining up eighty kids and lodging in St. Sauveur, getting the teachers, checking the weather and snow conditions. With hardly any snow that winter, she recalls, her committee had up and left for Florida. And so one morning she woke up to look in the mirror and saw that she had put on fifteen pounds in seven days. "I had nephritis [a kidney inflammation]," Rhoda says. "All the liquids were staying in." Rhoda was holding everything inside, including perhaps her emotions. "I took too much on without any help," she says. "So I ran everything from bed." That lesson at least she had learned from

Christopher takes the role of father, 1958. From left, Margie, Christopher, Nancy, Jere.

Millie Hutchinson back in the 1940s, who had worked out of bed for the Red Cross Nursing Corps.

By May of 1960, first Edgar would succumb to his illness, then, in August, the twins' father, Hunter Wurtele, passed away.

In Oregon Rhona hadn't been able to go back to Quebec for Edgar's funeral. Her father's death came at exactly the same time when Gene was "torturing himself and me," Rhona wrote in her diary. She had made it back for her father's funeral. Already she was alone with the children, all of them falling sick or getting hurt, and she was alternately sad and mad. A month after her father's death, in September of that annus horribilis, she received a letter from Gene telling her it was over.

She was still trying to digest the information that her husband wasn't coming back, ever. While she tried to keep the family

Rhona with Christopher, Margie, and Rhoda's John, in Boise, Idaho, 1955, during a visit from Rhoda.

going and continued to teach Sunday School and play golf, she also noted in her diary that when she spoke with a friend about Gene she fainted. She told herself she would wait it out and live from day to day. Her diary entries from the time talk more about golfing and the kids than her mental anguish. "Gene needs time," she wrote. But in the next sentence: "My mind is cracking."

Gene had now moved east to develop Stratton Mountain in Vermont; the woman he was with, having some experience with divorce, apparently counselled him to leave his children while they were young and not keep in touch with them. It was so unlike him, Rhona felt, to leave four young children, never mind leaving his wife. He had been a fine and loving husband, but then "his personality changed, and the dregs were left." She blamed the changes on the many severe concussions he had suffered during his career.

Now Rhona was truly on her own, with four children, and stricken with all manner of illnesses. A doctor prescribed Benzedrine pills "for morale." Friends and the local minister counselled her not to leave town because she was still sick. Instead, Rhona got heavily involved with church activities, and began taking the kids to Sunday School. Somehow, incredibly, the church also got her to do things for them—she taught Sunday School and even gave skiing exercise classes at the church.

In Montreal, Rhoda instinctively knew something was very wrong. She phoned their brother George in Vancouver: "Would you kindly go and see her and bring her home," she said. "Oh, you women," George answered, "you always get excited over nothing." But he finally went. Seeing the situation was serious, he first brought Rhona to Vancouver, then on to Montreal.

"Did you even have your skis with you?" Rhoda asks.

"I had four kids anyway," Rhona answers.

"I think she had her skis," Rhoda says.

Rhona arrived in Montreal with her kids, but found it nearly impossible to rent an apartment—in those days no landlord would take on a divorced woman with four kids (although Rhona would never legally divorce). After spending the summer in Acton Vale with Rhoda and the kids, she finally found a tiny basement apartment near her mother and Jean, "an awful place," she says. "I had a little income. I hated being back in Montreal, everything was terrible. It was a struggle to adjust and do what was best. I became a fifth wheel at gatherings and felt it."

Her aging mother and sister Jean were unable to help much with the kids; when Rhona moved again to the Town of Mount Royal to be nearer Rhoda and Arnold, she hoped Arnold could be a father figure for the children. Rhoda laughs loudly; "Whatever made you think that?" she says.

"I know Mom would have loved to put all her problems, all her worries, on somebody's shoulders," says Margie, "but she couldn't, so she carried it herself."

"That was the biggest challenge of my life," says Rhona, "raising four children on my own. I didn't even know how to pay a bill."

Cooking up **a storm**

Much of the groundwork for the coming women's lib movement was laid the decade before the 1960s. While the top seller of 1950 was the *Betty Crocker Cookbook*, in 1953, two books came out that shook the foundations of the traditional home: Simone de Beauvoir's *The Second Sex*, and Alfred Kinsey's landmark research in *Sexual Behavior in the Human Female*. Kinsey's report was such a hot bestseller the year it came out that it permanently knocked Betty Crocker off her cake pedestal.

"WE LISTENED TO OUR HUSBANDS"

Living in Quebec made it even more difficult for Rhona. In those days, thanks to the social and political climate, says William Weintraub in *City Unique*, "Like minors and lunatics, married women were not legally capable of entering into contracts." They couldn't buy or sell goods, nor borrow from a bank, nor undergo surgery, without their husband's permission. As a separated woman without a divorce, Rhona got the short end of both sticks. It had only been a few years earlier when husbands could get a separation on the grounds of their wife's adultery; but for a woman to get the same decision, the husband had to have kept his concubine on the family premises. There was no federal divorce law in Canada before 1968, and in Quebec, due to the Catholic preeminence in the province, there was no provincial divorce legislation either; the only way to dissolve a marriage was by seeking a private Act of the federal Parliament.

Not only were legal strictures an impediment to women in the 1950s and '60s, society also had lopsided expectations for a couple. The ideal marriage was imagined as one where the woman kept the man happy: wives were advised to have dinner ready when their husbands came home, and to be pretty, and interesting, and to keep a clean house and cleaner children; they should put the children to bed early so they wouldn't disturb the man, and were not to talk about their own problems, but speak softly and listen to all his problems; above all, the king should be comfortable. For all their kingly attributes, however, men apparently had super-fragile egos, and women who wanted to live up to this wifely ideal had to manipulate and tiptoe around their husbands to get what they wanted.

This formula for success led to many marital break-ups, which seemed all the more shocking given the placid exterior some families presented. Some of that outer calm may have been due to tranquilizers coming on the market in 1955; their biggest market was women. But while there was nothing wrong with taking care of someone, women soon found that filling just one role left them unfulfilled, and that their own needs and desires were left behind. Could it be possible, some dared to wonder, that men might be able to look after their own egos, and their own laundry?

When Rhoda came back from her long stay in Europe she was surprised: "Oh look, these kids know who I am." Arnold, Bruce, David, John and Rhoda on a family outing to Mount Royal, 1959.

The changes that began in the new decade were slow and probably imperceptible to many, including Rhona and Rhoda. Rhoda says of her husband Arnold, "He had his job and his interests. Arnold has always done his thing, he's got a great sense of humour, very loyal, but his life is very important." Rhoda had never been one to curl up at home because things were difficult, though. When she was running the ski school and Arnold would refuse to come out and help, Rhoda simply began an instructor training program so she'd have more help. And while Margie Gillis says Rhona was more traditionally "girly" than Rhoda, Rhoda "busted her ass" to keep her marriage working.

"Still," says Rhona, "we listened to our husbands."

"We went along with anything with them because everything was happiness and darling," says Rhoda. Not that going along was always such a bad thing. Around this time, Arnold encouraged Rhoda to participate in his bridge club; Rhoda took on one of her mother's hobbies of painting watercolours, going on "sketch picnics" with friends like Libby Elder (and their ever-present dachshund dogs), and eventually took up oil painting, which she still enjoys.

Rhona uses her considerable energy to tame the Ski Chicks, the eight to 12 year-old skiers in her class. Hill 68, St. Sauveur, 1963.

THE TWINS GET BACK INTO THE SWING OF THINGS

With Rhona back in Montreal and slowly recovering from her physical and mental pain, and Rhoda dealing with the loss of men in her way too, the twins took their usual approach to their problems: they got busier.

With the encouragement of Rhoda, Rhona got back on her skis and went to help with the Ski Jays. Only the twins didn't simply leave it at that. Now at the St. Sauveur ski hill every weekend, they began offshoots of the Ski Jays in order to reach all ages of children. Rhona directed the Ski Chicks, for girls from eight to twelve years old, putting all of them through slalom courses and directing about 100 girls.

Although Rhoda surely appreciated finally having help with the Ski Jays and Chicks from her "big sister," at the beginning Rhona still found it laborious. Each time she went up to the Laurentians she had to organize someone to take care of her four young children. Then, perhaps because she was distracted or exhausted, she became accident-prone on the slopes. During a CSIA course at Mont Tremblant, her feet bled in her ill-fitting ski boots; she got smacked in the nose by the T-bar, causing the man next to her to nearly faint when he saw the result. Then, in 1963, on the first day of the Ski Chicks Club, Rhona had another tumultuous moment: Gene chose that day to show up and see his family. "Nice day to come!" Rhona says now, "Once in thirty years..." Gene in fact visited three times throughout the years. And yet she still calls Gene her husband; he is still "the love of her life."

The business of running a weekend ski school kept the twins busy during the winter months, but there was still the summer to take care of. Luckily, Gene had introduced Rhona to golf when they were living in the American northwest, and now in Montreal Rhona started to bring Rhoda along to hit balls. The pastime they had derided when they were young girls began to look much more attractive. Soon they played (and won) championships at Acton Vale, Summerlea, and Drummondville, and later were on the Quebec Seniors Team several times. Soon the twins were neck and neck in competition, recalling the one-two punches of their ski racing days. While Rhona would eventually hit three holes-in-one, three eagles and have a handicap of six, her favourite story comes from a four-day event they played in Drummondville. "We each came in with a score of 81, so played off the best of three holes. Well, I won the first and Rhoda the second hole. So now we're standing 155 yards from the flag, on a hill, through the trees, over a stream, and up in front of the club to the green. Rhoda hits and lands three feet from the pin. 'Well,' I said, 'there's only one thing I have to do and that is to put it in the hole.' So I carefully aimed with my five iron and hit and the crowd yelled—it's probably behind the flag I thought—but it was in! My first hole-in-one and I called it!"

Skiing goes **mainstream**

The twins' expansion of the ski clubs was perfectly timed. The popularity of skiing was growing every year, keeping pace with improvements in equipment and better access to the Laurentians. The first successful fibreglass skis came on the market, and new techniques such as counter-rotation (where the upper body remains facing the same way while the lower body does the turning) soon followed. This was the first major change in technique since the Arlberg and Allais methods, and using it skiers could make short, sharp turns. Skiing got safer and more fun, and more and more parents began sending their children up the new highway to St. Sauveur. The 1960 Olympics in Squaw Valley (where Gene Gillis was coaching and reporting on radio) helped skiing too: it was there Anne Heggtveit began to strengthen the Canadian tradition of internationally competitive female skiers when she captured the country's first gold medal in skiing.

Anne Heggtveit and her Olympic gold medal, 1960.

PHYSICAL FITNESS WAKES UP— **AND GOES BACK TO SLEEP**

The 1960s saw a slow reawakening of interest in physical fitness, just as the twins were beginning their classes for children. The previous peak of public interest had been during the Second World War, when the Government proclaimed the National Fitness Act, largely intended to keep people ready for wartime; but bureaucracy and politics eventually squashed its objectives. Since then, postwar Canadians (and Americans) had adopted an affluent and leisurely lifestyle, to the point that when children were tested for fitness, more than half failed at tests like leg lifts, sit-ups or toe touches. By contrast, only eight percent of their European counterparts failed the tests. While European children walked miles to school, rode bicycles, hiked and chopped and hauled wood for home heating, North American children were driven around in cars by their parents, stayed in their neighbourhoods, and had to perform chores no more strenuous than walking the dog.

Because of this, Canadians' fitness levels were decreasing, Canadian athletes weren't winning in international competitions (except for a few shining examples like Wheeler and Hegtveit), and health care costs were actually rising due to sluggishness.

Alarmed and shocked by the trend, the US government launched the President's Council on Youth Fitness in 1956 to counteract the trend. Canada soon followed in 1961, when new legislation introduced the Fitness and Amateur Sport Act, to "encourage, promote and develop fitness and amateur sport in Canada."

The battle for fitness seems to be repeating itself. A 2001 report from the Canadian Medical Association Journal showed an "alarming" rise in child and youth obesity, with numbers tripling since 1981. Today, children often perform chores no more strenuous than manipulating the TV remote control or jiggling joysticks on video games.

SEVEN CHILDREN TO TAME: "OTHER PEOPLE WERE NOT LIKE US"

Almost nothing can get the twins as excited as when they talk about sports; those pursuits kept them sane through the various ups and downs of their lives. The only thing that gets them more excited is talking about their children.

Their children, too, have been excited about sports and other physical pursuits all their lives: two were pioneers in freestyle and acrobatic skiing, one played professional hockey in the NHL, one is a golf pro, and they've all been ski instructors; two of the children became internationally renowned dancers. All of them were infused with the Wurtele spirit, complemented by the natural Gillis sport instinct or the Eaves drive. And although the children, particularly the Gillises, would experience upheavals, all would go on to excel at their chosen sport, art, or business.

Rhona, the mother hen of the Ski Chicks, 1960s.

Before all that happened, however, Rhona and Rhoda had their hands full trying to channel their offspring's energy. "Everyone in our family was so physical," says Margie, "I had to learn that other people were not like us."

With Gene gone, "I got terribly involved with the kids," says Rhona. "And I was very strict with them, I was in charge."

Margie has a different perspective. "At our house, it was a democracy—and Rhona lost. There were four incredibly strong kids at home, and she just got vetoed. We listened to her if we felt she was being reasonable."

On arriving in Montreal, Rhona quickly looked around for a sport that would keep the children occupied—besides skiing, which the children began before they could walk. She'd made a back yard ice rink, and the kids seemed to like that, so she thought they might like "fancy skating." She took Christopher to a shop run by Doug Harvey, the former illustrious Montreal Canadiens player. "And I asked him if he'd make some fancy skates for this

Nothing gets the twins as excited as talking about their children. The twins and most of the kids, Bend, Oregon, 1960. From left: Margie, seven years old; Nancy, five; David, ten; Jere, three; Chris, nine; Rhona, Rhoda; John, seven. Bruce was in Montreal.

kid. And he said, 'Fancy skates for a boy!' He made a lot of fun of it; and of course I was feeling pretty low at the time and I didn't need that." Further research showed her that to get a little square of ice at five in the morning with an instructor would cost what to her was a fortune: that was the end of that career.

But then the twins found gymnastic camps and diving classes, and their kids excelled at them, soon winning provincial competitions. Christopher, in particular, seemed well suited to the sports. "He was very agile," says Rhona, "very artistic, he did beautiful things. Once I was pushing him in this baby buggy and taking a shortcut across a field when I hit a rock. Well, he did a somersault out of the buggy—and landed on his feet. Another time I took him skiing and took a rope tow with him on my shoulders. When I grabbed the rope he did a backflip off my shoulders."

"Chris was a very gentle person, incredibly creative," says his sister Nancy. "He was also almost blind. Mother didn't realize at first, until she saw him doing handstands in the field while all the other boys were throwing a ball around. When he got into diving in the provincial championships he couldn't see the end of the diving board! He had to judge it beforehand." Chris eventually got glasses, and later contact lenses.

John also showed early promise. He ski raced until he was twelve, then dropped it. But after competing in gymnastics and diving, he got back on skis again and began imitating those acrobatic skills on the slopes. Hardly anybody was doing that in those days; beginning in the next decade he would win over fifty World Freestyle titles.

The Gillis kids, from left, Jere, Nancy, Margie, and Chris at Elgin gymnastics camp near Quebec City in 1966: "Other people were not like us."

Nancy personified the natural talent that flowed in both families. Once Nancy came back from a competition and cried in her mother's arms. The problem? She had won everything. "She hadn't even tried," Margie says, "she hadn't enjoyed it. She was astonishingly gifted. It came so easily to her, what we struggled for."

The youngest boys, Bruce and Jere, were golf caddies for their mothers, and while the twins collected their trophies the boys chipped and putted until they became excellent players; Jere was six years old when he missed a hole-in-one by an inch ("A natural like his father," Rhona says). Jere was also attracted to hockey ("He could do anything," brags his mother), and was so good he always played with the big boys; within a few years he would work his way up to the pro leagues.

NATURE OR NURTURE?

How was it that both families were able to produce such super-children? How is it that one year, all the members of the Eaves family—David, John, Bruce, plus parents Rhoda and Arnold—were ski instructors? Is it nature, a matter of genetics? Or nurture, the environment they were brought up in? A little of both, it turns out.

Rhoda with Bruce, John and David, in 1966. One year, all members of the Eaves family were ski instructors. Was it genetics?

Growing up in these two families, says Nancy, means that "I'm surrounded by people who have over-achieved. I'm happy to be around them. It's exciting, and makes you realize the potential in life." The families are close, and get together frequently. Her cousins, says Nancy, are like brothers and sisters.

"We're all blessed with a certain genetic makeup," says Nancy. "But it's taken us all in different directions. We all excel in things that we love."

David, the eldest of all the children, believes the way they were brought up was the biggest influence. "Any time my mother was really pissed off at me," he says, "she never held a grudge. It was like she acknowledged that I did something bad, but not that I *was* bad; and that gives you confidence."

Of course, much of the children's success probably comes from years of trying to keep up with their mothers, who enjoyed their company; Nancy recalls when she was sixteen, Rhona would wake up the kids early in the morning to ask who was coming running with her. Early on, both twins' children were taught to "physically cope with our bodies in space," says Nancy, simply by watching their mothers and also by going to gymnastics camp at an early age (Nancy was eight when she first went). She stuck close by her mom (after her rebellious teenage years), who, she says, instilled in her the importance of trying to accomplish something every day. "If she was running I was running. We often trained together. Even now I

From left, John, Arnold, David and Bruce, at Lennoxville College, 1967.

update her training programs, we go for walks. When she was fifty-eight she ran a marathon, and I happened to live across the street, so we trained together. We'd do our running out on Mount Royal, and I'd look out the window in the morning and see the snow blowing sideways and call her and say, 'I'm not going out in this storm.' And she'd say, 'Well, I'm going.' So I had to go, and we'd stuff plastic bags in our running shoes and put on balaclavas."

Today, Nancy says, "I can't seem to stop moving. I'm turning into my mother."

Margie experienced much the same thing with her aunt. "I tried to do as much as Rhoda did, one day," she says. "I ended up in bed for three days. But now I can do it—now that she's in her eighties." Yet Margie, who has always danced to her own tune and to great acclaim, is very much like her mother and aunt. "I find I'm often doing *can't* things. In dance you can't dance to silence, you can't dance to poetry. I'm doing these things because otherwise I'm bored. I get into trouble, and then I learn my way out."

HAIR: DEALING WITH THE SIXTIES

Sometimes it sounds as if Rhona and Rhoda's families were so blessed with athletic abilities that everything came easily to them. That wasn't quite the case. Rhona, especially, had to deal with four headstrong individuals on her own; for years her children substituted for friends of her own age. She'd been ostracized as a single mother, and felt quite alone. "The 1960s were the years of learning," Rhona says. "I had so much to learn, I felt like a stupid mother. But the children were my life and I adored them."

Although Rhona had done well to convince the kids to take up sports, she was less successful in convincing them to go to her Anglican church. The children resisted, and eventually, say Margie and Nancy, she "gave up on religion" too. More importantly, says Margie, her mother gave them a "belief in life; she gave us courage."

The sixties were a cauldron of change. Many of those changes would touch the Wurtele families directly. After decades of slow simmering, feminism would come to the forefront; the push for gay rights began in the 1960s as well. Marijuana use grew popular. The twins' children grew up in that decade of change, most of them impressionable teenagers during the era. It was difficult for adults to keep track of all the changes happening around them, never mind to keep track of the changes in their children.

Margie Gillis was perhaps the most affected by the upheavals the Gillis family went through, yet she went from being a wild child of the sixties to an internationally renowned dancer. It was partially thanks to the new acceptance of psychiatry that Rhona and Margie got through the difficult times.

"I think I was grounded for four years straight," recalls Margie. It was what she called her "wacko" phase, from age seven to thirteen. After Rhona brought the family back to Montreal, she put Margie and Christopher in a dance class. While Christopher took well to working in a group, Margie's passionate personality may have led her to solo dancing. "She would be the one telling everyone else what to do," says Rhona, "but doing her own thing on the other side of the room."

That passion also meant that Margie was deeply affected by the breakup of her parents' marriage when she was seven years old. In an interview with *Maclean's* magazine in 1980, she confessed that she felt responsible for it. "My mother was involved in her own horror, her own pain, and it was just...an extremely difficult time. I was screaming, banging on the windows, refusing to get out of bed, having hysterics every day. I was a horror to live with. One of the reasons I'm afraid to have children is [the fear] that I'll have one like me."

"Well, her hair fell out," says Rhoda. "She did go through hell."

"Margie went through hell," admits Rhona, "but she certainly let us know about it."

"Well, her hair fell out," says Rhoda. "She did go through hell."

"Well, so did I."

It was true: while during the 1960s the most obvious way to rebel was to grow your hair long and wild, by 1965 Margie's hair began falling out—first a small spot on her head, then her eyelashes. Rhona took her to a specialist ("With big bushy eyebrows"), who surprised Rhona by diagnosing the problem as emotional. It was acute alopecia, the loss of hair due to extreme stress, and the best thing for it, he recommended, would be family psychiatry. So the family "traipsed up to the Jewish General Hospital, not knowing what we were getting into," Rhona recalls.

The psychiatrist was unable to wave a magic wand and make all the hurt go away, of course. It was a long and difficult process involving eight years of sessions. Meanwhile Margie was still losing her hair, until she had to begin wearing a kerchief. One day Rhona met one of the mothers at the school who said, "It's too bad what happened to Margie." "What do you mean?" Rhona asked. The teacher had given Margie a hard time at school for wearing the kerchief, and had forced the twelve-year-old girl to take it off in

THE TIMES **THEY ARE A-CHANGIN'**

Neil Armonstrong walked on the moon.

Their spirited approach to life would serve the twins' families well in the coming decade: the 1960s would be one of the wildest periods in the century, and the one that saw most social changes. In the US, the decade began with the rise, then the death, of the Kennedys, the escalation of the Cold War, and the construction of the Berlin Wall; soon the war in Vietnam became American, too. The Pill revolutionized sexuality, and the Beatles, Bob Dylan, and Jim Morrison revolutionized music. The civil rights movement grew stronger than ever, then lost Martin Luther King, Jr. Neil Armstrong walked on the moon, Nixon was elected, and thousands of kids (including John Eaves, in his mother's car) flocked to Woodstock after the summer of love. But peace and love turned to riots, shootings of students, anti-war demonstrations, and the horrors of Charles Manson.

Canada went from stuffy Diefenbaker to the charismatic Trudeau (just three years older than the twins) during the decade, and Quebec was at the centre of many changes. Expo '67 came to a cleaned-up Montreal, and the baby boom and economic strength revived Montreal for a while. With the death of Duplessis, French-Canadians asserted themselves to become Québécois and "maîtres chez nous" during the Quiet Revolution; the province nationalized Hydro-Québec (Hunter Wurtele, who had built much of its infrastructure, passed away before it happened). French General Charles de Gaulle declared *Vive le Québec libre!* and the Parti Québécois was created with René Lévesque as their leader. But as in the US, the Quebec experiment with radical freedom ended badly. In 1970, Trudeau used the War Measures Act to deal with kidnappings and murder by the FLQ.

John Lennon, Yoko Ono, Pierre Elliott Trudeau

front of all her classmates. "So the poor little thing—no wonder she wouldn't go to school. I'd bring her to school and she'd sneak back."

Rhona was horrified at the psychiatrist's suggestion that Margie be taken out of school and put up with a foster family—keeping the family together was far too important for her to give up her daughter even for a short time. But she let Margie go to Arizona to stay with her father for a while after the incident at school, though Margie eventually felt she had to come back home. After she returned Rhona put Margie in a private school, but Margie only got sick again. "Actually," says Rhona, "Margie closed the school down. They couldn't take it. I think it's a hotel now."

Before that, however, Rhona tried to enroll Nancy in the same school; her youngest girl was beginning to clash with her mother too. The first thing Nancy did was run away. She didn't like going to see the psychiatrist either.

"I didn't appreciate it much," she says today. "I don't see that he helped me. Every time we sat down in his office, Mom would burst into tears, and she'd bawl for an hour and then we could leave."

As if things weren't difficult enough, on the way to the psychiatrist's office one day the family drove through an area where a bank had been robbed, and after a chase the police "shot the robber in the head right in front of us," Nancy says. Rhona and Margie "freaked out, but I didn't know how to react because it was so surreal," she says. "And they picked on me and said how I could be so cold and unfeeling. Well, that was another hour in the psychiatrist's office..."

During these difficult years, Rhona was also trying to teach skiing up in the Laurentians on Saturdays—and would leave her oldest teenage children alone at home. Margie and Chris were "supposedly going to gymnastic classes," Rhona says. "I don't think so. They'd go out in their bare feet downtown. Earlier Margie, at about four years old, had insisted on going around without any

John's stint
as a movie star...

"I ended up quitting my job to continue working on Willy's [Bogner's] dream, a film called *Fire and Ice*," says John. "Three years and another Bond film later (*A View to a Kill*) we released *Fire and Ice*. Not only was it a success as a ski film, but it also went to the number two highest grossing box office hit in the German-speaking countries of Austria, Switzerland, and Germany. It lasted twenty-two weeks in the theatres. This film ran as long as *Dances With Wolves* and *Titanic* did when they were so successful in America. It was fun being a movie star. We ate it up. We took the film all over the world for the next two years. In Canada it had a full house every day during the Calgary Winter Olympics."

John Eaves suited up to double for Roger Moore in the Bond film, A View to a Kill, Swiss Alps, 1985.

clothes on. She'd run down the street naked."

Meanwhile, Christopher had his own way of dealing with the family's turmoil—and no doubt with his own personal life as a young gay man in an era that was only beginning to understand and accept homosexuality. When his father had left, Chris was eight years old. Gene had told him to look after everyone. He had tried, as shown by his dressing the children in their pajamas and reading to them when his mother passed out.

And how did he handle his father's leaving? "Well, he didn't," says Nancy. "He left home really young." By 1966, a fifteen-year-old Christopher had had enough. He quit gymnastics and diving, and looked back towards the dancing he had done as a child. After hearing of some auditions for dancing, Chris won a scholarship to go to the Banff School of Arts. But then Rhona found a "nice little note" under her pillow: Chris had run away, but not to Banff, and wondered if he could take some money out of his account.

Today Rhona says, "He was old enough to know what he was doing," but at the time she spent two weeks "freaking out." Finally she heard from him when he was in New York, and from there he went to Amsterdam. He joined a dance company there, then came back to study dance in New York. The following summer he returned to Montreal to teach diving, then got a job with the opera at Expo 67.

Later, both Christopher and Margie became well-known professional dancers and choreographers; Christopher preferring group work with New York troupes, and Margie selling out solo shows and drawing comparisons to Isadora Duncan (and within the family, drawing comparisons to the twins' sister Jean). Margie would even use her dance skills to coach the Canadian National Freestyle Ski Team. Margie was going through "her stages," says Rhona: the Death stage, the Naked stage, the Funny stage. But now they were literally *on stage*. All of that turmoil turned out to be artistic grist for the mill.

Later, both Christopher and Margie became well-known professional dancers and choreographers

"Oh my god, some of her stuff," says Rhona. "I must say I

prefer the Funny stage. And her mother has to sit through some of those things." Rhona would sit uncomfortably beside her friends while Margie exposed her body and soul on stage; "Well, it's just Margie," Rhona would chuckle. "It's art...it was a little different from what I thought it'd be!" But, Rhona says, Margie had had to watch her mother go through *her* own stages: anxiety, depression, ulcerated colitis, back operations. It was hardly a coincidence that one of the most distinguishing features about Margie when she reached the peak of her career years later was her long, flowing, extravagant hair.

WHAT TWINS CAN AND CAN'T DO FOR EACH OTHER

"I think I owe my life and our lives to [the psychiatrist]," says Rhona, "I actually do. He went to Margie's show one time; came over to me and gave me a kiss; I haven't forgotten that."

"He was brilliant and helpful," Margie says. "Mom was adrift and lost, and he gave her a sense of self, reminded her that she had talents and gifts. Rhoda was her shoulder to lean on, but Rhoda was busy with her own family, and she suffered equally. She figured it was terrible for Rhona to have a child like me. But they both held strong not to commit me. Today Rhoda is my dearest friend, genuinely open."

For many years Rhona didn't tell anyone she was seeing a psychiatrist, "because they'd all think I was nuts. I guess I was anyway." Apparently, she even kept the secret from her twin sister.

THE TWINSKI MYSTIQUE: 1963

Throughout the tumultuous years of bringing up their own children, the twins were doing very well bringing up another thousand or so children in their Ski Jays program. However, a few developments were slowly coming together to point them in another direction.

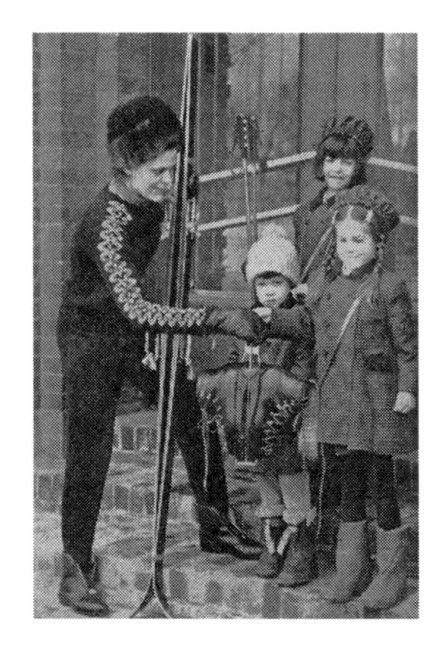

"All these ladies need is confidence." Photo from a *Montreal Gazette* article on Twinski and the phenomenon of women leaving their families to go skiing, from February 1966.

Rhona's regular visits to the psychiatrist were giving her back the natural confidence she'd always had—the freedom to do what she wanted, when she wanted. Women across North America were also beginning to rediscover themselves. In 1963 Betty Friedan published *The Feminine Mystique*, which became a huge bestseller. She espoused what seemed then a radical theory: women, who had no outlet for expression other than finding a husband and bearing children should be able to seek their own identity rather than the one defined by husband and society.

Although the twins have never defined themselves as feminists—and never read the Friedan book—their actions the same year fit precisely with the changes in the collective consciousness. Suddenly (after seven years!), Rhona and Rhoda noticed that bringing the hundreds of children to the ski hills were innumerable mothers; and these women would sit in their cars, knitting or reading, patiently being good mothers sacrificing for their children. "And we figured a lot of housewives needed to get away from the sink and get some fresh air and learn how to cope with skiing," Rhona says, no doubt identifying with the mothers. So the twins began to offer courses for women at Murray Hill in Westmount and Mount Royal; the classes would eventually evolve into Twinski, the club that continues to this day.

It was exactly what the housewives needed. The enthusiastic reaction of the women surprised even Rhona and Rhoda. "Frankly, we were astounded at the instant response and outright desire not only for lessons, but for some racing as well. Many members never skied before their marriage, others skied for pleasure and a few had race experience from 'a long time ago.'"

The women at the bottom of the hill were ostensibly only being offered the opportunity to learn or re-learn how to ski. But just as their children were not only learning ski skills but also social skills on the hills, so these women were now ready and willing to expand their lives, to branch out, to create new friendships—to become something other than just a mother and "darling housewife."

One of the first advertisements for the "Ladies' Ski School" which led to Twinski: December 1962.

"All these ladies need is confidence," the *Westmount Examiner* said in 1963, "and a chance to brush up on technique—and before they know it they will be skiing with their friends and family."

In the fifteenth year of the club, Betty McNeill remembered exactly how Twinski came along at the right time. She had a case of the "Uglies," she said; and "When I found myself putting martinis into the steam iron, I figured I'd better quit and go skiing."

Others were thrilled to go racing while their children went to school. A few years later the twins' favourite chronicler from their early days, Myrtle Cook, wrote an article on the growing club: "Grannies among skiing housewives in racing action," was the headline. Cook, ever a supporter of women wanting to expand their horizons, found that one skier had seven children at home; most had from one to five.

The club grew quickly, and soon every Wednesday the women were going to the Laurentians, Lachute, and the Eastern Townships. The twins began an inter-city racing competition for the club, challenging the women of the Ottawa Ski Club to a giant

Twinski group (with bear) on their regular Wednesday outing at Sun Valley Farm in the Laurentians, 1967.

slalom that became an annual event, the Silver Thimble trophy.

So, without espousing anything more radical than giving women the opportunity to enjoy themselves, the twins once again affected women's lives in Canada (the government would take longer to catch on; the Royal Commission on the Status of Women was established in 1967). Rhona and Rhoda had been born in the middle of the first wave of the women's movement, when the suffragettes of the 1920s pushed for the vote; forty years later they unknowingly took part in the second wave of the women's movement. And along the way, they would once again recapture that freedom of their childhood.

TWINSKI KEEPS GROWING

As interest in Twinski and skiing in general grew, the club took in a whole round of ski hills in the Laurentians: Belle Neige, Mont Gabriel, Alouette, Chantecler Olympia, Sun Valley, Shawbridge, Morin Heights, Mont Roland, Habitant, and St. Sauveur; once a year they would go to Mont Tremblant. Some of those hills are gone now, and so too, since 1964, are the ski trains. With the introduction of the autoroute and the ubiquity of the car, everybody preferred the personal freedom that came with driving. In fact, Twinskiers would reach even further. By 1967, the twins were taking their club out on two yearly trips, one to the Rockies in the Canadian West, and one to the Alps of Europe. From the beginning, it was Roger Tanguay of Voyages Sportsmania who arranged the trips to Europe. He has done it now for 38 years. That year they took a group to Lech, Austria, and to Davos in Switzerland, where they had trained and raced during the Olympics (the trip cost less than $500 each). [For a full list of all the Twinski travellers trips, see the appendix at the back of this book.]

Like anything the twins began, the club too began expanding. By 1969 there were two hundred women and over twenty instructors with Twinski, and the twins began a cross-country section of the club. It certainly called to mind the earliest days of skiing in the Laurentians; the women in the club took the tow rope to the top of a hill, then went bushwhacking with several instructors—not the least of them the then ninety-four-year-old true pioneer of Laurentian skiing, Herman "Jackrabbit" Johannsen.

The twins would also capitalize on their families' skills, until almost all of their kids would help with instructing.

Canada's fastest growing **sport**

Some of the Twinski club's quick growth was due to the increased interest in skiing after the war—"Canada's fastest growing sport," according to the *Gazette*. From 1955 to 1965, the number of ski resorts in the US had leapt from 78 to 662, and the growth in Canada was just as explosive. The introduction of Lange plastic boots gave those who were unsure an extra push, with their safer and more comfortable fit. Television made ski racing an international spectator sport, and the first World Cup competitions in 1967 coincided perfectly with the ascendance of television-viewing. It was also the year Canada's winningest skier Nancy Greene won the first women's World Cup championship; the next year she would win it the second time, and also take the gold in the giant slalom and silver in the slalom at the Grenoble Olympic Games.

The original club name was the Wurtele Twin Ski Club, which eventually got shortened to Twinski. The twin figures in the logo formed the "W" of Wurtele.

Jackrabbit Johannsen, middle, with Rhona on the left and her sister Jean Wurtele on the right. "The Chief" became an honorary member of the all-women's ski club in 1968.

WHAT IS FAME? THE KIDS' CAREERS

In 1969, a few years before their fiftieth birthday, Rhona and Rhoda were inducted into the American Ski Hall of Fame. Whereas in the last few decades Canada had always beaten the US down the ski hill—being the first to have ski clubs, trains, and tow ropes, for instance—now the US became the first country to properly honour its ski pioneers. It would take another thirteen years for the twins to be recognized in the Canadian Ski Museum. In 1985 they were named to the Quebec Ski Hall of Fame; the next year they were inducted into the Laurentian Ski Hall of Fame.

That kind of recognition has never been the twins' obsession; it's nice to get, they admit, but they rarely raise their voices about it. Their children have experienced a good dose of fame too, but are predictably blasé about it. "I didn't know Mother was famous when I was growing up," says Nancy. "But they always told us they were." Even in their daily lives the twins crossed paths with famous people, from Salvador Dali to Jackie Robinson to Emile Allais.

"My mom was incredibly famous, but fame never made a difference in our lives," Margie says. "It never stopped my family from having an extremely difficult time of things and it never stopped us from having financial problems: we had fear, poverty, struggle. The twins weren't in their heyday then, but already we knew that fame wasn't important.

"I thought it wouldn't make a difference to me, but I was unprepared for how demanding fame is [in Canada, Margie was known as the "Goddess of Dance"]. I've had guns and knives pulled on me backstage. People want things from you, demand things, expect things. You're in isolation, on a pedestal. That's why Mom never remarried—a woman's fame is intimidating to a man. It's different if the man is famous, of course."

Nancy feels that her mother and aunt's fame did have some benefit. Her mother's greatest contribution to sport was not so much in what she has won, but more generally in what she has done to promote skiing and as a role model for women in sport. But, Nancy says, "If you don't speak up about it, nobody will know. They're also pretty humble. We were at Tremblant recently and the staff were trying to get Rhona to pay for skiing there. Well, I had to explain to them, first of all she's over eighty, and you don't know who you're dealing with here, and I had to explain everything she had done. Rhona would never have said anything. She's a little shyer than Rhoda."

Despite the humility the family espouses, as early as 1960 the effects and pull of fame were already having an effect on the twins' children. As a young girl missing her father's affections, Margie had just wanted to be *adored*. Rhoda's John had a reputation as a cold fish during his peak as a freestyle skier, but those

A Wurtele **weekend**

When Jere Gillis was traded in 1980 to the New York Rangers, Rhona had the unique yet typically Wurtele experience of going to New York City for a weekend to see almost all her children perform: Jere played hockey that weekend in Madison Square Gardens, Christopher performed with the Paul Taylor Dance Company, and Margie danced *The Garden of Earthly Delights*. "Margie was hanging by her hair in that one!" Rhona laughs. Along with her on the trip and completing the family was Nancy—presumably happy to be out of the spotlight.

Advertisement for the Paul Taylor Dance Company, featuring Christopher: just one of many Gillis children performing in New York that weekend.

Years later (around 1985), the twins' kids hung out at the same Acton Vale copper mine swimming hole as their mom and aunt—and did equally daring dives. Diving from top, John, Jere, a friend of John's, Bruce, David. Seated on the left, Nancy, right, John's future wife Brigitte.

who knew him laughed at this perception. Somehow, whether instinctively or through watching his mother and aunt, John knew how to deal with the demanding public. In an interview from the 1970s he said, "A competitor can't give himself up 100 per cent to the public. Controlled emotion or nervousness can be a great source of strength. If you let that adrenalin run haywire, it ebbs away, giving the public a great show and you nothing."

Certainly, in both twins' families, the fame and public attention drew them tighter to each other. "My children were very close," says Rhona. "They had this web around them that I'm sure was very intimidating for a lot of people. Not that they were conscious of it. Someone would bring a boyfriend or girlfriend to Acton Vale, and to see all the activity and all the crazy people there at the house, it must have been pretty weird. Some of them backed off."

The twins were kept busy with activities outside of their own sporting pursuits, especially those of their increasingly successful children. From early childhood the twins' ferried their children to gym, dance, swimming, and diving classes, then hockey games and various sport competitions, and of course Rhoda and Rhona brought them along to golf and ski. When the kids reached adulthood, the twins loved to go see every show, game, and event they participated in.

CHRISTOPHER

As the eldest child of Rhona's family, Christopher had at the beginning of the 1960s been given the role of "father" when Gene left. In some respects, the responsibility made him grow up early. He always had a deep connection with his sister and sometime dancing partner Margie, and a *Dance Magazine* article from 1991 says he retained an "engagingly youthful manner" into his forties; he and Margie gave "the impression of being as vulnerable as they are intense."

Christopher tries out some skis at a tender age, 1951.

Chris kept his mother hopping with his early gymnastics and diving. But when he left to dance in Europe and New York, the family began to see a lot less of him. Chris travelled the world, seeing his family when they came to New York. In the late 1970s Chris was asked to join the Paul Taylor Dance Company in New York. He hoped to stay, he said in *Dance Magazine*, "Until I no longer look good onstage." He stayed with them the rest of his life—fourteen years.

By 1991 Christopher had become the mainstay and unofficial spokesman for the company, and Taylor was grooming him to eventually take over. Among some of the highlights in Chris's dancing career were performing with Mikhail Baryshnikov (friendly and easy to work with) and Rudolf Nureyev (haughty and disrespectful). Chris also danced in four premieres in New York with his sister Margie, with whom he always shared a deep trust. "He was every little girl's dream of a beloved big brother," says Margie. "Dancing with Chris, it was astonishing," she remembers. "He was legally blind. He would sense other people through body heat; he knew where they were in space. The twins taught us that."

Rhona says Margie noted Chris's disability and used it for her own dancing too: before a performance she moves around the stage with her eyes closed until she knows where everything is.

Chris had the added struggle when he was young of being gay.

Rhona had to make adjustments to the news he brought home. "Mom wanted the best for Chris," says Margie. "And the prevalent thought at the time was that being gay was an illness. She tried to cure him, but of course it didn't work." But Rhona was just doing what any mother would do: she wanted the best for her children. "So when I solo danced," Margie says, "and was naked on stage, and when they saw that Chris was gay, she would just say like most mothers: do you have to? She knew that these were routes that would ostracize us, and as a mother she was concerned." Rhona too had been ostracized to an extent when her husband left her, and had suffered through that. The reaction from Chris's Marine father was more severe: he completely cut him off when Chris was twenty-one. "It was very sad the way Chris was treated," Rhona says. "It wasn't healthy. Chris wrote to his father and said here are the tickets, why don't you come and see me, Dad, and I'll pay for your trip to come out. And his father said, give the money to your mother and let her go. Things were different then."

Christopher on the cover of *Ballet Review*, a New York magazine, Summer of 1985.

But years later, when Chris died and the whole family was in New York, Rhona said, "If only the heterosexual community could have such genuine caring and respect."

"She went from being phobic," says Margie, "to doing a 180-degree turn. And now I think she's heterophobic," she says with a laugh.

By the time brother and sister were featured on the 1991 cover of *Dance Magazine*, Christopher was already using that sense of space to choreograph dances for the troupe. The *New York Times* was smitten. "*Icarus at Night* is not the first work that Christopher Gillis, long one of the best dancers in the Paul Taylor Dance Company, has created for the troupe or under other auspices," they wrote. "But this premiere signaled his arrival as a first-class choreographer." When it was presented in 1992, Christopher's choice of theme—the *Times* wrote of the dance's "recurrent deaths" and men taking care of men," was very timely: AIDS was killing some of the brightest stars in the arts during these years. Yet Chris's work, said the *Times*, remained infused with hope and joy.

MARGIE

Margie Gillis, like Christopher, had risen above the early trials of her childhood to achieve international recognition for her art. But she did it very much her own way. "She just kept on dancing," says Rhona, "and finally she was in some things locally."

Margie was led by emotion and impulse.

While Christopher preferred classical shapes, forms and lines, Margie was led by emotion and impulse; Christopher was happiest working in a group of dancers, while Margie doggedly pursued a solo career. At eighteen, having rejected formal dance classes, Margie auditioned for a dance troupe, "more to be seen and applauded than for anything else," she says. "Then she and her boyfriend went to China, and she danced in the parks and the people there discovered her." Rhona is giving the condensed version of events; what is missing from her description is the intensity and stubbornness Margie brought to perfecting her dancing. Margie inherited her mother's and aunt's passion, energy, and refusal to be told she couldn't do something. When Margie went to China, Rhona relates, a crowd of curious people gathered to watch her perform. At the time Margie was dancing in costumes that were raggedy and ripped, accentuating the emotion of the dance. "But after she performed the Chinese took her costumes and mended them for her! I don't know how many hundreds of dollars the costumes were worth before they got through with them...but the people were very sweet."

Throughout the decade she slowly built up her art and career, putting on solo shows, even teaching ballet at freestyle skiing camp.

Just as Margie always danced by herself in the corner of the studio when taking dance lessons as a child, she remained convinced of the worth of her individual vision and her own creations. In the next decade her stubbornness and dedication would pay off: she would become the most renowned dancer in Canada.

"She's got a cult following now," says Rhona. "She got many

Photo by Cylla von Tiedemann

Margie dancing on the coast of Cortes Island, B.C., 2005.

offers [to dance with companies] but she didn't like the strings attached. Both she and Chris did what they wanted to, and certainly it opened up a lot of wonderful doors." And yet there was a price to pay for her independence. "They're dedicated people, dancers, but they suffer," Rhona says. "Margie's had many awards, including the Order of Canada, and strings of boyfriends. She's been unlucky in love, but it's a difficult life."

Today Margie works full time, dancing, choreographing, and teaching; she is the artistic director of the Margie Gillis Dance Foundation. While she has travelled extensively for her dance, throughout North America, Europe, the Middle East, and Asia, and choreographed major dance numbers such as two solos for the Beatles tribute *Love* in Las Vegas presented by Cirque du Soleil, teaching and performing are still closest to her heart. She has taught at the Julliard School in New York, and performed in *Sacred Ellington* with the soprano Jessye Norman, as well as with many of the greatest dance artists of our day and age. She is an Honorary Cultural Ambassador for both the Quebec and Canadian governments.

NANCY

When Nancy was a child, it didn't look like she would follow her family members into sports. Rhona was convinced she would be a vet because she loved animals so much. In the early 1970s she was "more interested in becoming an airline hostess," a Mount Royal newspaper story on the family said. But she did get into sports, inevitably. She excelled at school sports, and took up speed-skating with her brother Jere, eventually placing in the top three provincially. She was also a top ski racer with Rhona's Ski Chicks for one year. But after a stint of meditation and yoga (and hanging with visiting Indian guru Swami Shyam at the Acton Vale rectory one memorable weekend) Nancy realized her physical potential and began entering freestyle ski competitions in the mid 1970s, her cousin John had already established himself in that new world. "I looked up to John, and hoped he would look after me," she says. "But his only advice was to jump higher, and go faster." Most mothers would have been worried sick if their daughter entered into freestyle skiing competition at a young age.

Nancy Gillis Andersen at the family church in Acton Vale before the Thanksgiving service, August 2007.

Those were the days even freestyle skiers didn't wear helmets; they were still making up the rules as they went along, literally. Nancy won a car at one competition, only to have it taken away from her when the rules were changed mid-competition. Still, she established herself very well in the freestyle world, touring the US with the Colgate Women's Freestyle Circuit in aerials; she was featured on *Wide World of Sports* and in a Labatt's Blue commercial, and was on the Rossignol freestyle team. By 1978 she had placed second in aerials at the world championships. She met with a good amount of injuries and surgeries over time; a well-meaning doctor told her she shouldn't be a freestyle skier, but would do better as a secretary—echoing the sentiments expressed by men in her mother's competitive days.

During the 1970s, Nancy began running with her mother,

Nancy learning to fly, at freestyle camp in Colorado, 1978. Her cousin John's only advice was "jump higher, go faster."

eventually earning the honoured title of "the other twin" for one summer as she competed in local races with her mother and occasionally Rhoda.

After a few injuries, by the early 1980s Nancy drifted more towards the burgeoning field of fitness training, a time when aerobics were booming and Jane Fonda's workout video hit the stands. When the YMCA offered the first classes for instructors, Nancy was there; she also received many fitness certifications from McGill University. It suited her better than the dancing at which her brother and sister excelled. "Each time I took dance classes they would just make me laugh," she says. For many years, Nancy taught fitness classes to "elite Westmount women." Today she is a personal trainer at a tennis and squash club in the West Island, where she lives with her Danish husband Henrik and twenty-year old daughter Kristina. She also continues to teach skiing with the Twinski Club, and "supports the twins in any way she can."

JERE

The youngest member of the two families also began a professional sports career during the 1970s. Jere Gillis had been playing Junior Major Division hockey with the Sherbrooke Castors as a star left-winger and one of the team's most popular players. By the age of twenty in 1977, Jere Gillis was drafted by the Vancouver Canucks and began his ten-year career in the NHL. Eventually he played for teams all over North America; after Vancouver he played for the New York Rangers, then Quebec, Buffalo, Vancouver again, and ended his NHL career in Philadelphia. He played four seasons in Europe and two as a player coach as well. Rhona came to see many of his games. She also watched him go through a tough time off ice.

Jere with the TMR Boomers, 1960... and with the New York Rangers, 1980-1981.

"Anybody who marries hockey players has to go along with it, that's the life. You should realize what you're getting into." Jere had to go through the pain of a divorce, something his mother had already suffered through. With his multi-sports background (besides early baseball, football and gymnastics training, he's also trained in Kung-Fu, skiing and rollerblading) Jere has since moved into another career pioneered in the family by his cousin John Eaves: since 1998 he has been a stuntman in movies. It's also a very physical job, but like his family members, Jere "likes to take impossible tasks and find a way to make them work." His first stunts were done in his cousin John's movie *Fire, Ice and Dynamite* (a sequel to Bogner's *Fire and Ice*), and he has since performed stunts in films such as *The Red Violin*, *Battlefield Earth*, *The Sum of All Fears*, *The Day After Tomorrow*, *Maurice Richard*, *Bon Cop, Bad Cop*, *Secret Window* and *Blades of Glory*.

DAVID

Rhoda's eldest, David in 1971, top; and in 1999 with the object of his passion, bottom.

Rhoda's three boys were just as sporty and successful as their cousins, but seem to prefer to stay out of the limelight. The eldest of them all, David, did well at sports but must have inherited genes from his grandfather Wurtele. He excelled in his studies at Lower Canada College, winning scholarships and graduating from Sir George William University in fine arts, going on to become a successful businessman, the only one of the twins' children whose work is not directly connected to either sport or dance (he calls himself "a lousy golfer"). Still, he managed the SkiCan office in Montreal in the 1970s, and has been with the Canadian Ski Instructors Alliance for twelve years. His life has been profoundly influenced by Twinski. In 1976 he accompanied the club on a trip to Whiteface Mountain in New York; on the same trip Twinski member Marjory Glassford had found her friend couldn't come, so invited her daughter Patsy instead. David and Patsy shared a chairlift, "and soon dumped their non-skiing partners," getting married in 1979.

As the eldest among the twins' children, David resonates with soundness: he lives with Patsy (Patricia) Glassford Eaves, two daughters and one son in the house that used to belong to Margaret and Wemyss Ironside, the godparents Rhona and Rhoda visited as children; out his back door he can see the place where the twins went swimming in the 1920s. Since 1984 he has been with the Nordson Corporation, one of the world's leading producers of precision dispensing equipment that applies adhesives, sealants, and coatings. The self-appointed historian of the families, he finds his most passionate outlet in historic trains.

JOHN

Perhaps the first child to start getting a lot of attention was Rhoda's John—his older brother David had never hankered for the limelight, and was content to go to university, get a fine arts degree, and be a ski instructor for awhile. His cousin Christopher, eighteen years old in 1969, was just beginning his forays into the dance world, including in Amsterdam and New York. John Ironside Eaves, fifteen going on sixteen, already had a reputation around town. He was "crazy about music," says Rhoda—what teenager could have resisted in those heady hippie days?—and used to bring friends home to practise music in the basement. Among them were Frank Marino and the kids from Mahogany Rush, a band that gained solid cult status in the following years.

John Eaves with the twins on a heli-hiking trip in the Bugaboos, 2005.

"John did the most awful stuff," says Rhoda, "but he always admitted he did it. So John asked to borrow the car for a couple of days. Where are you going? I asked. We're going down to this music festival, he said." Rhoda's car was her lifeline, an integral part of her freedom—and she needed it to get back and forth to the ski hills. But she felt John knew what the car meant to her. She let him take it.

"The next day I open the paper and what do I see—down in New York state there's this huge music thing where everyone is walking around dopey and naked and rolling in the mud..."

"Woodstock? Three days of peace and music?"

"Yeah, my car went to Woodstock with these crazy kids. My god, I thought, I'll never get it back. But it came back in about three days. And the kids cleaned it out. They didn't say too much about it. Then *Life* magazine comes out about this festival."

The festival and hippie culture affected youth across North America, and it left its mark on John. He immediately began growing his hair long, then went to Europe and the Swiss Alps: he knew that like his mother and aunt he wanted to ski for a living.

After a few years he came home and began instructing at the twins' ski school. With his early training in gymnastics, John naturally gravitated towards "hot dog" skiing, now called acrobatic or freestyle skiing. While working in Whistler in 1973–74, he met freestyle skiing pioneer Wayne Wong; Wong liked his style, and encouraged him to go further. The first pro event John entered he won; by 1974 he was the Canadian freestyle champion and had placed second in the European championships. By 1976, John made his big breakthrough when he won the combined title at St. Moritz, the site of his mother's earlier disappointment. In 1977 and '78 he won the world trophies for freestyle skiing. These were the days of "ballet skiing" as well, something that didn't last too long. John had kept his love of music alive, and composed and recorded his own songs for his routines in Nashville, Tennessee.

The early days of their children's careers kept the twins hopping during the 1970s, no matter what the season. In summer the twins pursued their own golf competitions, then their kids', including John's freestyle camps when there was no snow—he built ramps at Ste. Agathe so students could do jumps into the lake. Another love of John's was windsurfing; he was instrumental in bringing the World Windsurfing Championships to Kingston, where Rhoda helped out—and surfed.

Rhoda also joined John again in 1976—she went to perform in a celebrity ballet skiing competition with him in Stowe, Vermont. The only instruction she got from John was "Just don't fall." They worked up a routine to music and did quite well. "And we won," Rhoda says. "I won a beautiful pair of skis and bindings, and John got a silver belt. John competed in aerials and moguls and ballet [the latter since omitted from World Competitions], and John won in all of them. He used to have twelve pairs of skis when he went on the freestyle World Circuit." Competitions continued to be family affairs, when Margie eventually choreographed ski ballet routines.

In his skiing career, John won six World Championships in the

John Eaves, Freestyler of the Year in 1977.

late 1970s and early 1980s, including Combined Freestyle Overall and Aerials, and over fifty World Championship titles. The wins led to him developing a mogul ski for Olin Skis, the Mark 4, which became the best-selling ski in the US during the 1970s.

John's fearlessness and flexibility, a direct inheritance from his mother and aunt, led him naturally into performing stunt work, usually using his skiing prowess. Earlier, John had found a sponsor in an old family friend, Willy Bogner. It began a lifetime of collaboration. Besides his ski apparel business, Willy Bogner Jr. had gone into movie-making. After John's astounding success in world championships, Bogner asked John to double for Roger Moore in the 1981 Bond film *For Your Eyes Only*. With interest in the Winter Olympics still running high (the Lake Placid games had been held in 1980), the makers of the film decided to use winter sports in the film, and shot many sequences at Cortina D'Ampezzo where the 1956 Olympics were held (and where Lucile Wheeler won Canada's first medal in skiing). Over one billion people saw Eaves careen down a bobsled run on skis, towed by an unseen bobsled. The stunt was as dangerous as it looked; on one run the bobsled left the tracks and smashed into a tree, killing stuntman Paolo Rigoni.

John would go on to do stunts for another Bond film, *A View to a Kill*, and later develop a friendship with Leslie Nielsen after snowboarding on an ironing board in *Mr. Magoo*. One of John's more dangerous stunts was in 1995 for Jackie Chan in *First Strike*: he jumped from a cliff on a snowboard and grabbed the skids of a hovering helicopter, coming within a metre of the blades. He also acted and was a camera operator for the film. Then he went over Iguazu Falls in Brazil on a life raft. Like his mother and aunt, John apparently knows no limits; in the Willly Bogner film *White Magic*, he skied down fifty-degree faces of icebergs in Iceland, then water-skied on his snowskis around the same bergs.

Today, John has got out of the stunt business and makes his own movies. He began with feature films, (his first was the 1988 *Skier's Dream*), and now makes a business out of filming other people's heli-skiing vacations around the world. But again, like his mother and aunt, age won't be the thing to slow him down. In 1999, at the age of forty-five, Eaves was the oldest sponsored athlete at the Canadian Freestyle Championships. He had been asked to sit on the judge's panel with a friend, but declined. He wanted to ski instead. "It's a little more fun, you know," he said.

According to the Canadian Ski Museum, John Eaves is still "arguably one of the most successful skiers to represent Canada in the freestyle disciplines." In 1988 he was inducted into the Canadian Ski Hall of Fame, only six years after his mother. He is married to his high school sweetheart, Brigitte Callary Eaves, and they divide their time between a house in Calgary and one in Fiji.

And a nephew **too...**

Besides the high level of achievement all of Rhona and Rhoda's children have attained, the larger family also boasts Canada's most famous coach. Glenn Wurtele is the nephew of Rhona and Rhoda, son of their brother George. Glenn was the coach of the Canadian Men's Ski Team during the "Crazy Canuck" era, when "Jungle" Jim Hunter and Dave Irwin, the original Canucks, and their teammates Dave Murray, Steve Podborski, and Ken Read took the international press by storm. By 1984, the skiers had had fifteen World Cup wins; throughout the '70s and early '80s they were almost always in the top ten. Glenn Wurtele (and former Austrian coach Heinz Stohl) were instrumental in finally getting Canadian men onto the podium, largely in the downhill. Podborski was the first North American male to win a downhill medal (a bronze), at the 1980 Olympics in Lake Placid, then took the World Cup Downhill Champion title in 1982, the first win by a non-European. Since 2002, Ken Read has rebuilt the Canadian Ski Team. Read has a Wurtele connection too: his mother Dee Read went to Trafalgar with the twins, then skied with the Penguins and Rhona and Rhoda. Today Glenn Wurtele is the Manager of the Race Training Venue at Panorama in the Canadian Rockies.

Bruce Eaves with sons Nicholas Bruce and Sebastien Hunter at Whistler in 2006.

BRUCE

Bruce played Junior B hockey as a young man, but discovered early on that his talent lay in teaching sports; he was ski instructing by the mid-1970s, and has since moved up to the highest possible level: he is a three-time member of the prestigious Interski Team that represents Canada at the international congress of ski instructors. And yet, Bruce competed for four years on the World Cup freestyle skiing circuit from 1977 to 1981, ranking 7th in the world in his last two years of competition. In wintertime, Bruce works at Mont Tremblant as a CSIA Level IV examiner; it is the top instructor level, meaning Bruce is qualified to teach expert skiers and instructors. Essentially, he says, "I teach teachers how to teach." Bruce is the technical director of Ski le Gap, a ski and snowboard instructor school that invites British students on their "gap year." When the snow melts, Bruce packs up his skis and takes up his clubs to continue his work as a golf pro at Golf Dorval. He has two sons, Sébastien and Nicholas. Sébastien, 15 years old in 2009, competes (and wins) in open class free ski professional competition.

Rhoda watches as Bruce teaches Junior Golf Camp, with his sons (from left) Sebastian 7 years old, Nicholas 10 years old, and nephew William, 15 years old, in 2001.

THE DANGERS—AND REWARDS—
OF THE PHYSICAL LIFE

The twins' dedication to a physical life—and their children's pursuit of them in some way or another—has led to innumerable rewards, but it hasn't been without its dangers. As the twins neared their fiftieth birthday in 1972, the problems Rhona had had with her back began to pile up. Since her accident-prone days after she moved back to Montreal, Rhona had gone through a number of operations and interventions. Finally in 1970 her back seized up and she had to have a serious operation.

In another classically Wurtele moment, then, at that time Rhona was joined by a number of other family members: Rhoda's Arnold was in the next room of the General Hospital recovering from two hip operations. "Then Margie comes in with her hip injury," Rhona says, "and Nancy's just had her gallbladder out, and Jere comes in with his hand in a cast from hockey."

Rhona was especially sympathetic towards Jere and the dangers of hockey. "It's very physical, it wears the players out. Anybody who marries them has got to go along with it, that's the life. You have to realize what you're getting into." She speaks of this as a way of empathizing with Jere over the break-up of his marriage. "He had a very difficult time," she says. "He really suffered, he's still suffering. He's got a beautiful child who's about fifteen now, and another two in their twenties. And now he's doing stunts for films: he had a broken nose yesterday. He's been talking of redoing his teeth; of

Rhoda jumps at Aspen in 1976 with Twinski: not without its dangers.

course he got hit from head to toe during hockey."

The other children had their share of broken bones too. "When I was fourteen I skied off a flat rock without a lip to give me the height I needed," John Eaves said in a 1974 article in the *Gazette*. "I landed flat on my back and had internal bleeding for three days." But he was soon back on the slopes again. "I don't disregard pain as much as I use it to my advantage," he said. "I perform better under pain, raising my concentration to treble its usual force."

The dancers in the family also had to deal with physical pain—Margie had danced with bare feet on a splintering wooden stage. "Pain is a part of life," she said in a 1980 *Maclean's* interview, "and you shouldn't avoid it with Valium and TV." In particular, she says, "Skiers are very physical people. They're proud of their physical prowess. But athletes are so competitive; I'm more concerned with sharing than watching the opposition."

And yet, Margie says, getting through her fears—physical, emotional, and mental—has allowed her to "accept greatness" into her life, to push herself to do whatever she wanted, when she wanted. It is no mystery where this comes from: "My mother gave us the courage."

For Rhona after her back operation, courage was crossing the street—while wearing a full body cast. For seven years after the operation she could not physically approach any sport—no skiing, no diving, no swimming, no tennis, not even any golf. During that time too, the twins felt another kind of pain when their mother Edith "Colly" Wurtele passed away. And yet, ten years after her operation, at the age of fifty-eight, Rhona ran the Montreal Marathon in four hours and fifty minutes.

During her recuperation period, she became interested in running as she watched her brother George take up jogging after a heart condition prompted him to get in better shape. "So I started walking, then became sort of a closet runner...an old lady running was a little odd, I thought." Then, like Forrest Gump, she just kept on running. She began running through the woods around

Canada **keeps winnning**

Meanwhile, back in the ski world, Canadian athletes were using the "Me Decade" to rack up more and more wins. And the men were finally catching up to the women! In 1974, Kathy Kreiner won the World Cup giant slalom race. The next year, Ken Read (whose mother, Dee Read, had been a member of the Penguin Ski Club) became the first Canadian man to win a World Cup downhill race; a few weeks later, another Crazy Canuck, Dave Irwin, won a similar race. Eventually the team, which also included Dave Murray and Steve Podborski, would win fourteen World Cup victories. In 1976 at the Innsbruck Olympic Games, three of the men's team placed in the top ten downhill event. But the women still took the top spot, as Kathy Kreiner won the giant slalom gold.

Kathy Kreiner, gold medallist, giant slalom, XIIth Olympic Winter Games, Innsbruck, Austria, 1976.

the house at Acton Vale (first clearing and clipping branches on her own with a chainsaw and Weedeater), perhaps remembering running through the same woods as a carefree child with her twin Rhoda. She began to subscribe to running magazines and bought books on running and setting goals. Soon she started entering competitions. At one ten-kilometre run in Montreal she remembers feeling all alone at the start line, doubly so because no one else spoke English, and she wondered if she might get lost on the course. "Beside me was a girl I spoke to, and asked her how far she ran each day. Eighteen miles, she said—to work. When we started, the girl took off with all the men. I certainly didn't have to worry about where to go. And it turns out she was our top racer who won the prestigious Boston Marathon! That was the year a woman took the subway part of the way and won, but this woman was declared the real winner after they found out." The woman who took the subway was Rosie Ruiz; the real winner was Quebecer Jacqueline Gareau.

Rhona kept training (sometimes with Nancy as she has described earlier, no matter how bad the blizzards were), running to the river and down its course, then around Mount Royal. In 1980, Rhona entered and completed the Montreal Marathon. After a lifetime of stellar achievements, she still calls it "the thrill of a lifetime."

Après-ski 1980–the present

FIFTY-NINE YEARS TO EIGHTY-FIVE YEARS...
...AND COUNTING

NEW CHANGES

Until they were twenty-six years old, Rhona and Rhoda had spent almost every waking moment together. Then love had separated them across the Great Divide. For another twelve years, each twin had to learn not only how to live with her husband, but also without her sister. When Rhona moved back to Montreal with her four children, the sisters were reunited. Things had changed, yet they continued to work together, still managed to fool a few people when they switched places, and were often perfectly matched competitors in skiing and, later, golf. Then nineteen years later, the twins would separate again.

> I celebrate myself,
> And what I assume
> you shall assume,
> For every atom
> belonging to me as
> good belongs to you.
>
> —Walt Whitman,
> *Leaves of Grass*

The province of Quebec where both lived had already been going through some separation anxiety of its own in the last few years. While North America was going through major changes in the 1960s, French Quebecers had struggled to keep their culture afloat in a sea of English. When the Parti Québécois came into power and introduced language laws favouring French, many companies packed up their head offices and began the trek "down the 401," the highway linking Montreal to Toronto. Between 1976 and 1981, more than 100,000 English speakers took the trip. Among the companies that moved was RCA Inc., the offices of Arnold Eaves. In 1979, Rhoda and Arnold joined the exodus west.

Although for her "everybody was in Montreal," the then fifty-seven-year-old Rhoda wasn't too worried. Since Arnold was already looking at retirement, she thought the move to Toronto would be for only three years. Arnold did retire in 1983, but by then the couple and their children were comfortably ensconced. "Now it's been twenty-six or twenty-seven years," says Rhoda. "That damn highway." Up to the present day, Rhoda has driven back and forth on the 401 a few times a month, first for the Ski Jays, then for Twinski events and to see family.

Back on the hills of St. Sauveur, things were changing too. After twenty-five years of teaching, in 1981 the twins decided to close down the Ski Jays Club. "It had more than served its purpose," they say. Thousands of Quebec youngsters had got their first taste of skiing and developed their skills under Rhona and Rhoda's tutelage. And running the clubs had taught the twins a lot too. At fifty-nine years of age, after untangling the kids and skis spilling from nineteen buses for innumerable Saturdays, they both thought it time to concentrate on their families and themselves.

Inside the Acton Vale church in their bathing suits, Margie Gillis (upper left) and Rhoda (upper right) prepare to scrape the ceiling. Here they push the scaffolding plank up a level with their heads. Rhoda painted the whole church and the lower reaches of the ceiling during the 1990s when she was in her 70s. On the floor, Rhona at left and Arnold at right survey the work.

That didn't mean they were about to slow down. A few years earlier in a newspaper interview, Rhoda had expressed an interest in a new craze: helicopter skiing in the Rockies. In the coming years, the twins would also try windsurfing, paraponting (skiing down a mountain with a parachute pack on your back that opens up to take you soaring, essentially paragliding on skis), and bungee jumping.

LOSING CHRISTOPHER... AND HIS FATHER

Like so many others at the start of the AIDS epidemic, Christopher Gillis was unaware that he was living at high risk: within the gay community of New York in the 1980s. And, like so many others, Christopher became infected with HIV, the virus that causes AIDS. By 1993, the symptoms of AIDS were impossible to ignore. "Mother, of course," Rhona says of herself, "was so stupid she didn't know anything. 'He has this thing but it's not AIDS,' I thought." She *hoped*. Rhona had heard of the illness. Just the year before, famed tennis player Arthur Ashe had revealed that he got the disease through blood transfusions during heart surgery; Ashe died in February of 1993. "Chris had had his appendix burst and they gave him blood," Rhona says, "so I thought he might have got it from the transfusion."

Rhona, Christopher, and Gene Gillis in 1952.

However he got it, that year Chris was in a New York hospital. "Mom was holding his hand in the hospital bed as he's dying," Margie says. "It's the last week. And he's not taking the morphine—or a fraction of what he could. Mom thinks it's great that he's decided to do that." It was just like old times. If Chris was going to fall, he was going to fall really well. Only then could he fly away.

"So they're discussing his illness like he took a fall and it was a sore knee," says Margie. "The pain threshold of Mom and Chris was incredibly high, like that of a cartoon character. And Mom just kept on handing out peppermints to Chris, which were her cure for everything. Of course, later on we find out that according to naturopathy, peppermint is used to speed recuperation." (According to natural healing practitioners, peppermint detoxifies and strengthens the body.)

By the end of the week, Christopher's physical daring, his sense of humour, and his calm and dignified centre were memories. The loss for the family was like no other, and left them "terribly affected."

Although Chris had always had the full support and love of his mother, even at Chris's death his estranged father kept his distance. "There was love waiting here for our father," says Margie, "but he did not come to it. He and his wife were just forty miles away from New York when Chris was dying, and they didn't come. It was Dad's loss."

Canine serenade: In recent years, Arnold and dachshund Max took to entertaining. 1989.

Before Chris' death, Gene had come back to see the family in Montreal; Margie remembers him showing up at her home just as she was being interviewed and filmed there by a television reporter; his timing, as on his last, rare visit, was impeccable. When Rhona saw her former husband again, "it didn't mean anything," she says. "Nancy saw him and he treated her like she was five years old, like when he left. It was like nothing had happened. By then he could hardly walk, all the old injuries, you know."

And yet, Margie tells of another time when Rhona wasn't quite so distant. It was around 2000, she says, when "Dad called Mom. He said, 'I want to come home.' And right away, Mom said 'Yes' without hesitation. After forty-six years. She never signed anything, you know. She never let him go."

With hindsight, the family now knows the phone call was the first symptom of the onset of Alzheimer's disease. Eventually, Gene's current wife intervened in the process of Gene trying to "come home." In 2005, at the age of eighty, Gene Allan Gillis passed away in Colorado. When an obituary in a ski magazine listed only his current family and children as mourners, Rhona and Rhoda had to send a letter reminding the Americans of their and their families' existence.

After years of being reluctant to travel, especially to Europe, Rhoda's husband Arnold eventually joined her on many ski trips to the Rockies, and to Austria and Switzerland. By the 1990s his

Margie and Chris dancing together, 1980s. If Chris had to fall, he was going to fall well. Only then could he fly away.

health began to fail. A quadruple bypass in 1994 and a third hip replacement in 1995 limited him to working out at the couple's condo gym and swimming pool. Today Rhoda usually makes the journey to see her family in Montreal alone.

Because of his health, Arnold was unable to travel to Holland for the observances of the fiftieth and sixtieth anniversary of the end of the war; he has not ever gone back to the country where he fought in a Sherman tank. However, the Government of the Netherlands presented him with a medal, which, says his son David, "He wore proudly with his other medals when he gave a speech at the local high school in November of 2005."

WHAT SKIING HAS BECOME TODAY

As the twins moved out of ski racing to instructing, then from instructing to skiing purely for the joy of it, the technology and even the psychology behind skiing changed drastically. In the 1930s and 1940s, skiing had been called "a great sport with great inconveniences." When they began skiing, the twins wore wool clothing, put leather boots with laces into flimsy bindings on heavy and long wooden skis. They had to wax their skis every few runs, and applying it was a long process that involved boiling tar and heating the skis over wood stoves. Then, skiers either had to tramp up the hill (sometimes for hours) to get to good skiing; when rope tows and early chair lifts appeared, wait lines still meant you had to wait for hours. The advantage was that there was hardly anybody else on the slopes: very few people were that dedicated, or that crazy.

Today more than two million Canadians own skis, with nearly a thousand ski areas and over fifty major ski resorts. The Canadian Ski Instructors Alliance has twenty thousand professional skiers. With ten million skiers and snowboarders in North America, skiing has become a multi-billion-dollar industry. And no wonder. Today's skiers step into stiff synthetic boots in safety-release bindings, all rigidly fastened to light, parabolic skis. Clothing fits well, keeps you warm and dry, and can make trail-blazing fashion statements. Trails are groomed and even the smallest ski areas have snow-making machinery. Gondolas and eight-chair lifts whisk you to the top of the mountain with very little waiting time. You don't have to be particularly daring to go skiing anymore—but the cost of lift tickets and ski equipment mean you still need to have a good amount of money.

Ski racing too is hardly recognizable as the same sport. In Rhona and Rhoda's heyday, racers climbed to the starting gate, often packed down the race course themselves by sidestepping up the hill, threaded through slalom gates cut from nearby Jack pines, and wore no helmets, goggles, or other protective gear. Of course, they didn't often reach speeds of 120 kilometres per hour either, which downhill racers regularly do today.

The appearance of a modern Canadian ski racer on the hills of the 1940s would probably have been greeted as an alien invasion. In their distinctive Spyder form-hugging suits, helmets, goggles, gloves and high-tech skis, bindings and boots, today's skiers do everything they can to shave hundredths of a second off their time.

It's not just appearances that have changed either. When Rhona and Rhoda represented Canada in St. Moritz, they were given ski equipment, outfits, and $50 spending money. For training, it was

Rhoda slaloming in 1943...

...and Brigitte Acton skiing today.

recommended they work outside at manual labour if possible. The Ski Team hoped to raise $25,000 for its ten-member team, but only scared up "a fraction of that." Behind the scenes in today's ski racing world, Canadian skiers receive far more attention—and money—than ever before. Right now the Alpine Canada team is gearing up for the 2010 Olympics in Vancouver. Once famous skier Ken Read, who heads the organization (and was "one of the principle architects" of Own the Podium, which is putting a total of $105 million towards all Olympic athletes), bumped up the total budget for the ski team in 2007 from $6 to $8 million dollars a year.

When Rhona and Rhoda raced, they were only allowed to use

The best **new invention**

When the twins are asked what is the most radical change they've seen in skiing since they began, they cite one thing: parabolic skis. Thin in the middle and wide at the ends, the skis "almost turn by themselves." Whenever a newcomer joins Twinski, Rhona and Rhoda immediately tell them to throw out their old skis and buy parabolic ones.

Speed

In today's downhill events, women average speeds of 112 km/h, men 136 km/h. The record is 156 km/h, set at Austria's Kitzbühel. The record for speed skiing, sanctioned by the FIS in 1960, is 251.4 km/h.

Photo courtesy GM of Canada

Canadian Alpine Ski Team member Brigitte Acton, of St. Jovite, Quebec, perfects her aerodynamic tuck position in General Motors' wind tunnel in Warren, Michigan, 2005.

the one pair of skis for every type of race (even if they burned them in applying wax). They were lucky to find one coach a few months before the Games. They also had a team manager. When their skis were late arriving in Switzerland, the twins had to borrow another pair from their US counterparts.

The Canadian Women's Ski Team today has nine racers, three of whom come from Quebec. It also has a full-time head coach, seven specialty coaches, four technicians, four physiotherapists, and four conditioning coaches. Most modern ski teams also include doctors, wax technicians, school teachers, and nutritionists. Sponsorship and fundraising organized by Alpine Canada has afforded them even more tweaking of performance, and is used for developing special clothing, wind-resistance testing in tunnels, and recovery programs for after races. The Canadian Men's Speed Team uses three trucks and two pick-ups to transport their gear to the training hill. World Cup skiers now arrive at practice hills with between fifteen and twenty-five sets of skis—each.

All of this concentrated push towards winning medals at the Olympics and World Championships bore early fruit: on the first day of the 2006 Winter Olympics at Torino, Jennifer Heil won a gold medal in the moguls. In speed skating, Cindy Klassen took an unprecedented five medals in one Games. That year saw Canadians take a record nineteen Olympic medals, fourteen of them won by women, a full 70 percent. Canadians have had a record thirteen World Cup and world championship Alpine medals this season (2006–2007); Jennifer Heil took the World Cup freestyle ski title in March 2007.

And yet, the program has found that there are not enough high-performance athletes in Canada, and are recruiting them from other sports. In-line skaters are being groomed for speed skating; and using John Eaves's example from so many years before, gymnasts are now recruited for freestyle skiing.

Rhona and Rhoda have watched these changes in the ski world. Some of the changes they've been thrilled with and embraced,

The Canadian Olympic Ski Team entering the parade at St. Moritz, 1948. At front, Rhona and Rhoda. Note Rhona checking Rhoda's left foot—which sports a non-matching ski boot a few sizes larger than usual.

like improved ski equipment. Some of the changes, notably in competition, leave them cold. There's so much pressure for team members now, they say; youngsters specialize in one field so early "that they're shutting the door on a lot of things," says Rhoda. The worst, the twins agree, is that it seems ski racing has "lost the sense of real fun." That was the driving force behind Rhona and Rhoda's career: they were thrilled to see which of them could make it down the hill faster.

"Kids are exposed to so much more now, and they're brighter and they're smarter," says Rhoda. "But they have to make decisions too soon, before they're ready. It becomes commercial so soon, with sponsors—the first thing after a race, up go the skis so people can see the brand. So you get kids egging each other on, scared but wanting to be the best, and they're getting hurt badly."

Contemporary racers reply to worries like this by saying that they're ready to work as hard as they have to anyway. They're also relieved that they're finally getting the attention. Not so long ago, some on the team had to go door to door raising funds for each race.

How would the twins have fit into today's training programs? They were doing "crazy things" themselves in the 1940s, the most memorable of which was going off the men's senior ski jump at eleven years old. During their racing years, they were always the first and last on the hill ("Why, they don't even wait until they have finished their apple pie and ice cream before they are back on the slopes," Hermann Gadner had said of their eagerness). On the other hand, the twins ran a ski school for children for decades; they learned a thing or two about pushing youngsters.

"I tried to do as much as Rhoda did in one day," says her niece Margie. "I ended up in bed for three days. But now I can do it—now that she's in her eighties."

"Look at aerials," says Rhoda. "John [Eaves] was in it early, and Bruce, and he had three somersaults with twists; now they have four and how many twists? The higher and farther they go, where are they going to end? Nancy did aerials too. I think she was the first girl to do a somersault. I think John taught her."

But for all the twins' (and their children's) ability to push their bodies and their minds to the farthest possibilities, they recognized that even they had limits. Before racing, the twins would always check the course, choose the right kind of wax, and make sure they were qualified to race it. John Eaves would make test runs of his stunts while attached to ropes before removing safety devices.

"But some of these kids aren't qualified to do things, and they dare each other and those are the ones that have terrible accidents. If they do it seriously, they do the tricks first in gymnastics or on a trampoline; then they do them landing in water so they're safe and don't get hurt. To do these things you have to be in such good condition."

All in all, says Rhona, "I'm not envious of skiers today. All the glamour, the television coverage, the stories made up—and not half of them true anyway."

And yet, Rhona and Rhoda's approach may be coming back in style. Recreational skiing, at least, is going through another sea

Rhoda and Rhona after a ninety-mile marathon at the Seigniory Club, Quebec, 1987. The twins had just reached retirement age. In 1985 both won gold medals for skiing seventy miles in two days in the Canadian Ski Marathon.

change. As skiing has become easier and easier to do, "Younger skiers and snowboarders are seeking more difficult ways to descend mountains." That's what John Fry, author of *The Story of Modern Skiing*, sees. Old equipment is being made anew. Adventurous skiers are avoiding ski resorts and their pampered trails, and instead heading for the kind of slopes Rhona and Rhoda found at Banff some fifty years ago—empty, full of powder, and riskier. Skiers are "unknowingly replicating the exploits of earlier skiers like Jackrabbit Johannsen and his friends, who bushwhacked their way down Mont Tremblant," says Fry. "Ski resorts have responded by constructing terrain parks bristling with halfpipes, bumps and jumps to hurl patrons in the air...the Laurentian pioneers would have approved."

The Laurentian pioneers Rhona and Rhoda certainly approve—if the skiers are qualified.

OLYMPIC SKI RACING
INTO THE NEW MILLENNIUM

Since the Wurtele twins were kept from the medal count in St. Moritz in the 1948 Olympic Winter Games, Canadian women began the long and difficult climb towards the podium to collect medals. Lucile Wheeler, Anne Heggtveit, and Nancy Greene began the wins in the late 1950s and 1960s. In 1970, Betsy Clifford took gold in world championship giant slalom, won the Alpine skiing World Cup in 1971, then took silver in the downhill in 1974. Kathy Kreiner won a 1974 World Cup giant slalom, then took gold in giant slalom at the 1976 Olympics. In the 1980s, Laurie Graham, Lisa Savijarvi, and Karen Percy gave the women's team a boost, with Percy taking two bronzes at the 1988 Calgary Games. Yet after Kerrin Lee-Gartner's prestigious gold in the downhill during the 1992 Albertville Olympic Games, Canadian women and men in Alpine skiing hit a slump—besides a men's bronze in downhill skiing in 1994, it was the last medal Canada won in Alpine skiing.

When Rhona and Rhoda went to St. Moritz, and earlier during the 1928 Games of the "Matchless Six," some thought women on the Canadian team would be a drain for the men. It turned out they were more of an embarrassment for the men because women won most of the medals. Women were still winning in 2006. Sixteen of Canada's twenty-four medals at Torino were won by women. In Albertville in 1992, one-quarter of the team were women; in 2006, they made up fully half of the team.

While today the Olympic ski teams are receiving a large push through programs like "Own the Podium" for the 2010 Vancouver Games (which Alpine Canada head Ken Read says represents $1.6 million of a total $8 million budget), today's women's Alpine ski team is still in a building process and many do not expect it to win big.

But Ski Alpine CEO Ken Read bristles when he hears talk like that. "It may have been the case in the Wurtele era that women were not considered important, but this was not the case when I was a member of the Team (1973 to 1983) and certainly is not the case today." With funding for the "ladies" team, in Read's words, the same as for the men's team, Alpine Ski Canada has a goal of four Olympic medals. "And we make no distinction as to who we hope lands on the podium—female or male."

"WE WERE PASSÉ"

In 1988, the *Montreal Gazette* ran a retrospective article on the Wurtele twins and their many accomplishments. Wrote Dick Bacon in February of that year, "Forty-four years later there have been women who have run faster, skied faster and won more medals [than the Wurteles]...But there have been none who did more things—athletically and artistically—better than these two laughing and delightfully identical twins. And certainly nobody can match their feats over the same span of time. And they're still going strong."

The living legacy of Canadian Women's Alpine skiing: at the Canadian Ski Instructors Alliance reunion with Rhoda, Lucile Wheeler, and Rhona; golfing at Gray Rocks, Quebec.

Yet, even as Canadian sportswomen continued to carry the torch initially lit by the Wurtele twins, Rhona and Rhoda were almost completely forgotten when the Winter Olympics came to Canada for the first time, in 1988 at Calgary.

Rhona and Rhoda were then sixty-six years old. Three of their children were scheduled to perform at Calgary: Margie had been asked to choreograph and dance a piece, and John and Bruce Eaves were involved in freestyle skiing as a demonstration sport. But as for the twins themselves, "We were passé," Rhona says. "People didn't think about us." Already visiting in Calgary before the Games, the twins waited patiently for an invitation. None came, but unfortunately it wasn't something new for Rhona and Rhoda.

> "The organizers of the Games probably missed the boat by not inviting them as special guests," Dick Bacon wrote in the *Gazette*. "The twins shrug off the oversight; they've been through it before. Two years ago [in 1986] the sponsors of the prestigious Harriman Cup races at Sun Valley, Idaho, marked the 50th anniversary of the

event with a reunion party of past performers in the race. They overlooked the Wurteles, both of whom were past winners.

"'That kind of hurt,' admitted Rhona, who once won the race by a full ten seconds in a sport that today measures victories in 100ths of a second.

"But being overlooked seems to come with the territory. They were members of the Canadian Sports Hall of Fame and the US and Ottawa Ski Halls of Fame long before their own Laurentian Zone accorded them the same honour last November."

Four pioneering ski stars today: from left, Peggy Johannsen Austin, daughter of Jackrabbit Johannsen; Lucile Wheeler Vaughn; Anne Heggtveit Hamilton; Linda Crutchfield. Penguin Ski Club reunion, November, 2000.

That same year, Rhona's daughter Margie Gillis was awarded an Order of Canada for her dancing. Attempts to get the twins nominated for the same honour have met with resistance. Ironically, three of their children were involved—one dancing at the ceremony, two others in exhibition events.

When at the last minute the twins finally did receive a call from Olympic organizers, they were already back in Montreal. Rhoda quickly suggested Lucile Wheeler as a special guest. "It hadn't occurred to them," Rhoda says. Wheeler had been the first Canadian skier to win a medal at an Olympic Games.

SHARING THE FLAME—KIND OF

The year before, as preparation for the first ever Canadian Winter Olympics heated up, organizers put together an Olympic Torch Relay called "Share the Flame." The longest relay in Olympic history, the torch (modelled after the Calgary Tower) was carried by noted and ordinary citizens across Canada (Canadians could enter a lottery to have a chance to run the flame for one kilometre). The relay began at Signal Hill in St. John's, Newfoundland, in November of 1987. None other than the twins' contemporary Barbara Ann Scott was the first to carry it, along with former Olympian Fred Hayward. The flame travelled 18,000 kilometres to Calgary, and arrived on February 13, 1988.

"Her two moms": Rhona, Margie and Rhoda during the 1988 Winter Olympics in Calgary, Alberta.

At least in this event, someone remembered the twins—kind of. They're still not sure which genius came up with the idea of asking only *one* of a pair of identical twins to "Share the Flame."

Eventually someone called Rhona to ask if she could run with the torch in Westmount; later he would call back and sheepishly wonder if the then sixty-six-year-old Rhona minded running with it in distant St. Eugene, *before dawn.* "Well, we were from Westmount," says Rhona, "and well-known here. So it was too bad. But I got up at four in the morning and went to St. Eugene and carried the torch."

"Why didn't you say, I'll carry it with my sister?" Rhoda asks her today.

"I don't know," Rhona says. "It was July. Whatever, you don't always think of all these things. But it was quite an experience because when I got out there I couldn't believe how excited these people were."

Predawn, St. Eugene, Ontario, 1988. Left to right, Rhoda, Olympic official ("He was there to make sure I didn't keel over"), Rhona carrying the flame.

Rhoda did end up coming along with Rhona, and Rhona's daughter Nancy came too. It shouldn't have been much of a problem for them to run one kilometre—after all, Rhona had just run a marathon a few years earlier, and had started running again to prepare for the relay. But "They get you so excited when you're out there with the torch. You kind of hyperventilate. At one point near the end of the run, I asked if I could walk the rest," Rhona admits. "I felt ridiculous. When I got in the van I felt sick. I was on such a high."

Fortunately, neither of the twins are the kind to hold grudges or spend their days wondering what might have been—skiing has always been too important to them to bother with official titles. For them, their record of wins says all you need to know. For others, their continuing work with beginning skiers, from four-year-olds to eighty-four-year-olds, is the mark of athletes truly dedicated to their sport.

There's something about the twins that is refreshingly anti-fame, yet they continue to attract people to themselves, inspiring loyalty all around them. Perhaps it has something to do with their being rough around the edges. They are well liked by friends and admired by colleagues, about the sweetest and most thoughtful superstars you'll ever meet; but as public relations people they may be too honest, too straightforward about what they like and don't like. And the public doesn't like celebrities to have rough edges. Normal people have rough edges. Celebrities are supposed to be different.

SLOWING DOWN, BUT NEVER STOPPING

When all is skied and done, the twins do not wait for accolades and recognition to come to them. After all, they didn't spend their lives waiting for the mountain to come to them either. By the time the twins were in their seventies during the 1990s, they were still trying new things; Rhona said she tried to do something active every day. Some days that meant going for a walk or short run. Other days, it meant kayaking or heli-skiing. Rhoda went windsurfing with her son John and his wife in recent years. Then there was the bungee jumping.

That was in 1995. Rhoda, at age seventy-three, didn't just take one fifty-metre plunge. No: the second jump was free, so she took advantage of that one too.

Always learning: Rhona and Rhoda heli-skiing and taking "skills drills" ski school in Panorama, B.C., 1991.

Around the same time, the twins tried paraponting in Europe. The sport involves skiing down a hill with a harness attached to a parachute glider until the skier rises into the air. Experienced paraponters can stay up in the air for four hours. The twins didn't go that long, but they did take off by themselves, under the direction of John Eaves.

A decade later, around Christmas in 2006, Rhoda's son John gave his mom and Rhona another gift. He appreciated that they were getting older and slowing down a little. The gift was a trip to the Caribous in B.C. Except it wasn't a tidy little sight-seeing voyage. They were going heli-skiing—at eighty-four years old.

Since then, Rhona especially has come to experience a few new limitations. Her eyesight has worsened, she has lost hearing in one ear, and still deals with a back injury. Besides skiing (they occasionally slalom race for fundraisers like the Breath of Life),

When Rhona and Rhoda went with Twinski to Corvatch at St. Moritz, Switzerland, in 1994, they ran into John Eaves filming *Fire, Ice and Dynamite*—a title that pretty well sums up their approach to life.

the twins still keep golfing. "It's a challenge, and something we can do," says Rhona. "Well, actually I don't do it properly now because I can't see well. And my balance is ungodly. But you see the birds and the bees and the flowers and the trees."

But apparently, the twins have kept the competitive edge that led to so many one-two wins in their racing days. "I'm still surprised by their competitiveness," says Margie Gillis, who calls Rhona and Rhoda "my moms". "When Rhona goes biking, she puts the edge on, she comes chasing me down. Then she passes me with a huge grin on her face. She takes great pleasure in beating Nancy and me."

Yet for Margie, the twins have something glowing from inside that is just as indomitable as their physical prowess. "Seeing their youth and beauty during their heyday is very special for me. They have a radiance, and you sense that they know the sun is always shining. They remained steadfast with lovingness," she says.

But while Margie says she inherited courage from her mother, there are still things that surprise her about Rhona. "I'm better at coping with the world than she is. My mom thinks she knows what hell is because of parking tickets. She's not good with numbers. And she surprises me sometimes, like with the way she and Rhoda dealt with car repairs—they felt a man had to do it. Why for only this area did they need a man, when in everything else they were equal? Sometimes," says Margie, "it slips out that they come from a different time."

Nancy still finds time to go with Rhona every week in the winter to instruct with Twinski; she drives her mother and helps her out. "I'd be a full-time ski bum if I could," she admits. Like her sister Margie, Nancy is still impressed with the indomitable spirit of her mother. "She has an optimistic hope that tomorrow will always be a better day," Nancy says. "If you want to feel good, or if you need sympathy, you call her."

In 2002 the twins were back at Panorama with Twinski.

THE SPIRIT OF FUN

When the *Montreal Gazette* looked in on the twins again in 1991, they found that "nothing has dulled their love of skiing, sense of humour, or infectious talent for bringing out the best in people." (At the time, their *older* sister Jean was still skiing with the club.) The same is true today, when the twins are eighty-five years old. It is that love of taking other people on the ride with them that will always be there. It was in 1938 that the twins first became certified ski instructors, almost seventy years ago. And they have led Twinski for more than forty years.

While the ski club started out helping housewives get out of the kitchen and onto the hills, the club has evolved to fulfill different needs over the years. As the club members' husbands retired, they began inviting them to the hill too—it was better

KEEPING UP **WITH THE TWINS**

Lou Lukanovich and his wife Jean on the far right with Rhona and Rhoda after a Twinski summer day of kayaking, July 2006.

In the 1960s, Lou Lukanovich helped Rhona and Rhoda teach skiing to the young Ski Jays. A former Olympian as well (he competed in the 1960 Rome Olympics in canoe/kayak racing), Lukanovich eventually left ski instructing to begin a business in Montreal and Europe. In 1989 he and his wife Jean joined Twinski after member Ami Bard told him about the club.

After twenty-five years, Lou then returned to teach skiing again with the twins. "I noticed that Rhona and Rhoda had not changed much," says Lukanovich.

"'It is good to see you, Lou,' Rhona said. 'I have a good class for you. But there are a few problems.'

"'What problems?'

"'There's one girl with two hip replacements, one with one hip replacement, and one had a stroke six months ago. But I think you can handle it.'

"I thought to myself, How can I handle this?" says Lukanovich. "Remember, this was the early '90s when very few doctors would think that skiing with hip replacements was okay. Well, the ladies, Mary Iversen, Joan Bonnet, and Elfie Valenta, were ready for it, so why not me? I said, 'Okay, sounds good, see you on the hill.'"

That was the big difference between Twinski and other ski schools at the time, Lukanovich says. It defined the spirit of the twins: Never give up, have a good quality of life, play and enjoy it.

"When I look around I can see that this makes us young," Lukanovich says. "We may not necessarily live longer, but we will belong to a like-minded group, have and make good friends, and contribute to having a good quality of life from fifty to eighty years old and beyond. This motivated me to begin with and it continues to motivate me to be with the twins for as long as I am useful and can physically keep up."

Lou Lukanovich is the owner of Simon River Sports, a canoe and kayak maker in the Quebec Laurentians. A member of the Order of Canada, he is also the Director of the Canadian Canoe Association.

than them staying at home resenting the women having all the fun. Today the club no longer takes on "rank beginners," and the twins let a group of carefully selected instructors (including Nancy Gillis Andersen) lead the teaching. Skiers come mostly from the Montreal area—West Island, NDG, Westmount, and the Town of Mount Royal, and a few come from the Laurentians or Eastern Ontario, Rhoda not the least of them. The club—these days numbering around 100 people—regularly meets at St. Sauveur and Mont Tremblant over the winter. Rhona runs the Wednesday ski outings in the Laurentians and the summer jaunts (one day a month the club goes golfing, biking, kayaking or swimming), and Rhoda takes care of organizing the two ski trips per season, one to the Canadian West and one to the European Alps. Those trips have been going on since the late 1960s, and the twins show no signs of giving them up. [For a full listing of Twinski Travellers voyages, see the appendix at the back of this book.]

There would probably be howls of protest if they tried to stop them anyway. With their unfailing energy and enthusiasm always evident, the twins inspire those around them to reach for their own personal best—and inspire devotion and respect from the youngsters around them. "It's sort of good therapy," says Rhona, "and an awful lot of good friendships are formed." With an emphasis on healthy living and a spirit of fun, the club attracts people at retirement age who want to get back into skiing; suddenly they find themselves on the ski slopes once a week. At a recent ski outing, the "girls" (that's how club members refer to themselves) announced a few birthdays in the group. Most of them were in their seventies or eighties. One man was turning eighty-nine, and had spent the day skiing in the light rain of a January morning.

Back in February of 1944, when Rhona and Rhoda were twenty-two years old, *Maclean's* magazine interviewed the rising stars. "The sisters expect to go on skiing until a day or so before they die," the magazine said, "believing firmly in the axiom that skiing is a sport enjoyed by people from eight to 80."

There is little else in the world like the sight of a full room of seventy-year-olds cutting loose after a day of skiing. At the St. Sauveur Ski Hill it is Twinski's Crazy Hat Day. To close off a season of skiing, members form groups, dress up in silly costumes, and perform skits or songs. It is, one imagines, a bit like attending an innocent and hilarious high school party back in the 1940s, except for the absence of bobby socks and saddle shoes. Two annual prizes are given out as well: the Doris Molson and the Libby Elder trophies (named after two of the twins' friends; Libby was the one who floated down the river with Rhona on an ice floe), to two members for their contributions to the club. The twins love giving gifts and prizes; they collected so many throughout the years themselves. But none of the awards are for who came in first (or second) in a race. They are rewarding those who have the most fun.

Despite the silliness, Rhona remains conscious of her physical conditioning, says her daughter Nancy. "She's been conditioning ever since the army finally came out with exercises for women; she always goes out for her walk, and has to get home and get on her bike. When she found out she was going to the Monashees for heli-skiing she over-trained, and got a cold. For her the hardest part of it for her was trying to see. She had to rip her goggles off and close one eye." After the trip Rhona felt she had to give her fitness trainer daughter some serious advice about having that kind of fun. "She said to me, 'If you ever go on a trip like that you make sure you're in shape.' Right. Thanks, Rhona."

In 2006, the Laurentian Ski Museum inducted the Twinski Club into their Hall of Fame, adding yet another prize to Rhona and Rhoda's trophy cases. The club was named because of the contribution it has made to skiing in the Laurentians. It may as well have been for promoting the enjoyment of life itself.

Shortly after accepting the honour, Rhona and Rhoda took forty youngsters under eighty, including some family members, to the Panorama and Kicking Horse ski resorts in B.C. Even John showed up; he had to leave early to go film a group going heli-skiing in the Indian Himalayas. The twins were happy to have their family with them, they said.

Margie Gillis saw the vacation from another angle.

"They were skiing, and Rhoda had a bad knee, and Rhona was hung up in a tree somewhere. They were tired. So Nancy and David who were with them said, 'Why don't you go back to the hotel and pack?' It was the last day.

"Later Nancy goes back to check on them. She sees them lying on the bed, packing a bit. And they're saying to each other, 'Yeah, I think you're right. Next time let's not bring the kids. They really put a damper on things."

Rhoda windsurfing at Lake Memphremagog, Quebec, 2000—at seventy-eight years old. "I love that sport," Rhoda says.

After a lifetime of racing, thrills, and celebrity, today "I like watching things grow," Rhona says. "I like being alone, I like the peace and quiet at Acton Vale." She'd much sooner putt around the yard and garden these days, exercise and bicycle. In the summer Rhona gets up at 5:30 a.m. and plays 18 holes five times a week when she's at Acton Vale; she also spends a lot of time keeping the 145 year-old house alive.

"She's a great idea person," practical Rhoda says. " 'Course, it's the follow-up that's important."

Rhoda is the follow-up person. She used to paint pictures more than she does today. But her excuse is not that it's too difficult. "It's not very inspiring in Toronto," she says. "And there's too many things going on now." One gets the feeling that there will always be too many things going on in Rhoda's life. That's exactly the way she likes it.

Some days more than others the twins will admit to a few fail-

FEAR **AND** **THE** FEARLESS

By Mary Iversen and Sue Godber

Photo courtesy of Sue Godber

Mary Iversen and Sue Godber, 1989.

"It was ten a.m. at the top of Blackcomb Mountain when Rhoda and Rhona met us beside a sign that read, 'Do not go beyond ropes. This area out-of-bounds.'

"They had two big smiles. 'Come on girls,' they said, 'follow us. We have to go quickly because at noon the snow melts and the avalanches start.'

"'We aren't good enough to follow you two,' we said, 'and anyway, we don't want to be air-lifted out at a horrendous cost and sent to jail.'

"'Come on, follow us. You can do it. It's easy and it's a fabulous run on the best snow field in the Rockies!'

"It was a cloudless day, the snow was sparkling, and Rhoda and Rhona were so convincing about us having the run of our lives. What else could we do?

"We climbed fifty or sixty snow stairs, holding onto our skis and poles, arriving at a narrow ledge that seemed to fall hundreds of feet away on both sides. Shaking with fear of heights, Mary led the way. Sue followed on her stomach. Voices from somewhere below us called.

"'Give us your skis and poles.'

"There were the twins, skiing along the sides of the drop-off, with camera equipment dangling from their necks and wanting us to give them our equipment to carry. What a fearless twosome, always ready to help anybody at anytime, anywhere.

"The mile-long (or more) snowfield beckoned us, and after adjusting our skis and bindings, we began our descent following Rhona and Rhoda. Fortunately they stopped to take pictures, thus allowing us to catch up to them and catch our breath.

"We didn't dare look south as we heard roars of snow falling down the cliffs. We were still numb with fear but elated at the same time. Never had we skied on three inches of virgin snow over a firm base. It was a once in a lifetime experience for which we were so grateful to the twins—they had faith in us and gave us a fabulous day to remember."

Mary Iversen and Sue Godber have been Twinski members since the 1960s.

ings. They have more trouble communicating than they used to. Ironically, because of that they find they need each other more. "Before we just sort of understood what was going on," says Rhona. "Not now. I don't hear what Rhoda says. She's got to look me in the eyes if she wants me to hear. And she doesn't."

"Works both ways," says Rhoda.

"I hear a quarter of what she says. But I can't do anything about it. I've got a tumour in my head that's killed the nerves in the ear. A hearing aid or operation wouldn't bring any hearing back. So being in crowds is nerve-racking; I can't figure out what's being said. And my eyes aren't helping." After several operations, her eyesight is still not what it used to be. "It's annoying, because it's limiting. And on the ski tours, Rhoda better not get out of sight 'cause I won't know where I am. I'm dependent on her."

For Rhona and Rhoda, being identical twins doubled the power that each woman had on her own. They pushed each other, they fought for things together, they doubled their enjoyment of everything together. In hard times they supported each other as best they could. When they were close, they were so close that during races they had identical finish times, down to the fraction of a second. Because of that, they achieved what no woman—never mind two women—had done before. And that taste of absolute freedom, the expectation that they could do what they wanted, when they wanted, would stay with Rhona and Rhoda forever. They always had each other, no matter where the other was.

It was that single-mindedness of twins that made them heroes for a generation—and almost unrecognized heroes for all women in Canadian sport today. In the first ski clubs that began around Montreal, women only came as guests of men. Because Rhona and Rhoda didn't care what people thought they became ground-breakers and pioneers in women's sport, and even in the women's movement in general. But they would never take the credit themselves.

"Oh, we were just having fun," they'd say, with impish grins that haven't quite worn off since their childhood.

But in the meantime, they changed the way women were seen.

"They were a force to be reckoned with—as a duo," says Margie Gillis. "They bounced off each other. They sheltered each other from the storm. And they would immediately drop something if it didn't work. The fun stuff, they believed, is where you can go the furthest. It's like they're dangerous children: you've got to keep an eye on them. I've seen them do miracles.

"I would be completely unsurprised if someone told me, 'The twins were up on the roof and walked off, stood in the air for three minutes, then turned around and walked back on the roof.'"

"Oh, we were just having fun," the twins would say, with impish grins—that haven't quite worn off since their childhood.

The end

Rhoda and Rhona celebrate their 85th birthday, at a party given by Twinskiers, Montreal 2007.

EPILOGUE

We lived in North Carolina and had never heard of TWINSKI. We knew nothing of Rhoda or Rhona – all we knew was that we were at the top of a mountain called Big White, it was our first time there, our first day skiing that year, -- and the fog was so thick you couldn't see five feet.

Trying to follow a trail map was impossible; we couldn't see to read the signs, so my husband and I stood there, not knowing where to go, or what to do. Suddenly a green ski-suit went by. I said, "Let's follow, just keep enough distance so we can stop if he goes over a cliff or something!"

We fell in behind this beautiful rhythmical skier, who went down the slope doing lovely even turns – a joy to follow! When he finally stopped we skied up to what turned out to be a lady with a great smile. We explained our situation and asked if we could keep on following her – to which she replied, "Sure, we're here with a whole gang from Montreal and you're welcome to ski with us." We couldn't see a 'gang' as the fog was still very thick, and all we tried to do was follow that green suit down the hill.

We skied behind her for quite a while – never worrying about where we were or what run we were on - just enjoying following a lovely skier. Suddenly the fog disappeared, the sun came out and we could SEE the mountain.

Feeling that we had imposed on her long enough, we thanked our green guiding angel and watched her ski off with her gang. We took off in the other direction, went around a corner, through some trees, when suddenly there she was again!! My husband and I were both stunned – I skied up to her and asked "How did you do that?" - "Do what?" asked the green-suited lady with the beautiful smile. "You went the other way. We watched you ski down – how did you get here?" "Oh, you must have been skiing with my twin sister." [I still don't know if it was Rhoda or Rhona that first morning] We had NO IDEA that there were two identical great skiers, in identical green outfits, so when we got over that first shock, we all thought it was a very funny situation and told that story to our friends many times over the years!

But we're not done yet!

As we lived in North Carolina and our skiing was limited to only one week per year – we went with SKICAN – they sent us a catalogue and did all the arrangements. The following year we tried a different area, and met the Twinski group AGAIN. We joined them for a few runs when we accidentally met on the hill, and chatted with them at the wine & cheese, saying what a lucky coincidence it was that we'd picked the same area and the same week.

To make this story shorter, I'll tell you that for four years we accidentally picked the same week and the same four areas as TWINSKI. We were accepted into their wonderful group, and made great friends. We decided that this was just too much fun to chance ever missing them, so we begged to be adopted by them as "out-of-country, unofficial honorary members". For the past 6 seasons we've made sure that our "one-week-a-year" ski trip is wherever Twinski decide to go. We'll be forever grateful that we followed a beautiful green suit on that socked-in morning at Big White!

Thanks, Rhona and Rhoda!

Elizabeth & David Lepore

APPENDIX

THE RACING YEARS

Note: a Combined event is the tallied results of the Downhill and Slalom races (sometimes the Giant Slalom race). Results given here are usually for 1st place unless there is a 2nd or 3rd place in a noteworthy race. For instance, Sugar Bowl's Silver Belt race, Sun Valley's Harriman Cup, and Aspen's Roch Cup were pre-cursors of the modern day World Cup Circuit.

PARTIAL COMPETITIVE RECORD, RHONA WURTELE GILLIS

1942 2nd place, Downhill event, Ladies' International Ski Meet, Mont Tremblant, Qc

1943 1st place, Downhill event, Ladies' International Meet, Lake Placid, NY, USA
1st place, Combined event, Ladies' International Meet, Lake Placid, NY, USA
2nd place, Taschereau Downhill, Mont Tremblant, Qc

1944 1st place, Downhill event, Kate Smith International, Lake Placid, NY, USA
1st place, Combined event, Kate Smith International, Lake Placid, NY, USA
1st place, Downhill event, Ladies' International Meet, Ste Marguerite, Qc
1st place, Combined event, Ladies' International Meet, Ste Marguerite, Qc
Winner, Colonial Airways Trophy

1945 1st place, Slalom event, Laurentian Zone Champ.'s, Gray Rocks, Qc
1st place, Taschereau Downhill, Mont Tremblant, Qc
1st place, Downhill event, Ladies' International Meet, Ste Marguerite, Qc
1st place, Slalom event, Alta Cup, Alta, Utah, USA
3rd place, Combined event, Alta Cup, Alta, Utah, USA
2nd place, Giant Slalom event, Teton Spring Ski Derby, Jackson Hole, Wyoming, USA

1946 1st place, Downhill event, Ontario Ladies Meet, Collingwood, On
1st place, Slalom event, Ontario Ladies Meet, Collingwood, On
1st place, Combined event, Ontario Ladies Meet, Collingwood, On
1st place, Slalom event, Ladies' International Meet, Lake Placid, NY, USA
1st place, Combined event, Ladies' International Meet, Lake Placid, NY, USA
1st place, Slalom event, United States Eastern National Champ.'s, Franconia, New Hampshire USA
1st place, Combined event, United States Eastern National Champ.'s, Franconia, New Hampshire, USA
1st place, Giant Slalom event, Alta Cup Races, Alta, Utah, USA
1st place, Downhill event, Alta Cup Races, Alta, Utah, USA
1st place, Combined event, Alta Cup Races, Alta, Utah, USA

1947 1st place, Downhill event, United States Eastern National Champ.'s, Pico Peak, Vermont, USA
1st place, Combined event, United States Eastern National Champ.'s, Pico Peak, Vermont, USA
1st place, Slalom event, Ladies' International Meet, Mont Gabriel, Qc
1st place, Combined event, Ladies' International Meet, Mont Gabriel, Qc
1st place, Slalom event, Laurentian Zone Champ.'s, Shawbridge, Qc
1st place, Taschereau Downhill, Mont Tremblant, Qc
1st place, Slalom event, Kate Smith International, Lake Placid, NY, USA
1st place, Combined event, Kate Smith International, Lake Placid, NY, USA
1st place, Downhill event, Dominion (Canadian) Ski Champ.'s, Mont Ste. Anne, Qc
2nd place, Slalom event, Dominion Champ.'s, Mont Ste. Anne, Qc
1st place, Combined event, Dominion Champ.'s, Mont Ste. Anne, Qc
2nd place, Downhill event, United States National Champ.'s, Ogden, Utah, USA
3rd place, Slalom event, Far West Kandahar, Mt Hood, Oregon, USA
1st place, Giant Slalom event, Teton Spring Ski Derby, Jackson Hole, Wyoming, USA

1948 Selected to represent Canada on the women's alpine team at the V Olympic Winter Games, St. Moritz, Switzerland. Rhona suffers a head wound and infection in training, then breaks an ankle halfway through the downhill race. She finishes the race.

1949 3rd place, Downhill, US Champ.'s, Whitefish, Montana, USA
Named to the US Federation Internationale de Ski (FIS) World Championship Team
3rd place, Downhill, Roch Cup Derby, Aspen, Colorado, USA
3rd place, Giant Slalom event, Silver Dollar Ski Derby, Reno, Nevada, USA

1952 1st place, Combined event, Golden Rose, Mount Hood, Oregon, USA
1st place, Giant Slalom event, United States National Champ.'s, Alta, Utah, USA
1st place, Downhill event, Harriman Cup, Sun Valley, Idaho, USA
Idaho State Diving Champion, and winner 100-yards freestyle swimming race

1954 3rd place, Downhill event, Harriman Cup, Sun Valley, Idaho, USA

1956 2nd place, Slalom event, Harriman Cup, Sun Valley, Idaho, USA

PARTIAL COMPETITIVE RECORD, RHODA WURTELE EAVES

1942 1st place, Downhill event, Ladies' International Ski Meet, Mont Tremblant, Qc
1st place, Taschereau Downhill, Mont Tremblant, Qc

1943 1st place, Downhill event, Laurentian Zone Champ.'s, Mt Baldy, Qc
1st place, Downhill event, International Ladies Meet, Mont Tremblant, Qc
1st place, Slalom event, International Ladies Meet, Mont Tremblant, Qc
1st place, Taschereau Downhill, Mont Tremblant, Qc

1944 1st place, Slalom event, Ladies' International Ski Meet, Mont Tremblant, Qc
1st place, Taschereau Downhill, Mont Tremblant, Qc
2nd place, Slalom event, Kate Smith International, Lake Placid, NY, USA
1st place, Slalom event, Laurentian Zone, Mont Gabriel, Qc
1st place, Downhill event, Laurentian Zone, Mt Baldy, Qc

1945 1st place, Combined event, Laurentian Zone Champ.'s, Mt Baldy, Qc
1st place, Downhill event, Ontario Ladies Meet, Collingwood, On
1st place, Slalom event, Ontario Ladies Meet, Collingwood, On
1st place, Combined event, Ontario Ladies Meet, Collingwood, On
2nd place, Combined event, Alta Cup, Alta, Utah, USA
3rd place, Giant Slalom event, Teton Spring Ski Derby, Jackson Hole, Wyoming, USA
Winner, Colonial Airways Trophy

1946 1st place, Taschereau Downhill, Mont Tremblant, Qc
2nd place, Downhill event, Ontario Ladies Meet, Collingwood, On
2nd place, Slalom event, Ontario Ladies Meet, Collingwood, On
2nd place, Combined event, Ontario Ladies Meet, Collingwood, On
1st place, Slalom event, Laurentian Zone, Mont Gabriel, Qc
1st place, Downhill event, Laurentian Zone, Mount Baldy, Qc
1st place, Combined event, Laurentian Zone, Mount Baldy, Qc
1st place, Slalom event, Great Divide Ski Cup, Banff, Ab
1st place, Silver Belt Trophy, Sugar Bowl, California, USA

1947 1st place, Slalom event, United States Eastern National Champ.'s, Pico Peak, Vermont, USA
2nd place, Combined event, United States Eastern National Champ.'s, Pico Peak, Vermont, USA
1st place, Downhill event, Ladies' International Meet, Mont Gabriel, Qc
1st place, Downhill event, Laurentian Zone Champ.'s, Mount Baldy, Qc
1st place, Slalom event, Dominion Champ.'s, Mont Ste. Anne, Qc
2nd place, Downhill event, Dominion Ski Champ.'s, Mont Ste. Anne, Qc
1st place, Downhill event, United States National Champ.'s, Ogden, Utah, USA
1st place, Combined event, United States National Champ.'s, Ogden, Utah, USA
2nd place, Slalom event, Silver Dollar Ski Derby, Reno, Nevada, USA
3rd place, Combined event, Silver Dollar Ski Derby, Reno, Nevada, USA
2nd place, Slalom event, Far West Kandahar, Mt Hood, Oregon, USA
1st place, Silver Belt Trophy Race, Sugar Bowl, California, USA

1948 Selected to represent Canada on the women's alpine team at the V Olympic Winter Games, St. Moritz, Switzerland. Unable to compete due to an injury during training.

3rd place, Arlberg Kandahar Downhill, Chamonix, France (First North American woman in top three)
1st place, Shot Put, Provincial Record, Quebec Track & Field Champ.'s (Olympic Trials), Montreal, Qc
1st place, Discus throw, Quebec Track & Field Champ.'s (Olympic Trials), Montreal, Qc
1st place, Softball throw, Quebec Track & Field Champ.'s (Olympic Trials), Montreal, Qc
1st place, High Jump, Quebec Track & Field Champ.'s (Olympic Trials), Montreal, Qc
1st place, Provincial Record, Javelin throw, Quebec Track & Field Champ.'s (Olympic Trials), Montreal, Qc

1949 1st place, Downhill event, Laurentian Zone Champ.'s, Mount Baldy, Qc
1st place, Slalom event, Laurentian Zone Champ.'s, Mount Baldy, Qc
1st place, Combined event, Laurentian Zone Champ.'s, Mount Baldy, Qc
1st place, Slalom event, Kate Smith International, Lake Placid, NY, USA
1st place, Downhill event, Kate Smith International, Lake Placid, NY, USA
1st place, Combined event, Kate Smith International, Lake Placid, NY, USA
1st place, Downhill event, Dominion Champ.'s, Mont Tremblant, Qc
2nd place, Slalom event, Dominion Champ.'s, Mont Tremblant, Qc
2nd place, Combined event, Dominion Champ.'s, Mont Tremblant, Qc
2nd place, Downhill event, US Champ.'s, Whitefish, Montana, USA
1st place, two Downhill events, Roch Cup Derby, Aspen, Colorado, USA
1st place, Downhill event, North American Champ.'s, Aspen, Colorado, USA
2nd place, Combined event, North American Champ.'s, Aspen, Colorado, USA

1951 1st place, Downhill event, Kate Smith International, Lake Placid, NY, USA
1st place, Slalom event, Kate Smith International, Lake Placid, NY, USA
1st place, Combined event, Kate Smith International, Lake Placid, NY, USA
1st place, Downhill event, Dominion Champ.'s, Mont Tremblant, Qc
1st place, Slalom event, Dominion Champ.'s, Mont Tremblant, Qc
1st place, Combined event, Dominion Champ.'s, Mont Tremblant, Qc
1st place, Slalom event, Quebec Kandahar, Mont Tremblant, Qc
1st place, Combined event, Quebec Kandahar, Mont Tremblant, Qc
1st place, Downhill event, Harriman Cup, Sun Valley, Idaho, USA
1st place, Combined event, Harriman Cup, Sun Valley, Idaho, USA
1st place, Giant Slalom event, Canadian Olympic Trials, Mount Norquay, Ab
1st place, Downhill event, Canadian Olympic Trials, Mount Norquay, Ab
1st place, Slalom event, Canadian Olympic Trials, Mount Norquay, Ab

1952 Selected to represent Canada on the Women's Alpine team at the VI Olympic Winter Games, Oslo, Norway; finished 9th place in the Downhill event.

1st place, Slalom event, Holmenkollen Races, Norway
1st place, Giant Slalom event, Holmenkollen Races, Norway
1st place, Combined event, Holmenkollen Races, Norway
2nd place, Downhill event, Parsenn, Davos, Switzerland
2nd place, Hannes Schneider Pokal, St. Anton, Austria
2nd place, Dorftalli Giant Slalom, Davos, Switzerland

1959 1st place, Giant Slalom event, Kirchberg, Austria
Named manager & assistant coach for the Canadian Women's Alpine team in Europe.

MAJOR SPORTS **MILESTONES**

Rhona and Rhoda's Sporting Life over Seven Decades

1941 Twins become members of Penguin Ski Club.

1943 Twins take Canadian Ski Instructors Alliance (CSIA) course—and are still updated members with their Level III.

1944 Rhona wins Colonial Airways Trophy, for the most outstanding skier, Laurentians.

1945 Rhona and Rhoda are jointly named Canada's Most Outstanding Woman Athlete (sic) of 1944 by the Women's Amateur Athletic Federation and receive the Velma Springstead Rose Bowl.

1946 Rhoda wins Colonial Airways Trophy for the most outstanding skier, Laurentians. Rhona and Rhoda are runners-up for the Lou Marsh Trophy, given by the Canadian Press to Canada's Most Outstanding Athlete.

1947 The twins are declared eligible for Class A competitive rating by the Laurentian Zone Ratings Committee. They are named to the Canadian Olympic Ski Team.

1948 Twins are the only members of Canada's first official Olympic women's alpine ski team and travel to St. Moritz, Switzerland. Injuries prevent Rhoda from competing; Rhona suffers a head wound and infection in training, then breaks an ankle halfway through the downhill race. She finishes the race.

1950 Rhona named to USA FIS World Championship Team. Rhoda named to Canadian Track and Field team for British Empire Games in Australia.

1952 Rhoda named to Canadian Olympic Ski Team, for the VI Olympic Winter Games, Oslo, Norway; Rhoda wins Holmenkollen Combined, Norway.

1953 Twins both inducted into Canadian Amateur Athletic Hall of Fame for both their skiing and swimming achievements.

1956 Rhoda begins to manage the Ski Jays, a girls ski school and club founded and run by the Penguins, which continues until 1982.

1959 Rhoda named as manager and assistant coach for the Canadian Women's Ski Team in Europe.

1961 Rhona joins Rhoda in directing the Ski Jay Club, taking over Ski Chicks.

1964 Twins begin Twinski Club for adult women.

1969 Rhona and Rhoda inducted into US National Ski Hall of Fame.

1972 Twins begin regular Twinski trips to Europe and Canadian West.

1981 Rhona runs the Montreal Marathon in 4 hours, 50 minutes.

1982 Twins inducted into the Canadian Ski Hall of Fame, Canadian Ski Museum.

1985 Both Rhona and Rhoda receive Gold Pin for completing seventy miles in two days in Canadian Ski Marathon.

1986 Twins inducted into the Laurentian Ski Museum's Hall of Fame.

1988 Twins inducted into the Musée du Ski de Québec. Twins featured in *Skier's Dream* movie, where they perform paraponting.

1998 Rhona and Rhoda receive the YWCA Award for "Women of Distinction."

2001 Named "Canadian Skiers of Distinction" by *Ski Canada* magazine's Honour Roll 2001.

2005 Rhona and Rhoda's Twinski Club is inducted into the Laurentian Ski Museum's Hall of Fame.

2008 Twins receive honorary 4th level pins from the Canadian Ski Instructors Alliance.

2009 Twins receive Trafalgar School for Girls Distinguished Alumnae Award.

TWINSKI CLUB **TRAVELLERS**

A legacy of trips to the top ski areas in the world

1967 With the Twinski Club in full swing, Penguin Club skier Anne Campbell and employee of MacGregor Travel asked if the Club would be interested in taking members on a European ski holiday. Rhoda was game, and got together a small but enthusiastic group, including Betty Galbraith Cornell Houghton, Sheila Naimen and old chum Libby Elder Taylor. The group spent four days at Lech am Arlberg, Hannes Schneider's skiing home in Austria. They then went to where Rhona and Rhoda had trained for the 1948 Olympics, Davos, Switzerland for another four days. The flight, motorcoach in Europe, hotels, breakfast, lunch and dinner, "heating charges," tips and taxes came to a grand total of $495 for each person.

1972 The next trip came in 1972 when the club was invited by Robin Nasmith of SkiCan to come to Banff. This time 28 people joined the twins at Sunshine, Norquay and Lake Louise for a week during March (cost: $239 each). That trip began the tradition of an annual ski voyage in early Spring, often with one trip to Europe and one to the Rockies in North America.

1973 "Twinski West" – Banff, Norquay and Lake Louise.

1974 *Europe*: Crans Montana and Verbier, Switzerland. Forty people attended this first European ski vacation.
West: Banff

1975 *Europe*: Lech, Austria, and Engelberg, Switzerland.
West: Banff

1976 *Europe*: Mirabel and Val d'Isère, France.
West: Snowmass Colorado. Attendance increased to 55 people for this trip.

1977 *Europe*: St. Anton, Austria and Laxx Flims, Switzerland.

1978 *Europe*: Les Arc – Meribel, France.

1979 *West*: Whistler, BC.

1980 *West*: Whistler, BC.

1981 *West*: Whistler, BC.

1982 *Europe*: La Plagne, France and Verbier, Switzerland.

1983 *Europe*: Val Thorens and Tignes, France.

1984 *Europe*: Lech, Austria and Davos, Switzerland.

1985 *Europe*: Schruns and Solden, Austria.

1986 *Europe*: Ischgl & Lech, Austria.

1987 *Europe*: Crans Montana & Grindelwald, Switzerland. On this trip the twins met up with their Swiss racing friends from 1948.
West: Whistler, BC.

1988 *Europe*: Bad Gastein and Kitzbühel, Austria.
West: Whistler Blackcomb, BC.

1989 *Europe*: La Clusaz and Val d'Isere, France.
West: Whistler, BC. At Whistler the twins took part in celebrity races.

1990 *Europe*: Canazei, Italy and St. Moritz, Switzerland. John Eaves was making his film ***Fire, Ice and Dynamite*** at the same place Twinski vacationed that Spring.
West: Whistler Blackcomb, BC.

1991 *Europe*: Grindelwald, Switzerland, and Neustif, Austria.
West: Whistler, BC.

1992 *Europe*: St. Gallenkirck, Schruns, and Zermatt, Switzerland.

1993 *Europe*: Deux Alpes and Val Thorens, France. At Val Thorens, Rhoda bungee jumped and the twins sent many of their club members paraponting.

1994 *Europe*: St. Moritz, Switzerland, and Lech, Austria.

1995 *Europe*: Venice and Cortina d'Ampezzo, Italy; Badgastein and Vienna, Austria.

1996 *Europe*: Grindelwald, Switzerland, and Chamonix, France.

1997 *Europe*: Val Thorens and Verbier, France.

1998 *Europe*: Solden, Austria, and Davos, Switzerland.

1999 *Europe*: Canazei, Italy, and Bad Gastein, Austria.
West: Big White and Sun Peaks, BC.

2000 *Europe*: Schladming & Lech, Austria.
West: Lake Louise & Sunshine, BC.

2001 *Europe*: Zermatt and Grindelwald, Suisse.
West: Fernie, BC.

2002 *West*: Panorama, BC.

2003 *Europe*: Kitzbuhel and Ischgl, Austria. Pepi Salvenmoser, coach of Canadian Ladies' Team in 1959, visited the twins in Austria.
West: Silver Star (Big White), BC.

2004 *Europe*: Canazei, Italy and Lech, Austria.
West: Panorama, BC.

2005 *Europe*: Les Crosets, Switzerland; Verbier, France. At this point the cost of the trip has risen somewhat to $3,598 for each club member.
West: Fernie, BC. A number of the Wurtele family turn out to join the trip, including Nancy Gillis Andersen and her husband Henrik, David Eaves and wife Patricia, John Eaves and wife Brigitte, and nephew Scott Wurtele and wife.

2006 *Europe*: Ischgl, Austria.
West: Panorama, BC.

2007 *Europe*: Lech am Arlberg, Austria.
West: Silver Star (Big White), BC.

2008 West: Sun Peaks, B.C.

2009 West: Panorama, B.C.

TWINSKI HONORARY MEMBERS AND TROPHIES

TWINSKI CLUB **HONORARY MEMBERS**

Chief Jackrabbit H. S. Johannsen
Barbara Campbell
Sue Godber
Betty Houghton
Jim Houghton
Audie Maclean
Betty Maxwell
Betty Polis
Olive Sinclair
Marg Legge Stavert
Ainsley Stephen
Libby Elder Taylor

THE LIBBY ELDER **TROPHY**

Awarded by Twinski for enthusiastic support and devotion to the Club.

1982 – Bev Burnham
1983 – Elfie Valenta
1984 – Marion Dunn
1985 – Sue Godber
1986 – Esther Frischknecht
1987 – Jane Hugessen
1988 – Jackie Munroe
1989 – Valerie Megeny
1990 – Ken Thompson
1991 – Mo Clouthier
1992 – Ann Madden
1993 – Claire Fraser
1996 – Mary Iversen
1997 – Jim Moore
1998 – Lou Lukanovich
1999 – Michael Ellwood
2000 – Joan Robertson
2001 – Shelia Marquis
2002 – Betty Polis
2003 – Pierrette Phoenix

THE DORIS MOLSON **TROPHY**

Awarded by Twinski to the person personifying the essence of the Club, with loyalty and devotion.

1976 – Jean Hampson
1977 – Barbara Campbell
1978 – Betty Polis
1979 – Audie Maclean
1980 – Ainsley Stephen
1981 – Olive Sinclair
1982 – Sheila Naimen
1983 – Roberta Hampson
1984 – Margaret Townsend
1985 – Margaret Legge
1986 – Martha Moyle
1987 – Mitzi Ogilvy
1988 – Sue Godber
1989 – Ann Boyle
1990 – Betty Houghton
1991 – Mo Boorne
1992 – Dorothy Bernard
1993 – Esther Frischknecht
1994 – Margie Knight
1995 – Joan Donnell
1996 – Mary Iversen
1997 – Joan Meyer
1998 – Maxine Parent
1999 – Doug Hall
2000 – Nancy Andersen
2001 – Bev Hamilton
2002 – Marion Dunn
2003 – Norma Sklivas
2004 – Bev Waldorf
2005 – Nicky Denis
2006 – Ron Walker
2007 – Nicky Denis
2008 – Barbara Johnson
2009 – Nancy Robinson

SELECTED **BIBLIOGRAPHY**

Kidd, Bruce. *The Struggle for Canadian Sport*. Toronto: University of Toronto Press, 1996.

Weintraub, William. *City Unique: Montreal Days and Nights in the 1940s and '50s*. Toronto: McClelland & Stewart, 1996.

Walter, Ann (editor), *The Penguin Ski Club 1932 - 1992*. Privately published, 1992.

McKenty, Neil and McKenty, Catharine. *Skiing Legends and The Laurentian Lodge Club*. Montreal: Price-Patterson Ltd., 2000.

Hotchkiss, Ron. *The Matchless Six: The Story of Canada's First Women's Olympic Team*. Toronto: Tundra Books, 2006.

Stewart, Robert, *The Trail Breakers: The Red Birds Ski Club 1928 - 2000*. Montreal: Privately published, 2000.

Dorothy Campbell Poole's Paternal Ancestry, Her own Narrative of: *The Campbells of Quebec*.

Fry, John "First on the Hill", *Walrus* Magazine, February 2007 author of *The Story of Modern Skiing* (University Press of New Hampshire, 2006).

Also thanks to:
Vic Pelletier Inc., film on *Gaby Pleau, la reine des neiges*,
and Radio-Canada's *Histoires oubliées*.

INDEX

Boldface numbers refer to photos and italics to short sidebars.

Achevé d'imprimer
à Montréal
en l'an 2012
par
Le Caïus du livre inc.